Violence in the Media and
Its Influence on Criminal Defense

Violence in the Media and Its Influence on Criminal Defense

CYNTHIA A. COOPER

McFarland & Company, Inc., Publishers

Jefferson, North Carolina, and London

LIBRARY OF CONGRESS CATALOGUING-IN-PUBLICATION DATA

Cooper, Cynthia A.
    Violence in the media and its influence on criminal defense /
Cynthia A. Cooper.
        p.   cm.
    Includes bibliographical references and index.

    ISBN-13: 978-0-7864-2951-6
    softcover : 50# alkaline paper ∞

    1. Violence in mass media.   2. Mass media — Influence.
3. Defense (Criminal procedure)   I. Title.
P96.V5C66   2007
303.6 — dc22   2007015856

British Library cataloguing data are available

Cover photograph ©2006 BananaStock

Manufactured in the United States of America

McFarland & Company, Inc., Publishers
    Box 611, Jefferson, North Carolina 28640
        www.mcfarlandpub.com

Contents

Preface   1

One. The Historical Context of Media Violence   5

Two. Social Science Research and the Search
for a Cause of Violence   33

Three. Media Regulation   59

Four. Media on Trial   87

Five. Lionel Tate and the TV Wrestling Defense   125

Six. The *Matrix* Murders   161

Seven. Lessons Learned and Future Priorities   181

References   191

Index   203

Preface

In 1994, I presented my first research paper at an academic conference. It was a regional conference so I knew that it would be small and more intimate but I was still nervous. After years of working in the business world I returned to graduate school and here I was, about to present a paper to an academic audience on the FCC's new rules for broadcast hoaxes. I managed to get through my presentation without too much incident and I waited patiently while the last speaker presented his paper. Then the moderator asked for questions and a woman in the front was the first to raise her hand and indicate that she had a question for me. I was nervous but excited nonetheless. She commented on one of the cases that I discussed which involved concern over the effects of media violence. She gathered from my presentation that I didn't agree that media violence could inspire real-life aggression and violence. I answered that she was correct, I didn't. And then before I knew it I was making a snide comment that people today blame everything on the media and that television violence had become the scapegoat for all social ills in America. I wasn't that clever. The scapegoat label had been used for decades; I just thought I sounded smart using it. I didn't.

She paused for a moment and then took a deep breath as though she were prepping herself to say something very difficult. She then told the whole room that just a month before she had buried her daughter who was killed by two teens claiming to be like the murderous couple Mickey and Mallory from the film *Natural Born Killers*. She believed that media could influence behavior and she had the personal experience of losing a daughter to prove it. Not only did I feel like an ass for my glib comments but I also suddenly realized that I had missed an important point in the media violence debate. Her personal testimony made it clear to me that opinions about media violence are influenced by personal experiences more than scientific research

1

results or criminal court verdicts. She was going to believe that media violence influences behavior no matter what anyone else said and I realized that that was okay. My opinion up to that point was shaped by the research literature which generally concluded that media violence correlates with aggression, but only with some people, under some circumstances. All of us are likely affected in subtle ways, such as we are desensitized to real violence after viewing so much graphic fictional violence in movies and on television. And most of us exhibit third-person effects, meaning that we believe others are affected by media violence but not ourselves. Sure, there were studies that found stronger correlative connections between media violence and aggression and some that claimed causal connections. But the research community as a whole stood firmly behind a more conservative, middle-ground approach. As new research is being conducted every year there is no doubt that the body of media effects research is growing.

Although I never saw the woman from the conference again I have carried the lesson learned that day with me ever since. I now look for anecdotal evidence in my own life that either supports or refutes the latest research findings and I ask people to tell me how much their own experiences impact their perspective on media violence. Many of those anecdotes appear in this book. What this book won't do is tell you everything there is to know about media violence research; I leave that to the textbooks. Instead, I try to present an overview of significant media effects research in context with the overall regulatory scheme governing movies, television, music and video games. Media are such a pervasive force in our life that it is impossible at times to separate reality from fiction. As more media embrace virtual reality technologies we may see a shift in the media effects paradigm and more substantiated claims of media influence on real-life violence and aggression.

This book also includes the words and stories of some of the people involved in the most prominent media violence cases in the past decade. Much has been written in newspapers and debated on cable television news shows about true crimes allegedly encouraged by media violence, but often these do not actually quote or otherwise involve anyone connected with the case. I wanted to that with this project because I think it is a crucial piece of missing information in the media violence paradigm. I chose two cases to explore in more depth: the television wrestling defense trial of Lionel Tate and *The Matrix*-influenced murders by Joshua Cooke. I am extremely grateful to Joshua Cooke for agreeing to share his thoughts and impressions with me and being so open with his comments. I also appreciate Cooke's attorneys Rachel Fierro and Benjamin Griffits for speaking to me and sharing their trial experiences for this book. I'd also like to thank Jim Lewis, Kenneth Padowitz, and Michael Brannon for spending several days with me to discuss the Lionel Tate case. Their help was invaluable in understanding the inner workings of this famous case. By sharing their stories I'm able to include many aspects of this case that were never reported in traditional news reports. To all of you I am grateful.

I'd also like to thank my colleagues at Salisbury University for their support in completing this project. I'm especially grateful to the Fulton School of Liberal Arts for granting me assistance and the thing I needed the most, time. To my family, you are the best. I'm buoyed by your never-ending belief in me and in my work.

ONE

The Historical Context
of Media Violence

In June 2004, Ronny Zamora walked out of a Florida prison after serving 27 years for murdering an elderly neighbor. In one of the first trials of its type, Zamora's lawyer argued that the 15-year-old teen was not responsible for his actions due to "television intoxication" brought on by years of watching violent network TV programming with unrealistic consequences. The jury rejected Zamora's defense but it was not the last time a "media made me do it" defense claim was made. The urge to blame media for someone's violent behavior has resurfaced throughout the decades in many different contexts: when President John F. Kennedy was assassinated; when a young child was burned to death after her siblings allegedly watched MTV's program *Beavis and Butthead*; when Dylan Klebold and Eric Harris murdered a dozen classmates at Columbine High School; and when 12-year-old Lionel Tate killed a neighbor while recreating wrestling moves he said he learned from TV wrestling. In fact, each time a violent act gains national attention the immediate and predictable quest for the root cause of violence in our society follows. Why do people hurt and kill others? Where do they learn to kill or that violence is an acceptable resolution to conflict? Most important, where do children learn how to inflict injury on themselves and on others? Often, media are the main culprit. A scapegoat for societal ills, media are seen as primary educators of violent acts and the use of violence as an acceptable means to solve conflict.

America clearly has a love–hate relationship with violent media. Even a cursory look at our most popular movies, video games, and music reveals a fascination with violence, or at the very least an acceptance of violence in our entertainment products. On the other hand, parents, critics and politicians often claim that media act as an educating agent for acceptable behavior in real life. If we willingly accept violence as a major part of our chosen entertainment products, does that not translate to a greater acceptance of violence in real-life situations as well?

The debate over media violence is not a new one. And television was not the first target of protests, despite the fact that the first court cases revolve around broadcast programming. In fact, many contemporary complaints over the effects of violent media products display remarkable similarity to parental and citizen complaints against radio, comic books and movies decades earlier. In short, little has changed in the past 70 years. Media may have changed with the advent of digital video and audio and the Internet, but the concerns over violent content have not. Concern throughout the years has focused on the effects of violent media on children. While societal effects of media have been studied, the most concern still revolves around children since there is a common belief that children are more susceptible to the influencing effects of media. Young children and teens are generally believed to be more impressionable and less able to distinguish between abstract concepts such as good and evil, reality and fantasy, and acceptable and unacceptable behavior.

Early complaints about the media's potential harm to children were spearheaded by parents, not by government or the law-enforcement community. For example, in 1933 the Fox Meadow PTA of Scarsdale, New York, called for an end to the "ether bogeyman," suspenseful radio serials that reportedly caused nightmares among young listeners ("Mothers protest 'bogeyman' on radio," p. 17). The group conducted its own primitive content analysis of forty popular radio programs and concluded only five did not contain unacceptable levels of violence and other objectionable content. The study was hardly scientific but it was enough to spur the group's efforts to attract a wider audience to their cause. The group publicly condemned radio hits *Betty Boop* and *Little Orphan Annie*, which drew the attention of CBS network officials who responded to the group. However, over time no real action was taken by the network as a result of the parents' complaints. Isolated campaigns popped up across the country but never had a real chance to effect change because broadcasters were more concerned with appealing to nationwide, broad-based audiences. Local groups had a much better chance of getting results if they joined forces with other groups across the

Early television was little more than radio with pictures. *The Milton Berle Show* was one of TV's first hits.

country. Until then, the "ether bogeyman" was safe from government intrusion.

Years later, the newly formed Radio Council on Children's Programs conducted a national survey of 100,000 parents that revealed predictable complaints about the effects of violent content on young listeners. The group used these results to start a campaign to rid the airwaves of the most offensive programs ("Radio reforms for youth," 1939, p. 4D). While the effort largely mirrored earlier campaigns, the Radio Council offered no explanation why parents continued to let their children listen to these programs. So while parents were voicing concern over the content of programs, they weren't stopping their children from listening to the programs. This contradictory behavior proved a difficult stumbling block in the campaign to force broadcasters to change programming practices. Without proof that the radio violence drove away listeners, broadcasters had little incentive to change anything. As the importance of radio as a mass medium grew during the Great Depression into World War II, the power of the radio was undeniable. How could the medium that brought together millions of families and neighbors to listen to the *Howdy Doody Hour*, *The Milton Berle Show* and President Roosevelt's *Fireside Chats* also be capable of such destruction to America's youth?

The Golden Age of Media Violence

With attention on the war and the government's appropriation of all available broadcast frequencies for military use, complaints about programming content dropped off. But the emergence of television in the late 1940s provided a catalyst for renewed concerns over violent media. Television delivered the visual excitement of cinema movies directly into the home, a convenience that made radio a staple. Suspenseful programs were now combined with visuals to transform the media experience of millions of Americans. The mix was irresistible to youth and adults alike, but particularly so after a drop in television prices helped bring the medium into more homes. Soon it became a fixture in American life, regardless of age, geographic location or socioeconomic status. Television's popularity renewed earlier complaints about programming content but also spotlighted the role parents played in allowing children's viewing. The National Council of Churches of Christ released a revealing nationwide survey in 1954 that reported favorable attitudes toward television because parents saw it as good way to occupy their children's idle time ("Too much bang bang," E1). Despite reporting concerns over violent content in Westerns and crime shows, parents in this survey were surprisingly honest about their use of television to entertain their children while they attended to other activities.

One significant change in the concern with television violence was the number of parents who reported it was a direct influence on their children's behavior. Unlike radio and comic books, parents reported a direct, and sometimes immediate, mimicking of behaviors witnessed in favorite children's programming. Often it was the mere imitation of television characters involving a relatively innocent reenactment of a favorite Western or cartoon. Other times it was a "gunfight" between the good guys and the criminals. But parents soon realized that the unrealistic consequences of cartoon violence didn't translate in real life. Neither did the fictional violence of physical comedies like *The Three Stooges* and *The Little Rascals*.

At the same time television was becoming an entertainment staple in most American homes, law-enforcement agencies began reporting a disturbing trend in youth misbehavior. The rise in juvenile delinquency coinciding with the growth of television's popularity led many to the inevitable conclusion that violent television programming was to blame for youth violence. A 1954 report released by the National Association for Better Radio and Television (NAFBRAT) reported that crime shows had increased fourfold in three years (Hill, p. 29). This led to renewed advocacy by parent and religious organizations concerned about the rise in juvenile delinquency. The National Council of Churches of Christ, the national PTA and the United Methodist Church all released reports that warned members of the dangerous influence of television violence on American youth. Many established advisory groups produced evaluative criteria for programming and yearly lists of acceptable and unacceptable programs. This is a practice that continues today with television reviews by the Catholic Church and many child advocacy groups.

Citizens were so alarmed over youth violence that the U.S. Senate directed a special body, the Senate Subcommittee to Investigate Juvenile Delinquency, to uncover the root cause of these growing crime statistics. Richard Clenneden, the subcommittee director, immediately cast his investigatory eye toward the growing medium of television, correlating youth viewership statistics with incidences of violent acts in programming. Clenneden reported the average elementary school child viewed 22–27 hours of television per week, about the same amount of hours each also spent in school. He also reported that the programs that were most popular with children contained 6.2 acts, or threatened acts, of violence per hour (*Juvenile Delinquency*, 83rd Cong., 1954). Clenneden claimed that proved children were drawn to violent programming.

Representatives from NAFBRAT and the National Council of Churches testified that their survey results also showed that television was saturated with violence. Officials with the California Youth Authority reported that juvenile crime increased 10 percent in two years with many offenders citing television as "inspiring" their crimes (*Juvenile Delinquency*, 83rd Cong., 1954, p. 66). The subcommittee's anecdotal evidence was damning to the entire television industry, but failed to prove a definitive cause-and-effect relationship between television violence and youth crime. Absent this smoking gun, regulators could do little but pledge to continue to encourage the industry to clean up its programming. Predictably, broadcasters vehemently rejected any correlation between television violence and rising juvenile delinquency rates and ridiculed critics for their unscientific conclusions.

The public reaction to the subcommittee's investigation was varied. While many advocacy groups readily embraced the notion of television as a corrupting force, others rejected the claims and turned focus back on the behaviors of the parents themselves. Adolescent psychologist Erik Erickson scolded those who "scapegoated" television as a quick fix to a problem that had not been fully investigated (Illson, p. 72). Harvard University lecturer Ellenor Maccoby testified at a subsequent subcommittee hearing that in her own interviews with 300 parents most reported a higher incidence of aggressive behavior after their children watched violent television programming. However, this was not enough to scare them away from the medium and most still embraced television as a convenient form of babysitting (*Juvenile Delinquency & Television Programs*, 84th Cong., p. 83).

The public debates highlighted opposing viewpoints inherent in any investigation of media effects. First, the lack of consistent scientific data proving a direct and immediate correlation between media violence and aggressive behavior made it nearly impossible to impose any type of content regulation on broadcasters. Programming content is generally protected under the First Amendment except those classes of speech which may cause harm (e.g., indecent and obscene expressions, libelous statements, fraudulent advertising). Consequently, producers of media are not obligated to alter programming content just because some people don't like it. There has to be a potential for harm in order to restrict content in any way. Unfortunately, the media industry typically responded to critics with the common retort, "If you don't like it, don't watch it." While that wasn't the most politically savvy response, it also wasn't entirely accurate. Telling parents to simply stop using radio and television altogether because they didn't like some programming would deprive them of important news and culturally significant entertainment programming. It didn't need to be an all-or-nothing proposition. This defiance also ignored the fact that government did have limited regulatory power over the broadcast industry and could order the Federal Communications Commission (FCC) to exert pressure on the industry. Upon remembering this (usually at the insistence of an angry legislator), network representatives often promised to police their programming and make corrections when standards crossed the line. Although the promise of self-regulation seemed more hollow gesture than earnest pledge, it was a start.

A second difficulty with the campaign to clean up media violence rested with the popularity of television itself. The explosive growth of television viewership among children and parents alike in the 1950s clearly hurt the credibility of concerns voiced over violent content. It's very difficult to complain about the dangerous effects of programming on one hand while embracing its use as a convenient babysitter on the other. It seemed that parents wanted it both ways. They wanted television to occupy their children's time and attention, but they also expected the content to conform to their specific standards. In many ways this argument remains even today. With working parents and a ubiquitous media landscape, the blaming of parents seems overly simplistic. Parents simply can't monitor a child's activities at all times, nor can they anticipate objectionable programming that may be embedded in programming without warning. While parental involvement was generally greater in the 1950s, especially among women, television also was a new and seductive medium. Parents did not have tools to know what content a show might have until they were actually viewing it. The vivid and exciting medium was attractive to children in ways not experienced before. But times have changed. With more tools available than ever before parents must find a way to take responsibility for policing their children's media use.

Faced with these obstacles, any hope for improvements in television programming seemed remote at best. While critics may have lacked legal grounding to force changes in broadcasting programming, they did have a public relations issue that favored their cause embedded in the Communications Act of 1934. Aside from the technical issues addressed (e.g., licensing, station operations and procedures) the Act included a mandate that broadcasters program their stations in the best interest of the public. The airwaves that broadcasters use to transmit their signal are owned by the American public. With the privilege to use these comes a responsibility to the public. The PICON mandate, as it is called, stands for *public interest, convenience and necessity* and means that broadcasters have an obligation to program their stations in ways that serve the public. That doesn't mean that all programming has to meet strict educational and informational guidelines. But, at the very least, programming certainly should not harm the public.

Where the Communications Act of 1934 was once a liability for critics of television content, PICON fortified a public relations campaign broadcasters found hard to ignore. Members of Congress publicly criticized industry leaders for not following up on promised self-policing. Advocacy groups encouraged parents to increase their monitoring and report any objectionable programming. These groups reminded parents of their obligation to monitor their children's viewing and even limit it if necessary. The American Council for Better Broadcasts and NAFBRAT took another crucial step by providing parents with tools for developing their own monitoring projects, as well as contact information for organizations that provided program evaluations (Wharton, 1956). The International Catholic Association for Radio & Television developed a code for parents that allowed them to rate programs and ultimately decide how best to incorporate television in their children's lives ("Educator's television code," p. 467).

Broadcasters had little choice but to respond to the newly fortified critics. No longer could parents be dismissed as unknowledgeable or complacent. And no one, not even the most fervent supporter of free speech rights of programmers, wanted to appear totally indifferent to the very audience that was making its network such a commercial hit. In an apparent concession to the continued criticism, the National Association of Radio and Broadcasters (NAB) amended its Television Code in 1956 to reflect sensitivity to children. The code was not a set of rules or regulations governing the actions of member stations, but rather an ethical guide of suggested rights and responsibilities. Without admitting a direct link between violent programming and aggressive behavior, the new code included an amendment that read:

> **Responsibility Toward Children**: The education of children involves giving them a sense of the world at large. Crime, violence and sex are a part of the world they will be called upon to meet, and a certain amount of proper presentation of such is helpful in orienting the child to his social surrounding. However, violence and illicit sex shall not be presented in an attractive manner, nor to such an extent such as will lead children to believe they play a greater part in life than they do. They should not be presented without indications of the resultant retribution and punishment [National Association of Radio and Television Broadcasters, Television Code, 3rd ed., p. 3].

While it could hardly be considered a victory for critics of television violence, the amended code was a subtle acknowledgment of the interdependence between broadcasters and their audiences. A network needs a large and loyal audience in order to attract advertising, the lifeblood of any broadcast property. And while parents found television a useful and exciting form of entertainment for their children, they could not fully expect programming to be aimed solely at their needs. For now, the advocates and networks would continue to keep a watchful eye on each other as the medium continued to grow.

While these groups were testing their new-found relationship, there still were unsettled accusations that juvenile delinquency crime rates were connected to the emergence of television as a mass medium. FBI chief J. Edgar Hoover blamed television for the increase in juvenile crime in the October 10, 1958, *Newsweek* cover story ("TV: dial anything for murder," p. 66) that proclaimed it television's bloodiest year ever. Murders, shootings, beatings, as well as robberies and property crimes were a staple in prime-time programming. At the same time the juvenile crime rate was at an all-time high. Law-enforcement agents began reporting that youth offenders admitted to learning the techniques of their crimes from television. Could it be that the two were positively linked and scientific evidence just hadn't caught up with the anecdotal claims? Is it true that children really didn't know how to commit crimes until television provided an explicit how-to for any wayward youth? Or was this just another example of scapegoating the media for the social ills that naturally emerged from a changing social and cultural structure in America? Was it simply too painful to admit the age of innocence was over without finding a singular, corrupting cause for the downfall of our youth?

The Vast Wasteland of Television

The 1950s were dubbed the Golden Age of television due to the tremendous growth of the industry and the almost magical way in which it brought together millions of people through the shared enjoyment of variety and entertainment programming. By the end of the decade, broadcasting's reputation clearly was tarnished by the newly popular crime, Western and action adventure genres. But viewership was also at an all-time high. Many criticized broadcasters for abandoning the happy, lighthearted fare of entertainment programming in favor of a violent, fictionalized portrayal of the seedy side of American culture. How could children help but wish to emulate this glamorous, exciting medium? For parents, social scientists and government officials asking these questions, the turbulent 1960s offered more questions with no real answers.

Critics found an ally in new FCC chairman Newton Minow, who seemed more sympathetic to the concerns over violent programming. In a famous speech to the National Association of Broadcasters Minow declared television a "vast wasteland" of murder, mayhem and violence, and encouraged the industry to do better (Minow, n.p.). The speech was reprinted in the print media and praised by many advocacy groups. Later, Minow received the prestigious George Foster Peabody Award for his then daring critique of the broadcasting industry (Adams, 1962). Of course, coming from the chief of the major regulatory body overseeing broadcasting operations and programming, Minow's comments were not well received by broadcasters, and many wondered if this signaled a change in regulatory policy toward more censorship of programming content. Broadcasters were put on notice by Minow and members of Congress that the honeymoon was over. No longer could the industry claim that its infancy afforded it less oversight in order to determine its own standards for acceptable programming content. Instead, Minow's critical comments seemed to reenergize the campaign against television. Critics questioned, for instance, the broadcast industry's repeated claim to advertisers that television was a powerfully persuasive medium that was particularly effective on children, who in turn influenced the buying habits of their parents. How then could it be that violent content had no effect on children as the broadcast industry claimed for so many years? How was it possible that television advertising could be so influential while fictional violence was not? Granted, the two content forms differ in some fundamental ways, but both share elements of fantasy, of unrealistic claims and qualities, as well as unrealistic consequences. Broadcasters seemed to be caught in their own game of doublespeak.

The issue of violence in programming was also becoming a moot point economically. With nearly a decade of scholarly studies and content analyses that defined and coded categories, incidences and degree of violent acts in shows, there was no denying the increased amount of violence in programs. Broadcasters pointed to the popularity of crime shows as proven by high viewership ratings of these programs. Broadcasters were merely giving the audience what it wanted, the industry argued. The appeal was widespread since crime and action programming did not appear to negatively affect adoption rates of television either. At the end of World War II television was in fewer than 10,000 households throughout the United States; by 1950 the number had grown to 11 million households. But a mere decade later, in 1960, television was in nearly 90 percent of all 54 million homes (Baran, pp. 46–47). This astonishing growth rate surely illustrated the medium's popularity even if some were displeased with its content. This also explains why it inspired so much concern and was often blamed for causing societal ills. What other institution invaded American homes so completely in such a short span of time?

If Minow and other critics believed television's fictional programming was too violent, few could deny the importance of the medium's candid, yet violent, portrayal of the Civil Rights Movement and the Vietnam War. Violent images of civil unrest, war and protest were a staple of network news throughout the turbulent 1960s. Many credit televisions's unvarnished coverage of the brutality enacted against civil rights marchers as helping win nationwide support for the Civil Rights Act. Night after night footage from Vietnam came into American living rooms, transporting the daily struggles, death and destruction faced by American soldiers to viewers half a world away. Images of antiwar protests were equally as dramatic, and President Johnson blamed the media, television news in particular, with influencing the change in the public's support of the war. Nowhere was television's impact realized more than with coverage of the assassinations of John F. Kennedy, Martin Luther King and Robert Kennedy. A nation's collective grief was shared through television, as live coverage of the events unfolded before our eyes. The decade's images were often brutal and violent. Yet, their coverage was essential. As broadcasters stated in the 1956 amendment to the Television Code, violence is a part of our American society; denying this would amount to censorship.

While news media may have been saturated with images of a violent decade, entertainment media countered the harsh images with fluff and fantasy themes. We sang along with Annette Funicello and Frankie Avalon as they frolicked in the sand in *Beach Blanket Bingo*. And escapist television programs like *The Munsters, The Addams Family* and *I Dream of Jeannie* were top-rated programs that provided a welcome respite from the hardships that plagued American life. The violent decade left a divided nation with a damaged sense of security, and after Robert Kennedy's assassination in 1968 President Johnson ordered formation of the National Commission on the Causes and Prevention of Violence. The committee was charged with finding the root causes of violent behavior in America, a daunting, if not impossible, task. After countless investigations, numerous hearings full of conflicting witness testimony, and volumes of supporting materials, the commission released its findings in December 1969. The commission concluded that media violence, namely television violence, encouraged aggressive behavior, although no causal relationship could be supported scientifically. The commission continued that television violence contributed to the widespread acceptance of violence and confrontation as a means of resolving conflict, even though unrealistic consequences were the norm in fictional programming. The commission's findings were controversial and had little real effect since Congress and the FCC had no regulatory power to force changes in television programming. Instead, what followed was a cycle of periodic government investigations into the impact of media violence, typically coming

The use of film freed television from studios and allowed violence filled shows like *Gunsmoke.*

after a particularly shocking crime that captured national attention. The hearings followed a predictable path: dozens of witnesses (physicians, social scientists, law-enforcement agents, educators and advocates) provided testimony to media's impact on violent behavior; industry representatives denied that impact; money was pledged to support research and investigations; citizens and the press reacted to the committee's findings and the issue quietly faded away until the next tragedy propelled the issue back into the national spotlight.

In the 1970s advocacy groups joined forces to gain more recognition of their concerns. A simple way to do that was to file formal complaints with the FCC. The FCC reported that complaints from citizens about excessive violence and sexuality in programming increased from 2,000 complaints in 1972 to more than 25,000 two years later (Federal Communications Commission, *Report on the broadcast of violence, indecent and obscene material*). FCC Chairman Richard Wiley met with broadcasters to develop a plan for reducing television violence and to designate an hour of prime-time television free of excessive violence and sexual themes. Succumbing to pressure from Wiley and the thousands of viewer complaints, the NAB Code was amended in June 1975 to adopt a "Family Viewing Hour" which actually lasted from 7:00 to 9:00 P.M. Although advocates and politicians praised the move as an earnest effort to respond to parents' concerns, television writers saw it more as a direct assault on their creative product. The writers' union sued and in 1976 a Los Angeles District Court judge struck down the family hour as government censorship (*Writers Guild of America West, Inc. v. FCC*). Although the District Court's ruling was later overturned for lack of jurisdiction, broadcasters honored the Family Viewing Hour for a while but reported that family-friendly programming drew poor ratings. Without a legal mandate to continue the Family Viewing Hour, broadcasters merely let the issue quietly fade away.

In 1982 the National Institutes of Health reported that 2,500 books and research reports exploring violence in the media had been published since 1970. By 1993 the number had reportedly risen to 3,000 (Clark, p. 3). Scholars have disputed that number and estimate that the actual number of studies is around 1,500. That is still an impressive body of work in such a short time. While no definitive causal connection has been established between media violence and aggressive behavior, the medical and psychological communities

18

generally support less direct or immediate impacts. Sociologist Mike Males (1999) summarizes the difficulties of pinpointing specific triggers within a diverse American population:

> The effect of violent media on all subjects (not just children) has been reported in four decades of laboratory studies. In particular, aggressive individuals evidently seek out violent media in a reciprocal, mutually-reinforcing pattern that appears to stimulate violent expressions and exacerbate other problems linked to violence, such as poor academic achievement. As a rule, however, exposure to violence through television, movies, toys, and video games is a poor indicator of violence in real life settings. Large-scale studies that attempt to correlate aggression levels among children with their exposure to media violence in fact reveal only weak correlation or none at all.... In short, media violence is an unreliable predictor of violence in society and, if ultimately found to be important, apparently affects children and adults alike [p. 231].

Of course others remind the public that the lack of strong correlations does not negate the presence of any effects. Researchers believe that there is strong evidence that the effects of media violence are developed over time and most pronounced, as Males points out, in individuals who already exhibit aggressive traits.

School Shootings and Violent Video Games

A rash of school shootings in the mid-1990s led to renewed calls to find the root cause of youth violence in this country. This time the debate didn't surround concerns over juvenile delinquency but rather a disturbing trend in individual acts by young men who were shooting up their schools in record numbers. In a landmark study, the Secret Service studied gunmen involved in school shootings in the United States and released the preliminary results in a series published by the *Chicago Sun-Times* newspaper. The study was based on interviews with some of the shooters and documents recovered in other cases. A list of the shooters studied by the Secret Service provides a powerful snapshot of a disturbing trend of youth violence. The shooters studied include:

Anthony Barbaro, 18, Olean, N.Y., Dec. 30, 1974. Honor student brought guns and homemade bombs to school, set off the fire alarm, and shot at janitors and firemen who responded. SWAT team found him asleep, with headphones playing *Jesus Christ Superstar*. Hanged himself while awaiting trial.

John Christian, 13, Austin, Tex., May 19, 1978. Son of George Christian, former press secretary to LBJ, honor student, shot and killed teacher.

Robin Robinson, 13, Lanett, Ala., Oct. 15, 1978. After a disagreement with a student, he was paddled by the principal. He returned to school with a gun; when told he would be paddled again, he shot and wounded the principal.

James Alan Kearbey, 14, Goddard, Kan., Jan. 21, 1985. Killed the principal and three others in his junior high school. Said he was bullied and beaten by students for years.

Kristofer Hans, 14, Lewiston, Mont., Dec. 4, 1986. Failing French, tried to kill the teacher but shot and killed her substitute. Injured a vice principal and two students. Had threatened to kill the French teacher.

Nathan Faris, 12, DeKalb, Mo., March 2, 1987. Teased about his chubbiness, Faris shot a classmate, then shot himself to death.

Nicholas Elliott, 16, Virginia Beach, Va., Dec. 16, 1988. Went to school with a semiautomatic pistol, 200 rounds of ammunition and three firebombs. He wounded one teacher, killed another and fired on a student who had called him a racist name.

Cordell "Cory" Robb, 15, Orange County, Calif., Oct. 5, 1989. Took kids hostage in drama class with a shotgun and semiautomatic pistol with the goal of getting his stepfather to school so he could kill him; the stepfather planned to move the family. Shot a student who taunted him. Had told several students what he planned.

Eric Houston, 20, Olivehurst, Calif., May 1, 1992. Former student was upset over losing a job because he had not graduated. Killed three students and a social studies teacher who had given him a failing grade; injured 13 people. Held students hostage.

John McMahan, 14, Napa, Calif., May 14, 1992. Bullied by other boys, he opened fire with a .357 in first period science class, wounding two students.

Wayne Lo, 18, Great Barrington, Mass., Dec. 14, 1992. At an exclusive college-prep boarding school, Lo killed two people and wounded four others. School administrators knew he had received a package from an ammo company and had decided to let him keep it. A student tried to warn counselors.

Scott Pennington, 17, Grayson, Ky., Jan. 18, 1993. Held his high school English class hostage after killing his teacher and killing a custodian.

Leonard McDowell, 21, Wauwatosa, Wis., Dec. 1, 1993. Former student killed an associate principal who had handled his long history of disciplinary problems.

Clay Shrout, 17, Union, Ky., May 26, 1994. Killed his family, then sat in class with a gun before surrendering.

Nicholas Atkinson, 16, Greensboro, N.C., Oct. 12, 1994. Suspended student shot and wounded assistant principal, killed himself.

Chad Welcher, 16, Manchester, Ia., Nov. 8, 1994. Fired two shotgun blasts into the principal's office, hitting a secretary.

John Sirola, 14, Redlands, Calif., Jan. 23, 1995. Shot principal in the face and shoulder; died of self-inflicted wound, which may have been accidental.

Toby Sincino, 16, Blackville, S.C., Oct. 12, 1995. Sincino was picked on by students. A week before the shooting, he had been suspended for making an obscene gesture. He shot and wounded a math teacher, killed another math teacher, then killed himself.

Jamie Rouse, 17, Lynnville, Tenn., Nov. 15, 1995. Upset over failing grade, fired at teachers, killing one, wounding another. When firing at a third teacher, he hit a female student, who died. Had told five friends that he planned to bring the rifle to school.

Barry Loukaitis, 14, Moses Lake, Wash., Feb. 2, 1996. Walked into algebra class with a hunting rifle, two handguns and 78 rounds of ammunition. Killed the teacher and two students, wounded a third. One of the students killed had teased him.

Name and location withheld by investigators, 16, Feb. 8, 1996. Wounded a student and killed himself. He had tried to commit suicide in the past. Other students knew he had been asking for a gun but didn't report it.

Anthony Gene Rutherford, 18; **Jonathan Dean Moore,** 15; **Joseph Stanley Burris**, 15; Patterson, Mo., March 25, 1996. The three killed a student at a rural Christian school for troubled youths. They thought he might intervene in an attack they planned on the school.

David Dubose Jr., 16, Scottsdale, Ga., Sept. 25, 1996. A student at the school for less than a week, Dubose shot and killed a teacher.

Evan Ramsey, 16, Bethel, Alaska, Feb. 19, 1997. Killed the principal and one student, wounding two, with a shotgun. Had told many students what he would do.

Luke Woodham, 16, Pearl, Miss., Oct. 1, 1997. Killed his mother, then killed two students and wounded seven. Was urged on by other boys.

Michael Carneal, 14, West Paducah, Ky., Dec. 1, 1997. Used a stolen pistol to kill three students and wound five in a prayer group, including his ex-girlfriend.

Joseph "Colt" Todd, 14, Stamps, Ark., Dec. 15, 1997. Shot two students. Said he was humiliated by teasing.

Mitchell Johnson, 13, and **Andrew Golden,** 11, Jonesboro, Ark., March 24, 1998. The pair killed four female students and a teacher after pulling the fire alarm. They had stolen the guns from Golden's grandfather.

Andrew Wurst, 14, Edinboro, Pa., April 25, 1998. Killed a teacher and wounded three students at a dinner dance. He had talked of killing people and taking his own life.

Jacob Davis, 18, Fayetteville, Tenn., May 19, 1998. An honor student three days before graduation, Davis used a rifle to shoot another boy in a dispute over a girl.

Kip Kinkel, 15, Springfield, Ore., May 21, 1998. After being expelled for bringing a gun to school, Kinkel killed his parents, then two students in the cafeteria, wounding 25. Father had given him the Glock.

Shawn Cooper, 16, Notus, Idaho, April 16, 1999. He rode the bus to school with a shotgun wrapped in a blanket. He pointed the gun at a secretary and students, then shot twice into a door and at the floor. He had a death list, but told one girl he wouldn't hurt anyone. He surrendered.

Eric Harris, 17, and **Dylan Klebold,** 18, near Littleton, Colo., April 20, 1999. The pair killed 12 students and one teacher, wounded 23 students, and killed themselves. They had planned far more carnage at Columbine High School, spreading 31 explosive devices. They had detailed plans, including hand signals for "use bomb" and "suicide (point to head w gun)."

Thomas Solomon, 15, Conyers, Ga., May 20, 1999. Fired at the legs and feet of students, injuring six. Had turned sullen after being dumped by his girlfriend, and had talked of bringing a gun to school.

Victor Cordova Jr., 12, Deming, N.M., Nov. 19, 1999. Shot a student in the head, killing her.

Seth Trickey, 13, Fort Gibson, Okla., Dec. 6, 1999. Wounded four students outside Fort Gibson Middle School. Surrendered.

Nathaniel Brazill, 13, Lake Worth, Fla., May 26, 2000. Had been sent home for horseplay with water balloons on the last day of school. Returned with a gun and killed a teacher.

The Secret Service report indicated that school shootings are rarely impulsive; rather, the disgruntled student carefully planned his attack (sometimes for years) and typically shared that plan with others. These "bystanders" rarely told anyone about the planned attacks and certainly did not tell an adult who may have prevented the shooting. Many of Barry Loukaitis's classmates did nothing to stop the shooting spree that he planned for more than a year. Loukaitis killed two students and a teacher at his school in Moses Lake, Washington, in 1996. Classmates reported knowing of his plan, but did not think he would really go through with it. When questioned by the Secret Service, one classmate reported: "He said it would be cool to kill people. He said that he could get away with it" (Dedman, online). Another replied that he just "blew it off" when Loukaitis showed him a sawed-off shotgun, thinking it was just another of his empty threats. Such threats likely would not have been taken seriously at home, either. At his trial Loukaitis's mother testified that she had told her son of her own fantasy of tying up her estranged husband and his girlfriend and forcing them to watch as she committed suicide (Ryan, online).

In other cases, friends and classmates not only didn't tell anyone who may have stopped the assault, they actively encouraged the shooter. In Evan Ramsey's case his classmates even showed up to see the shooting. Ramsey, 16, who killed his principal and a fellow student in Bethel, Alaska, explained: "I'd called three people and asked them to go up to the library. [Two boys] told [one boy's] sister what was going to happen, and I guess she called some of her friends, and eventually there was something like two dozen people up in the library" (Dedman, online). During the two weeks of planning before the shooting, Ramsey told his friends he would take a gun to school to scare his tormentors. He made a list that consisted of three targets, but his friends suggested 11 more, including the principal.

The Secret Service report also indicated that few gunmen suffered from diagnosed mental illness, although almost all had experienced depression and 75 percent had threatened suicide or tried to kill themselves prior to the shootings. Many expressed this despair in poems, dairies, online journals and Web sites. Bullying by classmates was the most reported source of the gunmen's anger, especially when school officials did little to address the problem. Loukaitis penned several poems, including "Murder," in which he imagined confronting his tormentor, a male student who called him a "fag":

> It's my first murder
> I'm at the point of no return
> I look at his body
> Killing a bastard that deserves to die
> Ain't nuthin' like it in the world. But he sure did bleed a lot.
> [Youth's poems, 1998]

Luke Woodham, a Mississippi teen who killed two students and wounded several others in 1997, wrote in his journal: "I am not insane. I am angry. I am not spoiled or lazy, for murder is not weak or slow-witted, murder is gutsy and daring.... I killed because people like me are mistreated everyday.... I am malicious because I am miserable" (Dedman, online).

Finally, the Secret Service reported that many of the gunmen had an interest in violent media and video games. Most notable were video games, especially first-person "shooter" games in which players assume the viewpoint of the game through their character. In other words, the image on the screen is from the perspective of the player as he places himself in the scenes of the video game. Eric Harris and Dylan Klebold, the Columbine killers, were big fans of the popular video game *Doom*. Harris programmed a new level of *Doom* patterned after Columbine High School and predicted on his Web site that he was going to make *Doom* a reality on April 19, the day of the murders. Michael Carneal was also a fan of *Doom*, along with *Quake* and *Final Fantasy*. In 1997, he opened fire on a before-school prayer group, killing three and wounding five more students. At his trial prosecutor Michael Breen marveled at the influence of first-person shooter games on Carneal's accuracy. Breen told the court: "Michael Carneal clipped off nine shots in a 10-second period. Eight of those shots were hits. Three were head and neck shots and were kills. This is way beyond the military standard for expert marksmanship. This is a kid who never fired a pistol in his life, but because of his obsession for computer games he had turned himself into an expert marksman" (Thompson, Interview on *60 minutes*). In 2005, Alabama teen Devin Moore grabbed an officer's gun while he was being questioned for suspicion of auto theft. He then shot three police officers and fled in a stolen police car. The act was very similar to a scene in Moore's favorite video game, *Grand Theft Auto*. As he was arrested Moore stated to police, "Life is like a video game. You've got to die sometime!" (Thompson, Interview on *60 Minutes*).

These same shootings were cited in a 2001 landmark study by Anderson and Bushman that attempted to show how and why violent video games affected aggression and arousal in players. The research on video games is admittedly in the early stages when compared with other media such as movies and television. Although video game technology has existed since the 1970s, there was little initial concern that early games such as *Pong* and *PacMan* would cause much harm. Concerns over the impact of video games really didn't emerge until the 1990s when violent themes merged with advanced, high-resolution graphics to make the games extremely lifelike. Anderson and Bushman conducted a meta-analysis, a comprehensive testing of the results of several research studies, that revealed preliminary evidence that violent video games could have negative effects on players. But the authors were also quick to point out that most video game playing by youths takes place with little oversight by parents. Anderson and Bushman cite studies in which young boys (ages 8–13) reported playing games an average of 7.5 hours per week (p. 354). In another study, 90 percent of all teens in grades 8 through 12 reported that their parents never checked the ratings before buying a game. By comparing the data from 35 separate research reports the authors concluded that the meta-analysis supported the hypothesis that exposure to violent video games was positively associated with "heightened levels of aggression in young adults and children, in experimental and nonexperimental designs, and in males and females" (p. 358). The researchers also found that exposure to violent games led to a temporary decrease in pro-social behavior, a measure of socially acceptable conflict resolution and a willingness to help others.

Anderson also told members of the Senate Commerce Committee that he believed the long-term effects of exposure to violent video games were just being discovered. Due to the relative infancy of video game research,

Some studies estimate that boys between ages 8 and 13 play video games 4–8 hours per day. First person shooter games are among the industry's top sellers.

no longitudinal studies have been done to track the behaviors of teens who were heavy users of these games. Nonetheless, Anderson told the committee with confidence that video games served as a learning tool for teens, and that over time their perception of the world is skewed by the abundance of violence they encounter. Testifying at the 2000 hearing, Anderson said:

> Children who are exposed to a lot of violent media learn a number of lessons that change them into more aggressive people. They learn that there are lots of bad people out there who will hurt them. They come to expect others to be mean and nasty. They learn to interpret negative events that occur to them as intentional harm, rather than as an accidental mistake. They learn that the proper way to deal with such harm is to retaliate. Perhaps as importantly, they do not learn nonviolent solutions to interpersonal conflicts.... There is evidence that such exposure increases general feelings of hostility,

thoughts about aggression and retaliation, suspicions about the motives of others, and expectations about how others are likely to deal with a potential conflict situation [*Impact of Interactive Violence on Children*, Testimony of Craig A. Anderson, p. 4].

The learning factor is heightened by the repetitive and addictive nature of video games, which cause a player to keep trying to get to the next level or earn more points. That probably isn't a whole lot different than in the days of the pinball machine when racking up the most points afforded you the honor of entering your initials on the display for everyone to see. However, as fun and challenging as that may have been, a player's enthusiasm lasted only until she ran out of quarters. With video game players, though, the drive to play appears to be far more complicated. Researchers typically explain that players, particularly young boys, are drawn to video games because they feed their enjoyment of competition and control. Jansz suggests that adolescent males like video games because of the emotional charge a player gets while playing them. Emotion theory suggests that we want to continue actions that bring us positive emotions and we quit activities that cause negative emotions. Consequently, a player who is doing well will likely want to keep playing, while one who keeps failing the same stage will become discouraged and quit. But Jansz suggests that video games players are different and play because of the wide range of emotions, both positive and negative, that the games afford. A player gets to assume an identity, place himself in situations, and experience firsthand the consequences of his quest. Therefore, he will continue to play even when faced with negative emotions (p. 236). This illustrates the thrill a player gets from experiencing the ups and downs of the game versus from simply winning the game.

This is not the same as the desperate gambler who continues to play long after he's lost his money because he's sure that the next jackpot is just a game away. The video game emotional thrill feeds a much more basic need, similar to someone who goes to a graphic horror film simply for the exhilaration of being scared. You know you're going to experience fear, relief, disgust, and maybe even be totally grossed out by the graphic violence throughout the film. But it's still fun to put yourself through the gauntlet of emotions. Of course, Jansz warns that the degree to which a player succumbs to his emotional charge from video games is dependant on many additional factors and can have various repercussions:

A conceivable negative effect of testing emotional experiences and identity options in a game context may be that it enhances tendencies toward social isolation. The violent video game may turn out to be too comfortable as an escape from the uncertainties of emotional confrontation in real life. In a positive sense, the actual experience of emotions, as well as the performance of particular identities in virtuality, may contribute to a better understanding of self and emotions in real life thus enhancing the gamer's potential to cope with the inevitable insecurities of adolescence [p. 237].

As increasing numbers of children are given unsupervised access to video games, the potential for anxiety related to their play increases. And by all accounts American children have more access to media than ever before. In 2000, Donald Roberts conducted an extensive nationwide survey of 2,065 teens asking about their media access and usage. Almost 70 percent of all respondents reported having a video game player, with 45 percent of these having the player in their bedroom (p. 9). Perhaps not surprisingly, boys (43 percent) were more likely to have the video game player in their room than girls (23 percent). Respondents reported playing video games for an average of three and one-quarter hours per week, with 55 percent of that time played alone. Thirty-six percent of game playing was done with friends or siblings while only 2 percent of the time was spent playing with parents (p. 13). In another survey done just four years later, the numbers of hours devoted to video games jumped to 13 hours per week for boys and five hours for girls (Stafford, p. A10). Most players also named at least one violent game among their favorites.

Although millions of American teens play video games and don't murder their classmates, the instances of teen violence and the increasing popularity of violent video games have led to repeated calls for legislation that would limit access to violent games. For instance, the Indianapolis City Council instituted an ordinance in 2000 that restricted access of minors to video games that depict violence. The ordinance specifically limited the access of unaccompanied minors to arcade video games with prominent violent themes that were believed to be harmful to minors. Teens could still play the games but only if accompanied by an adult who gave consent to the arcade's management. Games cited by the city included *The House of the Dead*, which pits humans against ax-wielding zombies with explicit and highly stylized violence. The interactive game depicts players spilling blood and guts (literally) as they ward off the demonic spirits that chase them. Of course, the more "undead" killed the more a player scores.

The interactivity of video games is a real point of concern for many critics because they believe this makes video games much more dangerous than passive media like television. By being a part of the game's action, including violent fights and shootings, the player is an active participant and helps dictate how the game proceeds. The realism of contemporary games also delivers a greater sense of concern to some critics. The same advanced graphics that are used to make video games an effective training simulator for military operations are also used in commercial-grade games, bringing the same violent virtual reality to impressionable young minds. Many of the creators of military training video simulators also produce games for the consumer market. Military officials have reported that video game technology is useful for teaching tactical skills, as well as helping to reduce anxiety about shooting or even killing another human being. One veteran commented about the games' similarity on an Internet message board. Roger Powelson wrote:

> As a Viet Nam vet and a father of two kids I am more than concerned by the similarity between the training I received in Fort Ord in 1972 as an Infantry-man and the traits of what I call "First Person Shooters." I'm surprised, once again, that no one else seems to notice the similarity. When I first saw two kids playing multiplayer *Doom* (two screens in a local store) I was amazed at the similarity of the adrenalin rush I had with what it felt like almost thirty years ago ["Violent Media," 2001].

Gilman Louie, CEO of In-Q-Tel, a manufacturer of military and consumer games, commented that it was the realism of video games that had the potential to save lives "in the training and mission ops sides of our business, and it sells on the games side" (Snider, p. D4). If the technology of 3-D virtual reality games is an effective training device for the military, why wouldn't it also be capable of desensitizing teens to violence?

The Indianapolis ordinance closely resembled obscenity prohibitions by defining the offending game as "an amusement machine that predominantly appeals to minors' morbid interest in violence or minors' prurient interest in sex, is patently offensive to prevailing standards in the adult community as a whole with respect to what is suitable material for persons under the age of eighteen, lacks serious literary, artistic, political or scientific value as a whole, and contains either graphic violence or strong sexual content" (*American Amusement v. Kendrick et al.*, p. 1). This definition merely folded violence into the obscenity standard because courts established long ago that obscene products are not afforded any First Amendment protection. The Supreme Court added the SLAP test (lacking serious scientific, literary, artistic and political value) in the landmark 1973 *Miller v. California* ruling to safeguard the First Amendment rights of sexually explicit products that have some social value. The Indianapolis council noted that many of the offensive video games were laden with sexually explicit themes and characters and that violence and sexuality were often intertwined in a game's plot. Further, the ordinance defined graphic violence as the "visual depiction or representation of realistic serious injury to a human or human-like being where such injury includes amputation, decapitation, dismemberment, bloodshed, mutilation, maiming or disfiguration (disfigurement)" (p. 1). The ordinance required operators with five or more video games to post warning signs and to partition the violent games in a segregated section. The council enacted the ordinance based on a belief that violent video games caused aggressive attitudes and behavior in teens that could lead to violent behaviors.

The U.S. District Court rejected the ordinance's restrictions on constitutional grounds and in part on the practicality of enforcing such restrictions. The court acknowledged that requiring vendors to segregate violent from nonviolent games and to secure parental permission for all teen patrons would force an undue hardship on arcade owners. Further, the court ruled: "we are not persuaded by the City's argument that whatever contribution to the marketplace of ideas and expression the games in the record may have the potential to make is secured by the right of the parent.... The right is to a considerable extent illusory" (p. 8). Requiring parents to actually be present for their child to play would naturally result, the court wrote, in a decrease in arcade attendance. Many teens are just negotiating independence from parental supervision at this age and would likely avoid the arcade altogether if required to bring along an adult. Likewise, busy parents and guardians simply may not want to accompany a child, preferring instead to avoid the loud, frenetic game arcade that their teen tolerates so much better.

From a constitutional standpoint, the court found that requiring parental consent to play these games infringed on the minor's First Amendment rights to expression. By restricting access to these games via adult permission, the ordinance bore little resemblance to other products with time, place and manner restrictions. Such restrictions are often placed on products that are legal but which society deems too risky for use by minors. Cigarettes, for example, are legal products accompanied by serious health risks. In theory, adults are mature enough to make the decision to smoke taking into account these risks. Children and teens, however, are not believed to possess the maturity or reasoning skills to make an informed decision to use a product that may bring about harm in later years. The Indianapolis City Council determined that video game violence was harmful to the extent that it should be restricted for minors unless a parent or guardian gives consent. Absent clear and convincing evidence that video game violence caused harm to teen players, the ordinance violated the rights of minors.

The court also ruled on Indianapolis's attempt to add violence to the obscenity class of restricted speech. The court rejected placing the two in the same category because each related to a different concern. Obscenity is restricted because it violates community norms and a shared sensibility about what is permissible regarding depictions of sex and sexual activities. Obscenity regulations are always determined with contemporary community standards in mind because the Supreme Court ruled that a national standard was unworkable and would unduly impose on a community's shared sense of decency. However, the Indianapolis statute attempted to restrict access to the video games not because they violate community standards but because they were believed to cause harm to minors. These are two entirely different standards of concern. The court drew upon *U.S. v. Thoma* (1984) to confirm that "depictions of torture and deformation are not inherently sexual and, absent some guidance as to how such violence appeals to the prurient interest of a deviant group, there is no basis upon which a trier of fact could deem such material as obscene." Consequently, Indianapolis was barred from prohibiting access to video games based only on the perceived harm of violence. While the teens and arcade owners in Indianapolis breathed a big sign of relief, it was not the last time government cast its investigatory eye on video games.

TWO

Social Science Research and the Search for a Cause of Violence

Scholars estimate that between 1,000 and 2,500 studies have explored media violence, although the real number is probably closer to the former. Social science researchers on media violence followed the concerns voiced by the public and government officials, but the bulk of research materialized as electronic media expanded from a news source into a giant and influential entertainment medium. As radio and television became more popular and prevalent throughout society, so did the concerns over the potential effects of these media. Congress offered financial support in the mid-twentieth century to support media effects research and today that research is done by a wide variety of investigators representing the fields of communication, mass media, marketing, psychology, sociology, anthropology, criminal justice and medicine, to name just a few. All of these disciplines developed a niche within the larger media effects paradigm because media influence so many different areas of contemporary life.

The Early Studies

One of the most famous early examples of media effects research was a series of studies done by Albert Bandura based on the basic tenets of social cognition theory and social learning theory. In an admitted oversimplification, social cognition theory seeks to explain human thought and behavior via a triad of factors: behavior, personal characteristics (intelligence, gender, race) and environment. All three factors interactively exert varying degrees of influence on each other, and ultimately on the process of learning itself.

Modeling is a key principle of social cognition theory because it is believed that people often learn from observing the behavior of others. We learn both acceptable behavior (positively reinforced) and unacceptable behavior (negatively reinforced). Infants and toddlers, for instance, are born with little innate knowledge of appropriate human behavior. They learn by watching others including their siblings, parents, playmates and teachers. Sometimes we teach children things by accident, such as the toddler who repeats the vulgar language accidentally blurted out by a parent. The child likely does not even know the meaning of those words, but is simply imitating an authoritative figure.

A key aspect to modeling is the type of reinforcement a behavior receives. If a child watches a parent open a door for another person entering a store and that action is reinforced positively (e.g., an expression of thanks, an acknowledging nod), a child will likely model her behavior in a similar fashion when approaching a storefront with other shoppers. If instead the parent gives no consideration to others entering the store and lets the heavy door go regardless of the consequences to the person entering behind him the child will still likely adopt the same behavior. That is unless that act is negatively reinforced. If the person following gets hit in the face by the door and unleashes an angry tirade, and the parent reacts by apologizing, the child should understand that it was not a good thing to do. Without this contrasting perspective, the child is simply mimicking the thoughtless behavior of the attending adult unaware of the potential consequences of the act. These effects of modeling are more likely with young children since they do not yet have the experience to know the potential effects of a given behavior or an understanding of the context of meaning. They are essentially a blank slate.

Bandura tested the modeling potential of media in the now famous 1963 "Bobo Doll" study. Nursery school children were divided into control and experiment groups and shown a film in which an adult acted out varying levels of aggression and violent behavior on the inflated vinyl punching-bag doll. The students were then allowed to go to a playroom with a Bobo Doll and other toys. In general, students who witnessed the film with the adult hitting the doll were more likely to imitate that behavior and to exhibit aggression with the other toys and toward other children in the playroom. Those who viewed the film with little or no aggression by the adult tended to beat the doll the least. Bandura believed the results exhibited the powerful modeling effects of media because children were heavy users of violent media. Because the children witnessed the adult beating the doll with no apparent negative consequences, the behavior was believed to be acceptable.

Of course there are some methodological difficulties with the study. There was no measure of the children's violent tendencies before they viewed the films, so it's difficult to determine if there was true change in their behavior. Some also questioned the choice of using a weighted, inflatable doll for the experiment since it is by nature something designed to be hit. Like a punching bag or the popular toy Weebles, a Bobo Doll was designed to be hit and then bounce back to an upright position. Despite these questions, Bandura's study showed that children are very capable of modeling adult behaviors, especially violent behaviors that are not negatively reinforced.

About the same time, Leonard Eron was beginning a landmark longitudinal study linking television viewing with aggressive behavior. To study the connection between aggression and child-rearing practices, Eron and his collaborators surveyed the parents of approximately 800 third-grade children in the town of Hudson, New York. The survey included questions that asked parents to estimate the amount of television their child watched and their favorite programs. Parents were also asked to assess their child's aggression. Eron found that children who favored violent programs were more likely to exhibit aggressive behavior at home. Eron returned to Hudson in the 1970s, '80s and '90s to continue to track the children's behavior. Although the number of participants who still lived in the area decreased each decade, Eron was able to trace a significant number of students through adulthood. Eron found that participants who watched more violent television as children were more likely to be convicted of serious crimes as adults and to use force with their children and spouses.

Eron's study was highlighted in a 1995 *Frontline* episode titled "Does TV Kill?" The film interviewed several of the men who had been a part of the original Eron study. Paul Abitabile was in the third grade when he participated in Eron's original work in Hudson. Abitabile admits that he watched a lot of violent television when he was young but rejects the notion that it made him a violent person. Abitabile said that television was for him then, and remains, just a fun way to pass the time and relax after a long day. Another participant in the study is more circumspect. Now unemployed, he looks back on a life full of drugs and unsteady employment, and attempts to analyze his own path in life. While he does not blame television for his lack of personal and professional success, he does concede that television occupied a good deal of his youth. It's a habit he's carried into his later years, he explains, because it's just easier to escape into the world of television when real life is not going so well.

Eron participated in a similar longitudinal study of Chicago-area students that spanned fifteen years, the results of which were published in 2003. Interviews were conducted at different intervals during their grade-school years, and again once they were in their early twenties. The participants' television viewing habits were recorded and their aggression levels were assessed through interviews with them, their classmates, and family members. The study concluded that childhood exposure to media violence was an effective predictor of aggression in young adulthood. The researchers also found that identification with aggressive same-sex television characters and perceived realism of TV violence predicted aggression in adulthood (Huesmann, Moses-Titus, Podolski and Eron, pp. 215–216).

In 2002 a team of researchers led by Columbia University professor Jeffrey Johnson released the results of a 17-year study of television viewing and aggressive behavior among 707 children. During this span, the children's television viewing habits were recorded and family members were interviewed and surveyed regarding the participants' aggression levels and behaviors. The researchers also used state and federal arrest records to track any arrests and criminal charges against participants into their adult years. The researchers discovered a "significant association between the amount of time watching television during adolescence and early childhood and the likelihood of subsequent aggressive acts towards others" (Johnson, Cohen, Smailes, Kasen and Brook, p. 2468). Like Eron's study, these researchers found that children who watched "extensive" television were more likely to commit aggressive acts against others as adults. Specifically, the study reported that 5.7 percent of children who watched less than one hour of television a day committed a violent act of serious consequence. The rate of violence increased to 22.5 percent for children watching 1–3 hours per day and to 28.8 percent among those watching more than three hours.

The researchers also found a significant association between childhood neglect, low family income, low parental education, neighborhood crime, psychiatric disorders and the amount of time spent watching television (Johnson, et al., p. 2469). These are important findings because they explain the likelihood that many factors contribute to a youth's tendency toward aggression. The acknowledgment that multiple factors determine a child's aggression level is a departure from many earlier studies that branded television a "magic bullet," capable of infecting youngsters with aggressive thoughts and actions. Indeed, after interviewing more than 200 grade-school students Gentile (2003) labeled media violence a "risk factor" in predicting future aggression. The researchers discovered that media violence, combined with other known risk factors for aggression (e.g., sex, prior aggression, hostile attribution bias), produced a greater predictor of later aggression than any single factor.

Media coverage of the Columbia University study was widespread and Johnson was quoted often as warning parents that more than one hour of viewing a day would increase the likelihood of aggressiveness (e.g., Stroh; Asimov, online; Mestel, p. A1). Detractors, including University of Toronto psychologist Jonathan Freedman, criticized the study and claimed that it proved no causal connection between viewing and aggression (Vedantam, p. A1). Freedman questioned why the researchers didn't report the types of programs the participants watched instead of emphasizing the time spent watching. The study's authors acknowledged that causation could not be proved with this type of study and Johnson later remarked in "Television Viewing and Aggressive Behavior During Adolescence and Adulthood" that causation was only possible through a longitudinal controlled experimental design. "To force people to watch a certain amount of television for a lengthy period of time would not be permissible. It's analogous to research on cigarette smoking... You couldn't force people to smoke a lot to see if they got cancer." Despite the criticism, longitudinal studies are extremely important because of their ability to observe development of human behavior.

Another important method in the media effects research paradigm is cultivation analysis. This field of study was pioneered by University of Pennsylvania scholar George Gerbner and his associates in the 1960s, although the methods are still widely used today. Cultivation studies use a message system analysis method to perform an extensive content analysis of programming content, coding the number and types of violent acts in a program, the characteristics of victims and perpetrators, and the consequences of each violent act. Gerbner's yearly content analysis found that television programming was saturated with violent images with children's cartoons among the most violent (Gerbner, 1976).

The results of the content analysis were then coupled with national surveys measuring the amount and type of television participants watched, as well as their opinions about the world in which they lived. Gerbner and his associates found that the more television people watched, the more they believed the world to be a mean and scary place. In other words, those who were heavy viewers of television, which was dominated by violence, were more likely to believe the world is violent and populated with people who are only out for themselves. People whose primary source of information about the world is filtered through the violence-laden world of television are more likely to fall prey to the cultivation effect and believe that the world is, in fact, dangerous. The effect is not immediate, but rather a longitudinal, unconscious effect that takes place over years of heavy viewing. A study of Miami TV news in the 1990s showed how the cultivation effect gripped many of the city's residents. NBC's news magazine *Dateline NBC* reported that Miami television news programs were resorting to more and more crime news to win the ratings race in a very competitive market. During some newscasts, crime accounted for one-third of all news stories. A survey of local residents found that most thought that crime had risen in Miami when, in fact, it was at a 30-year low. The more television news people reported watching, the more they believed Miami was a dangerous place to live.

The Difficulties Studying Human Behavior

While these studies received much attention from advocacy groups, the medical community and government leaders, the support from the research community has been less enthusiastic. By the late 1970s the controversy over the science of media violence effects research had fully erupted. Because the field was relatively new, the works by scholars such as Bandura, Eron and Gerbner were initially heralded as groundbreaking. However, the methodological techniques used in these studies were often scrutinized by the larger scientific field. Gerbner's team was criticized, for instance, for its definition of violence, or, more importantly, what it did and did not count as violence.

Eron's link between television viewing and adult crime was suspect to many based on his techniques and the small number of research participants that were actually tracked over the three decades. One of the genre's biggest critics, Jonathan Freedman (2002), dismisses most of these studies based on their methodology alone. While it is always prudent to hold researchers to the utmost scientific rigor, Freedman's acerbic style of labeling others' research as "junk science" and "ridiculous" has earned him few points for collegiality. Researchers respond to his criticism by questioning his motives and discrediting his qualifications, pointing out that Freedman himself has never actually conducted any media violence research, and that his most substantive critique was underwritten by the motion picture industry (Huesmann and Taylor, 2003). And so the cycle continues.

The plethora of studies focusing on modeling, cultivation and cognitive effects has been far from conclusive. It seems that for every study that finds a significant link between media violence and aggression there is another that finds no link or a very weak link. For instance, Barry Gunter (1987) and others have found that a person's view of the world is more likely to be influenced by the types of television programs he or she watched rather than the aggregate hours of viewing overall. These studies hypothesize that two people who watch the same amount of television would be affected differently based on the genres of programs they watched. A person who watches mostly violent and crime-oriented programs would be more likely to believe in a dangerous world than the viewer who watched the same amount of television but chose cable programming on home improvement networks instead.

These studies reveal the possibility that viewers actually seek out programs that reinforce their view of the way things are, thereby fueling a viewpoint that may not even be accurate. And it is equally possible that those who exhibit aggressive behavior, for whatever reason, may be more attracted to programming that reinforces these tendencies. Consequently, the child who is neglected at home or bullied at school may seek out violent media (in television, movies and video games) simply because it reinforces the anxiety and anger caused by his abuse. The selection of media reinforces the agitation or anxiety one feels rather than providing a cathartic release. While we are taught that exercise is good for the reduction of stress, violent media may not have the same reductive value. Rather, violent media may provide a welcome environment for these feelings, a safe haven that tolerates, if not fosters aggression. This is especially true for desensitization to violence. A child may scream with glee as he watches a violent explosion in a film kill a villainous character. But imagine the concern if the same child exhibited joy when seeing a player on an opposing baseball team get hurt on the field. Violent media provide a safe environment for expressing our aggressive and violent selves.

Andrea Martinez, a professor at the University of Ottawa, and adviser to the Canadian Radio-Television and Telecommunications Commission, summed up the lack of consensus regarding media effects in three intrinsic constraints of the research (Media Awareness Network, online). First, media violence is hard to operationally define and therefore hard to measure. And there is little consensus among researchers on a definition. Some studies define violence in physical terms while others also include verbal or mental abuse. Some recognize only actual harm as violence while others consider threats as violence. In addition, violence has been defined in various studies as acts perpetrated by man against man, man against animal, animal against man, even acts of God (nature) against man. With such a divergent array of definitions it is nearly impossible to compare findings of one study with another. Martinez's second conclusion is that researchers generally do not agree on the type of relationship established between media violence and aggressive behavior. Some find that media violence leads to aggression while other studies find no causal connection whatsoever. Other studies reveal the presence of many factors but not necessarily a causal connection among them. For instance, some studies reveal that aggressive children watch more violent programming. But the presence of those two qualities does not prove that media cause aggressive behavior. It's possible that these children are simply using media violence to reinforce their aggressive thoughts and actions. The third block to an agreement on media effects is a disagreement over how media violence affects aggression. Researchers have alternately identified media violence as having a psychological, physiological or sociological effect on humans and human behavior. The lack of consensus is more an indication of the difficulty of studying human nature than a blanket condemnation of the validity of media effects research. Martinez concludes that most studies support "a positive, though weak, relationship between exposure to television violence and aggressive behavior" (Media Awareness Network, online).

Ellen Wartella, a co-principal investigator on the National Television Study, summarized perfectly the difficulty in gaining consensus on the effect of media violence on aggression. Even though researchers have conducted thousands of studies, Wartella believed that there are really only three major findings that are close to gaining consensus. In a 1996 lecture she outlined the three findings:

1. Viewers learn the aggressive attitudes and behaviors depicted in the programs they see — known as the learning effect;

2. Prolonged viewing of media violence can lead to emotional desensitization toward real violence and real victims, which may result in callous attitudes and a decreased likelihood that desensitized individuals will take action to help victims when real violence occurs — the desensitization effect;

3. Viewing violence may increase our fear of being victimized, leading toward self-protective behavior and an increased mistrust of others — the fear effect.

Desensitization studies reveal that years of viewing and using violent media may make us less sensitive to real instances of violence and more accepting of violent acts. That is not to say that we welcome violence in our society. But after watching an estimated 11,000 violent acts by the age of 18 we are rarely shocked by violent acts in real life. This desensitization is often so subtle that we do not even recognize its existence. In graduate school I witnessed desensitization firsthand when I was teaching a section on news decision making in a freshman-level media class. To illustrate the complex interaction between news values and ethics, I planned to show the class a video clip of a shooting which they would then decide to include or exclude in a fictional local newscast. I selected a tape of a murder that was captured by a film crew during an interview for a Spanish-language cable network program on the effects of divorce. The exact segment featured a woman being interviewed at the grave of her daughter, who had committed suicide earlier in the year. Shortly after the interview began the woman's ex-husband arrived at the cemetery. Without warning he walked up to her and shot her in the head. The entire incident was captured on film and was featured on the cable network's evening newscast. Broadcast news networks reacted by covering the story as an example of ethical decision making and had to decide themselves if they would feature the clip in their coverage.

I debated for a long time whether to actually use the exercise. Was it exploitive or unfair to subject the students to a murder? After consulting with several colleagues I decided to go ahead with it. I braced myself for the potential fallout from the exercise but believed it to be an important project for these aspiring news reporters and producers. I prepped students the class before and I allowed any students who did not want to participate to do an alternative project. Much to my surprise almost every student showed up for class the next time, and no one asked for the alternative assignment. I soon discovered that all of my worrying was unnecessary. After I showed the two-minute clip there was an audible, if not collective, sigh in the room. One student after another expressed relief that the video was not as bad as I had made it out to be. Some even complained that it didn't look real, that it wasn't nearly as *realistic* as the gory violent acts they had seen in the movies or on television. Most gave vivid accounts of movie violence that was much more graphic than what they had just viewed. They had no problem watching it because it didn't look real. Because the gun used was a small-caliber pistol there was very little blood and the camera crew ducked when they heard the shot so the immediate scene was more frenzied than graphic. Virtually all students said they would show it on a television newscast with no hesitation. When I reminded them repeatedly that this was a *real person* who had really been murdered they didn't understand my concern. It was, they explained, nothing in comparison visually to the explicit depictions of crime they witnessed on most television crime shows every night. I realized that their unwavering attention was on the depiction of the murder, not on the human experience underlying the act. I was so stunned by their responses and their clear desensitization to real-life violence that I never used that exercise again. It wasn't their fault; I just couldn't take it.

The Major Studies and a Potential Solution

At the height of the debate over media violence, the cable television industry agreed to underwrite one of the largest television studies ever done. The National Television Violence Study was an ambitious three-year study encompassing five separate studies conducted by research teams at major research universities across the country. One of the studies involved coding

10,000 hours of television programming in the entertainment, reality and children's genres. The project revealed surprisingly consistent results throughout the three years regarding the amount and context of television violence. Among the findings in the study's final report were the following:

• Across the three years of this study, a steady 60 percent of TV programs contained violence. The typical violent program contains at least six violent incidents per hour. This means that, on average, a viewer watching American television will be exposed to at least six different violent interactions between a perpetrator and a victim per hour. Furthermore, each of these violent interactions can entail multiple acts of aggression. In fact, it is rare for a perpetrator to hit, stab, or shoot someone only once.

• Much of TV violence is still glamorized. Good characters are frequently the perpetrators of violence, and rarely do they show remorse or experience negative repercussions for violence. Another aspect of glamorization is that physical aggression on television is often condoned. For example, more than one-third of violent programs feature "bad" characters who are never punished anywhere in the plot.

• Most violence on television continues to be sanitized. Television often ignores or underestimates what happens to the victims of violence. Over the three-year period, less than 20 percent of the violent programs portray the long-term damage of violence to the victim's family, friends, and community.

• Much of the serious physical aggression on television is still trivialized. Violent behaviors on television often are quite serious in nature. Across the three-year study, more than half of the violent incidents feature physical aggression that would be lethal or incapacitating if it were to occur in real life. In spite of very serious forms of aggression, much of this violence is undermined by humor.

• Very few programs emphasize an antiviolence theme. A program can include violence in a way that is actually educational rather than harmful for the audience.

• Certain depictions can be labeled "high risk" because several plot elements that encourage aggressive attitudes and behaviors are all featured in one scene. These high-risk portrayals involve: 1) a perpetrator who is an attractive role model, 2) violence that seems justified, 3) violence that goes unpunished (no remorse, criticism, or penalty), 4) minimal consequences to the victims, and 5) violence that seems realistic to the viewer.

• The average American preschooler who watches mostly cartoons is exposed to over 500 high-risk portrayals of violence each year. Research indicates that the typical preschooler in the United States watches about 2–3 hours of television a day. Our study shows that there is nearly one high-risk portrayal of violence per hour in cartoons. Extrapolating from this, a preschooler who watches 2 hours of cartoons daily will see over 500 of these hazardous portrayals that encourage aggression each year [Federman, *National Television Violence Executive Summary*, pp. 26–29].

This content analysis showed an alarming increase in television violence, although parents did not seem to be so bothered by it that they stopped their preschoolers from watching 2–3 hours per day. Perhaps this was because parents didn't care, but more likely it was because they didn't really know the extent of violence in programming.

Another major study was conducted at the request of the National Institute of Mental Health in 2000. A panel of academic experts assembled to provide the U.S. Surgeon general with a comprehensive report on the effects of media violence. The panel members were all accomplished media violence researchers who compiled an incredibly detailed and well-documented review of the media violence research. The panel's report concluded that there is compelling evidence that media violence increases the likelihood of aggression, and has both short-term and long-term effects. This is all the more troubling when these results are combined with the NTVS content analysis showing that violence is a staple in television programming, and the surveys that reveal that children and teens are spending more time than ever in front of a television. Although video game research is still in its infancy, the panel wrote that early studies show that violence in video games can be expected to have the same effects as television and films (Anderson, Berkowitz, Donnerstein, Huesmann, Johnson and Linz, p. 93). The degree to which children are affected by media violence is likely to be influenced by other characteristics such as parental supervision and mediation, and identification with violent media characters.

In closing, the panel offered suggestions for improvement in media violence research as well as strategies for mediating the harmful effects of media violence. The panel called for more laboratory and field studies on media violence since these methodologies are well suited for studying the underlying psychological processes of media influence (p. 81). These, coupled with more longitudinal research, would certainly strengthen the body of media violence research and would force leaders in the media industry to take note of the potential harm associated with their products. Perhaps most important of all, the panel encouraged parents to pay more attention to what their children are consuming. Exposure to media violence is just one risk factor underlying aggression. But it is certainly one of the easiest to deal with if parents would simply take a more proactive role in monitoring their child's media exposure (p. 105). Sadly, many do not.

One specific way to combat the harmful effects of media violence is to teach viewers to be critical consumers of media. The campaign for media literacy promotes a proactive, rather than reactive, strategy for mitigating media effects. Media literate consumers are critical users, meaning they can identify, understand and interpret the codes, processes and technologies of media messages. Specifically, media literacy programs aim to provide children and adults with the skills to understand how and why media messages are created, as well as the technical and production values of those messages. With these skills consumers can better judge the relative truth and importance of information embedded in news and entertainment media. The Center for Media Literacy's educational philosophy articulates guiding principles for media literacy which include:

• Media literacy is education for life in a global media world.
• The heart of media literacy is informed inquiry.
• Media literacy is an alternative to censoring, boycotting or blaming the media.

For instance, many movie producers now actively engage in product placement, the practice of featuring real products in a program. No longer does a character drink a generic can of beer, which literally had a label on it that said "beer." Now a brewer may pay large sums of money to get its new product into the hands of a character in a film. Spending even more money will actually get the product written into the script. By doing this the brewer's product gets noticed by millions of viewers without resorting to traditional commercials that many viewers ignore. A media-literate viewer knows that program producers accept product placements as a revenue source and that the show is delivering the viewer to the brewer's product. The character's enjoyment of the beer is not a coincidence, and the viewer can see the placement for the cleverly disguised advertisement it really is.

The same manipulation of viewers takes place with media violence. Television news is a visual medium and therefore has technical considerations that are very different from newspapers and magazines. Sometimes television news programs will feature stories simply because they are visual, with little consideration given to traditional news values such as newsworthiness and localness. For example, a local news station may run a story about a police officer in England who is hit by a car while performing a routine traffic stop because the violent accident was caught on tape by the officer's dashboard camera. That same story will not be included in the local newspaper because it's not considered newsworthy to its local market and the newspaper doesn't place a premium on the visual value of a story. Media-literate viewers know they are being manipulated and that the television news organization only picked the story because it is visual. They'll still watch the program but at least they'll understand why one medium considers this a newsworthy event while another does not.

An Alternative View: Media Violence Is Not Always Harmful

Despite the overwhelming support for the theories supporting a link between media violence and aggressive behavior, several researchers argue that the violence paradigm is misguided. Some scholars do not debate the scientific rigor of various studies; instead they call for a reframing of the entire media violence model. For example, University of Southern California sociologist Karen Sternheimer in her book *It's Not the Media* (2003) identifies several fallacies of media violence effects she believes have persisted over decades of uncontested blame placed on media. Her concern is not with the studies themselves, but with the misinterpretation of the results in news coverage that ultimately condemns media as the cause of all social ills. News reports often use declarative headlines that don't fully report the complexities of media violence research or coverage only includes the results that are highlighted in a press release about the study. A quick search of news articles reporting on Jeffrey Johnson et al.'s March 29, 2002, *Science* journal article yielded numerous doomsday headlines: "TV today, violence tomorrow" in the *San Francisco Sun*; "Study ties television viewing to aggression" in the *Washington Post*: and "Adolescents' TV watching is linked to violence behavior" headlined the *Los Angeles Times* story. None of the reports fully explained the intricate research design involved in the 17-year study or the long list of statistical correlations made between various concepts within the study. Each article included only minimal challenges of Johnson's conclusion although criticism was abundant within the larger research community.

This is not totally the media's fault: it is incredibly difficult to distill such a large and complex research study into a one-page (or less!) article that is accessible to a mainstream newspaper audience. But even this one case illustrates Sternheimer's concern that "most of us do not realize that the research is not nearly as conclusive as we are often told or that the research suggests only a weak connection" (p. 62). The cumulative effect of such news reporting may lead the general public to believe that the media's role in cultivating a violent society is quite strong and well-supported throughout the research community.

Sternheimer also warns that flawed news accounts mislead the public about the true nature of violence in society and about the media's role in causing that violence. She debunks the common cry that media growth has led to an increase in youth violence by citing FBI statistics that show a steady decrease in youth violence. Sternheimer also cites crime statistics that show an increase in adult arrest rates while arrest rates among youths 15 to 17 years old steadily decreased. But she points out, "we seldom hear public outcry about the declining morals of adults," [an outcry that is so often resurrected after a highly publicized incident of juvenile crime] (p. 65). We have a need to explain criminal behavior by children since we are often so shocked when a child kills or assaults another. We simply need to know why it happened so that we can prevent the same circumstances in the future. News reports that simplify media violence studies only serve to energize the campaign for an easy answer to such a complicated behavioral issue.

James T. Hamilton (1998) also tackles some of the oversimplifications of television violence, particularly the claim that networks program a lot of violence because that is what the audience wants. Programmers claim they are merely following a market economy by responding to television consumers' demands for more violent programs. How viewers "demand" more violence is a relatively simple process: A violent program gets high ratings, meaning that a large number of viewers like the show's content and therefore tune in each episode to see more of their favorite action; high ratings catch the attention of other production companies and networks and soon more and more violent shows are added to network schedules; eventually, the majority of television shows are full of violence because networks are merely giving viewers what they want.

The problem is that surveys consistently show that viewers believe there is too much violence in programming and that it likely is responsible for lawlessness and a breakdown of social norms. For example, a 1975 Gallup poll reported that roughly 66 percent of all television viewers polled believed that there was too much violence in programs. Almost twenty years later, in 1993, a Times Mirror Center for People and the Press Poll found an equally cynical audience. Seventy-two percent of all respondents believed there was too much violence in non-news programming, with 47 percent overall ranking violence as "very harmful" to society. Interestingly, 91 percent of women 50 years old and above responded that there was too much violence on television while men 18–34 offered the least agreement (54 percent) with that statement. In every demographic (male–female, age brackets 18–34, 35–49, 50+) a majority agreed that there was too much violence on television. This would seem to debunk the theory that programmers are merely giving viewers what they want because a clear majority of viewers agree that there is too much violence in programming.

Looking at the responses closely, Hamilton points out that younger viewers, especially those who are characterized as heavy users (4+ hours per day), reported the least concern about media violence. Men 18–34 were least likely to believe that TV violence impacts society negatively, followed by males 35–49 and females 18–34. Given that advertisers covet the all-important 18–49 demographic, and those viewers are also less likely to believe that television violence is a major cause of lawlessness, there is less risk involved in promoting products on shows with violence (p. 73). While polls show that it is not true that audiences want more violence, there is less risk of angering viewers when running ads during violent shows that appeal to younger demographics.

W. James Potter brings a similar approach to the media violence debate by addressing public misconceptions surrounding media violence. In his 2003 book *The 11 Myths of Media Violence*, Potter takes on the established, yet misguided, societal views that have pervaded the public debate about media violence for decades. He carefully dissects the scientific data to dismiss such long-held notions that violence in the media does not affect me, but others are at high risk (Myth 1); there is too much violence on television (Myth 4); and that reducing the amount of violence in the media will solve the problem (Myth 8). The problem, according to Potter, is not merely the frequency of media violence but how we as consumers use it and interpret it. Unrealistic portrayals of violence have a higher potential for negative effects on the audience than those which show the consequences of violence in more realistic terms.

Despite Potter's attention to dispelling popular media violence myths, he does not let the media off the hook completely. He rejects the argument that producers of violent media are merely giving the audience what it wants because an "equally important function of businesses, that is, media, [is to] also shape demand. Businesses are not simply passive receptors to demand; they are also actively creating and reinforcing that demand" (p. 115). Film production companies and television networks create a buzz about new products the same way a fast-food restaurant chain markets a new product to create consumer interest. The successful advertising campaign that brings the masses in for a new hamburger (that we probably really don't need) can be equally as effective at delivering audiences to an action-packed murder thriller. According to Potter (2003), it is unrealistic to believe that audiences are demanding more violent films. It's more likely that we are responding to other elements of the film that attract us (e.g., actors, special effects, plot) or we just want to see the latest blockbuster film.

> Another reason for the complexity (of media violence) is that attraction is not determined by violence alone. Factors such as interesting plots, popular actors, exotic locations, fancy clothes and costumes, intriguing sound tracks and so forth all contribute to attractiveness. When all these elements work together along with violence, audience members feel pleasure, and the size of the audience is likely to be large. But when the violence appears in an

unattractive context, it does not foster pleasure, and the audience is likely to be small. So the key to understanding audience size is the content's ability to evoke pleasure — not how much violence appears in the content [p. 119].

Potter's concepts are all the more compelling given his long career as a respected researcher of media violence, including his role as a principal investigator on the National Television Violence Study. Potter brings his practical research experience to the larger philosophical and political debates over media violence while challenging the research community to improve the rigor and scope of effects research. Potter (2003) acknowledges that the focus of most studies is potentially limiting the efficacy of the research paradigm. In the early years of media effects it is understandable that scholars disagreed over such things as the definition of media violence or what counted as a behavioral effect from media violence. But today the "overlap in definitions is substantial. When researchers add unique elements to their own definitions of violence, this allows them to determine how the widening (or narrowing) of the definition affects the subsequent counts of how much violence appears in the media" (p. 86).

One scholar often found in the middle of these methodological arguments is Jib Fowles, an outspoken critic of media violence research. Fowles (1999) has often been a self-professed "odd man out" who has endured much criticism from other social science researchers and child advocacy groups (p. ix). Fowles himself is particularly critical of the methodology used in many media violence studies and has challenged the general acceptance of findings based on these so-called faulty studies. He stands with many other critics of cultivation studies, claiming that Gerbner and his associates failed to properly control for intervening variables that might impact a person's amount of viewing, a major variable in cultivation's causal link between media violence and fearfulness (p. 123). Many other researchers have shown that when these variables (e.g., city crime rates, socioeconomic class, age and gender) are accounted for, television violence's sole impact on cultivation is weak.

The research community's willingness to accept and promote flawed research is another of Fowles' criticisms. He explains the acceptance of dubious findings by news media, advocacy groups, and the general public as a result of the need to find a simple explanation for the often unexplainable act of violence. Instead of addressing the complex host of factors that lead to a rash of school shootings or teen suicides, politicians and pundits find it easier to attribute all of society's ills to a single, yet pervasive, cause, television. Fowles explains that television is the perfect "whipping boy" for three primary reasons:

> First, it is a large target present in one form or another in every household every evening and every weekend. It is not elusive. Second, if one puts on blinders, there might seem to be some correspondence between the mayhem on the television screen and aggression in the palpable, living mode. Both televised entertainment and the real world deal in hostilities. Third, and most signally, television violence performs ideally as a whipping boy because the issue attracts no supporters. Virtually no one speaks out in defense of television violence — the very idea seems silly to most... Even television industry representatives, whose companies' well-being absolutely depends on the delivery of animosities in symbolic form, rarely get beyond conciliatory statements when compelled to address the matter [pp. 54–55].

Fowles is also a believer in the cathartic effect of media violence, which argues that fantasy violence in media can act as an agent for releasing tension and aggression. Because of this media actually perform an important function in society because they act as an escape valve for anger and aggression. While most believe the cathartic effect of media is minimal, there is anecdotal evidence in our society that anger is used as a motivation device in sports and athletics. During a recent classroom discussion on media violence, one of my students recounted how her softball coach encouraged players to imagine the face of an enemy or someone they disliked on the ball. That way they would be motivated to concentrate and hit harder, and they would feel better for beating that person with their hit. Other athletes in the class told of similar discussions with their coaches. One famous business guru says that he goes to the driving range to whack his frustration when a business deal goes wrong. If we use aggression as both a motivational tool in athletics and a way to relieve pressure after a stressful day, could violent media also provide a cathartic effect in our lives? Why isn't it possible to relieve some aggression with a fierce gunfight in a video game?

In *Killing Monsters* (2002), comic book author-turned scholar Gerard Jones makes a similar argument that fantasy and make-believe violence are an essential part of childhood. Through these, Jones says, children work through their own fears and difficulties and conquer the insecurities that naturally arise in maturing young adults. Through fantasy games, whether it's realistic first-person shooter video games or a neighborhood game of "war," children act out their need for control and test their strategies for dealing with conflict in a safe, nonthreatening environment. Jones believes that children's experiences with violence and fantasy are more about their own development of self than about modeling violent behaviors and aggression. It is a mistake to lump all children together when discussing the concerns over media violence as if every player reacts, and interacts, with a game in the same manner.

To illustrate this point Jones writes about Jimmy, an eighth grader living with his grandmother after being removed from his mother's house because she had a drug problem. Jimmy had asthma and dyslexia and performed poorly in school. All of this left him with many fears and insecurities. To cope, Jimmy became the class clown, finding that humor and the attention it brought helped him feel less isolated and different. In junior high school, Jimmy's grandmother reported that he discovered first-person shooter games and became an avid fan of *Doom* and *Quake*. His grandmother believed the games had a calming effect on him, reporting that he was more confident after playing them. But school officials were concerned when they discovered Jimmy's passion for these games. School officials expressed their concerns and warned his grandmother that he should stop before it caused him to do something serious. Even worse, two teachers and the principal told Jimmy on separate occasions that the video games would have horrible effects on him, desensitizing him to real violence and making him believe that he could kill without consequence. In short, they previewed for him the monster he would become if he kept playing the video games.

Jimmy's grandmother told Jones that this only compounded Jimmy's worries because "instead of helping him with his fears, they send a message that they're afraid of him — and they make him even more afraid of himself" (p. 18). The grandmother encouraged his teachers to get past the generalizations about violent video games and instead talk to him about why he liked the games and what he was getting from them. When Jimmy was able to articulate what he got from playing these games, the teachers' concerns lessened. Most importantly, they learned to see him as an active participant in media rather than a passive receiver of all the horrible effects they feared. Jones points out that with no other media theme do we apply this standard of uniformity and pervasiveness. Like a magic bullet, we expect that all children who play first-person shooter games will be affected in an identical manner and infused with uniform negative consequences.

In our anxiety to understand and control real-life violence, we've tried to reduce our children's relationships with their fantasies of combat and destruction to vast generalizations that we would never dream of applying to their fantasies about love and family and discovery and adventure. We don't usually ask whether game shows predispose our children to greed, or whether love songs increase the likelihood of getting stuck in bad relationships. But when aggression is the topic, we try to puree a million games and dreams and life stories into statistical studies. We ask absurdly sweeping questions like, "What is the effect of media violence on children?" as if violence were a single, simple phenomenon of which sandbox play-fights and mass murder were mere variations, as if the evening news and *Reservoir Dogs* and Daffy Duck were indistinguishable [p. 19].

Jones makes a very good point that our society ascribes different degrees of influence to different media. There is no singular effect of first-person shooter games, but it is still difficult for many to accept that any game that involves shooting human characters can ever be a positive form of entertainment. Does shooting prostitutes and police officers as players do in a popular video game really help children test their conflict resolution skills? Or can gunning down a scary creature be enough to satisfy a child's need for control? Many parents report that they don't allow any shooter games that have life-like human characters, only those with monsters or alien life forms. They just can't get behind the notion that killing humans for entertainment is a positive value to teach their children.

New Approaches to Violence Research

There is a new chorus of voices from the medical and academic fields that think we have the whole thing wrong. These scholars argue that it's not the content of media that is the main problem, but the mere act of engaging with media for hours at a time that should be our top concern. Renowned child psychologist Marie Winn writes in *The Plug-in Drug* (2002) that the overwhelming amount of research and public criticism aimed at the content of media is misplaced. Winn argues that we should focus our attention on the fact that children spend so much time watching television or playing video games, thereby reducing their involvement in other activities that would better stimulate their minds and their social interactions with others.

What are the effects upon the developing human organism of spending such a significant proportion of each day engaged in this particular activity (television)? How does television affect a child's language development, for instance? Creativity? ... How does watching television for several hours a day affect the child's ability to form human relationships? What happens to the family life as a result of family members' involvement with television? [Winn, pp. 4–5].

Winn's questions underscore the developmental concerns that have nothing to do with the content of the media. It stands to reason that any amount of time in front of a television or playing a video game takes time away from other activities. Medical associations, for example, blame television and video games for childhood obesity. The mere passivity of television and video game playing severely reduces the physical exercise that we can get with more vigorous activities. In 1996 The American Medical Association developed the *Physician's Guide to Media Violence* that suggests parents keep *screen time* (television, Internet and video games) to only 1–2 hours per day (p. 21). Reading specialists and child development experts also worry that reading and language skills are negatively impacted by the lack of time spent reading in favor of watching television or playing video games. In *Endangered Minds* (1990) psychologist Jane N. Healy writes that the time spent with media is replacing family conversation and reading, activities that allow a parent to help children develop language and reading skills. Children have little opportunity to develop strong problem-solving skills if they engage primarily in the passive activity of television viewing (p. 196).

If video games and television make us fat they apparently do little for the exercise of our brains either. While cognitive and neurological research into media is still in the early stages, there is support for the idea that television affects brain development, especially the left hemisphere functions of language comprehension and development, logic, and analytical reasoning. Healy warns that "abilities to sustain attention independently, stick to problems actively, listen intelligently, read with understanding, and use language effectively may be particularly at risk" (p. 216). The frenetic images, music, graphics, fast edits and flashes of color populating today's electronic media stimulate the brain reactively rather than analytically. The brain is noting these flashes of color or jump cuts because they scare us or jar our sensory perceptions.

In popular culture this complex neurophysiologic reaction is commonly reflected in complaints that television and video games cause our children to have short attention spans and to be too impatient in play and in learning. A child who is routinely stimulated, if not overstimulated, by media will hardly be engaged by a book or by the endless possibilities of his own imagination. It's not because children are stupid or that they necessarily have short attention spans; it's because reading and imaginative fantasy play just aren't as neurologically stimulating as television and video games. Older viewers complained when television news channels added a moving crawl of news snippets at the bottom of the screen. Critics complained that it was distracting and difficult to comprehend moving written and audio information at the same time. But news officials claimed they were merely responding to the younger demographic who found television news boring. Any adult over 30 has watched as their local television weathercast evolved from using a plain map with simple icons into a choreographed maze of whirling graphics, flipping maps and zooming satellite views. There's no doubt that the day's temperature is not affected by its presentation, but it does grab one's attention when it comes flying onto the television screen.

Television viewing does not appear to improve our reasoning and analytic skills either. Watching television requires virtually no interaction by viewers and little or no analytic skills because most programs follow carefully crafted programming formats that have been found to fulfill viewers' expectation. For example, a typical episodic crime drama follows a predictable arc: a dead body is discovered; law enforcement investigates the crime scene; clues are pieced together to determine the nature of the crime and possible suspects; a leading suspect turns out not to be the murderer; a sudden discovery leads to the real killer, who is apprehended and dispatched for justice all within the 48–51 minutes of actual show time. The formulaic nature of television programming is not the result of lazy or uninspired television writers as much as it is a response to viewer demand. If a crime show diverges from this formula, such as leaving the crime unsolved or the perpetrator unidentified, viewers typically experience discomfort with the show. This happens because the plot runs counter to our expectations and beliefs of how a crime show should progress. Consequently, few television shows of any genre stray far from these program formulas. As viewers, we are relatively content being spoon-fed similar plotlines with similar resolutions week after week. Perhaps that is why many of us enjoy watching television at the end of a long day. All we have to do is sit in front of the television while the images, sounds and action come to us. We do nothing but absorb it and even that we can typically do without giving the program our undivided attention. Our brains are stimulated by the action but not challenged because the plot is familiar and easy to follow.

The pursuit of mindless entertainment in lieu of stimulating, mind-challenging information is probably okay for the adult looking to unwind after an exhausting day at work. But what are the implications for young children? Especially those whom scholars estimate spend upwards of six hours a day in front of a television or video game. Since so much of early learning is predicated on experimentation and knowledge gained through trial and error (e.g., a hot stove will burn your fingers), what happens to the child who is fed a daily dose of predictable, noninteractive media? How are problem-solving skills affected if so little reasoning is required for television viewing? Healy warns that heavy viewing in early childhood may create passive learners with little patience for reasoning or follow-through. Dr. Jennings Bryant, a famed communication scholar, recounted these very findings from his research on young television viewers.

> One thing that we know is that it (television) reduces vigilance [the ability to remain actively focused on a task]. If they watch lots of fast-paced programs then we give them things to do afterward such as reading or solving complex puzzles, their stick-to-it-iveness is diminished; they're not as willing to stay with the task. Over time, with lots of viewing, you're going to have less vigilant children [Healy, p. 201].

Researchers often say that fast-paced television and video games actually make us *more* adept at processing lots of information at once. Bryant's comments aren't about multitasking but rather about processing complex information that is found in common, everyday situations. It's one thing to be able to take in information from a number of sources simultaneously and another to process all or part of it in order to assess a problem and solve it quickly.

Another area that researchers are looking at is the role media play in the contemporary family. During a recent car trip with several friends (all in our early forties), we reminisced about our favorite television shows growing up. With some collective jarring of the memory we were, for example, able to piece together the Saturday night comedy lineup on CBS in the early 1970s. For us, the act of watching television on Saturday night was a family event, planned around the collective activity of watching this lineup of television shows. But my ten years of teaching college media courses have provided ample anecdotal evidence of a dramatic shift away from this ritual of television as family event. I'm typically met with blank stares (and even some giggles) when I teach about the communal nature of early radio and television, a practice so famously portrayed in the depression-era drama *The Waltons*. Most of my students report that they rarely watched a program with their family and many even had a television in their bedrooms. Instead of having to decide as a family what to watch, many of today's youth simply retreat to the privacy of their own rooms to watch a favorite program without the interruption, or company, of others. What for many in my generation was a family activity is now a solitary, highly individualized activity. That is not to say that communal viewing has disappeared altogether, but certainly the days of the single-television household, where parents and children came together to watch, are no longer the norm. In homes where television and video game players are used as tools to keep young children preoccupied while busy parents attend to meals or other household chores, the hours of unattended and unmediated viewing can be a powerful educational force. Many studies report that children between 2 and 11 spend from 18 to 28 hours per week watching television, more time than some spend in class or doing homework. This leads to an undeniable decrease in the amount of time spent interacting in family activities that can motivate both language and reading skills.

Faced with growing evidence that television and video games aren't particularly healthy activities, there is good reason to abandon, or at least diminish, the emphasis on improving the content of these media. While few would argue that graphic violence and explicit sex are positive, these issues may not be the most dangerous. The real issues to be dealt with are the physiological and cognitive harms associated with the sheer amount of time children spend watching television and playing video games. The continued vigilance over media content ignores the very basic dangers inherent in hours of media use each day. Improving the content will in no way address these inherent dangers. In fact, cleaning up television and video games may have the unintended effect of making each a more attractive electronic babysitter for parents.

THREE

Media Regulation

Faced with the knowledge that media violence, in all forms, is at least a contributing risk factor for aggression, the next question is, what can and should be done to reduce the risk to the general public? While some argue that we should ban all forms of violence because they are harmful to children, the law on this matter is less clear-cut. All media are fully protected from government censorship by the First Amendment of the U.S. Constitution. In addition, the broadcast media are further sheltered from content regulation by Section 315 of the Communications Act. There are two valid competing interests in the debate of regulation of violent media. The contest pits the well-intentioned effort to protect children from potentially harmful violent media versus media content that is protected from censorship by the First Amendment.

In general, the First Amendment protects all expression, even entertainment media such as video games, movies, music, and television programs. Although free expression is typically given a preferred position of protection, the First Amendment is not absolute. Modern society does not condone expressions that are potentially harmful to members of society, especially children. For example, obscene speech and child pornography are not protected in any medium because both are void of any socially redeeming value and are inherently harmful to society. The courts have also ruled that other forms of expression such as libel, fraudulent advertising and solicitation of a crime fall outside the scope of First Amendment protection.

Content Regulation

Aside from the above categories of unprotected speech, there are other times that speech may be restricted. A series of important Supreme Court rulings determined that speech or expression that by its very nature may bring about harm to society may be prohibited. In *Schenck v. United States* (1919) the court ruled that speech that presents a clear and present danger to the public's safety is not protected by the First Amendment. Historically this standard was applied to political speech that promoted the overthrow of the government or violence based on ideology. But later the clear-and-present danger doctrine was tested by a number of nonpolitical expressions and various forms of media. In 1927, Justice Louis Brandeis attempted to model a practical definition of what constituted a clear and present danger in *Whitney v. California* (1927). Brandeis voted with the majority to uphold the criminal syndicalism conviction of a woman who belonged to the Communist Labor Party and attended its meetings. Although Brandeis voted with the majority on technical grounds, he condemned the censorship of speech and thought imposed by the verdict. In his concurring opinion Brandeis wrote what some legal scholars consider to be one of the most eloquent defenses of free speech ever written.

> Fear of serious injury cannot alone justify suppression of free speech and assembly. Men feared witches and burned women. It is the function of speech to free men from the bondage of irrational fears. To justify suppression of free speech there must be reasonable ground to fear that serious evil will result if free speech is practiced. There must be reasonable ground to believe that the danger apprehended is imminent. There must be reasonable ground to believe that the evil to be prevented is a serious one. Every denunciation of existing law tends in some measure to increase the probability that there will be violation of it. Condonation of a breach enhances the probability. Expressions of approval add to the probability. Propagation of the criminal state of mind by teaching syndicalism increases it. Advocacy of lawbreaking heightens it still further. But even advocacy of violation, however reprehensible morally, is not a justification for denying free speech where the advocacy falls short of incitement and there is nothing to indicate that the advocacy would be immediately acted on. The wide difference between advocacy and incitement, between preparation and attempt, between assembling and conspiracy, must be borne in mind. In order to support a finding of clear and present danger it must be shown either that immediate serious violence was to be expected or was advocated, or that the past conduct furnished reason to believe that such advocacy was then contemplated [p. 377].

The clear-and-present danger test remained difficult to apply in the rapidly changing world of communications. While freedom of speech was historically linked to political expression, the growth of ideological groups tested the limits of the First Amendment. Hate groups, antiwar protesters, and members of different religions all tested the boundaries of the clear-and-present danger test. Forty years after *Whitney* the Supreme Court recognized the need to set a strict definition of dangerous speech. In *Brandenburg v. Ohio* (1969) the court ruled that a KKK leader could not be prosecuted for incitement under an Ohio criminal syndicalism statute. The leader presided over a Klan meeting at which he lashed out at the typical Klan targets — blacks and Jews — in his speech. Against a backdrop of a burning cross and Klansmen armed with guns, the leader also indicated that the group was planning future rallies that had the potential for violence. The leader's speech was recorded by a television news crew that he had invited to attend the event. The text of his speech outlined the group's future plans:

> This is an organizer's meeting. We have quite a few members here today which are — we have hundreds, hundreds of members throughout the State of Ohio... The Klan has more members in the state of Ohio than does any other organization. We're not a revengent (sic) organization, but if our President, our Congress, our Supreme Court, continues to suppress the white, Caucasian race, it's possible that there might have to be some revengence taken.
>
> We are marching on Congress Fourth of July, four thousand strong. From there we are dividing into two groups, one group to march on St. Augustine, Florida, and the other group to march into Mississippi. Thank You [pp. 444, 447].

The Supreme Court ruled that the First Amendment protected speech unless the advocacy was directed at inciting or producing imminent lawless action and that it was likely to incite or produce that action (p. 444). The KKK leader's speech was inflammatory, but because it did not incite imminent lawlessness it was ruled to be protected speech. *Brandenburg* became the test by which all laws and ordinances restricting speech were judged. While the court ruled that only speech that was likely to bring about imminent lawless behavior could be banned or punished, it did not offer much guidance on exactly what constituted *imminent*. Did it mean immediate? In the near future? Tomorrow or later today? Or was the question really about the likelihood of harm being caused? These issues were at the forefront of some key cases testing the culpability of potentially harmful media.

Weirum et al. v. RKO General (1975) involved the death of a Los Angeles driver because a teenager was participating in a radio station's scavenger hunt. On July 16, 1970, Los Angeles radio station KHJ held a contest in which listeners were given clues to find Donald Steele Revert, known on-air as "The Real Don Steele." Steele was a KHJ disc jockey who was driving around the metropolitan area. Steele would stop at different locations and the first listener to find him and complete a task (e.g., answer a trivia question) would win a small cash prize and be interviewed on the air. Steele gave occasional clues throughout the contest to help listeners find him. While his updates did not explicitly encourage listeners to drive in an unsafe manner, there was a lighthearted acknowledgment that listeners would race to be the first one to arrive at the location:

> 9:30 and The Real Don Steele is back on his feet again with some money and he is headed for the Valley. Thought I would give you a warning so that you can get your kids out of the street.... The Real Don Steele is out driving on — could be in your neighborhood at any time and he's got bread to spread, so be on the lookout for him.... The Real Don Steele is moving into Canoga Park — so be on the lookout for him. I'll tell you what will happen if you get to The Real Don Steele. He's got twenty-five dollars to give away if you can get it ... and baby, all signed and sealed and delivered and wrapped up....
>
> 10:54: The Real Don Steele is in the Valley near the intersection of Topanga and Roscoe Boulevard, right by the Loew's Holiday Theater — you know where that is at, and he's standing there with a little money he would like to give away to the first person to arrive and tell him what type car I helped Robert W. Morgan give away yesterday morning at KHJ. What was the make of the car. If you know that, split. Intersection of Topanga and Roscoe Boulevard — right nearby the Loew's Holiday Theater — you will find The Real Don Steele. Tell him and pick up the bread.
>
> 11:13: The Real Don Steele with bread is heading for Thousand Oaks to give it away. Keep listening to KHJ... The Real Don Steele out on the highway with bread to give away — be on the lookout, he may stop in Thousand Oaks and may stop along the way... Looks like it may be a good stop Steele — drop some bread to those folks [pp. 40–41].

Two teenagers, in separate cars, followed Steele for a while. When they were not the first to find him at the Canoga Park location they both decided to follow Steele's car as he proceeded to the next location. The teens drove at speeds up to 80 m.p.h. to follow Steele to the next location. In the process of exiting the freeway one of the teens hit another car, which overturned, killing the driver. The driver's family sued the radio station and the drivers for wrongful death.

The California Supreme Court, and later an appellate court, upheld a judgment against the radio station stating that it should have foreseen that its contest would lead to lawless behavior. The court also ruled that the station was no less culpable simply because the accident was caused by third parties, rather than by their own employee. The court ruled that, but for the station's contest, the teens would not have been recklessly pursuing the DJ and would not have caused an accident that killed another driver. That made the station at least partially responsible for the driver's death (p. 43).

In *Rice v. Paladin* (1997) the courts also found that a book with step-by-step instructions for committing murder was outside the scope of First Amendment protection. The book *Hit Man: A Technical Manual for Independent Contractors* detailed methods for killing people and then destroying evidence. In 1993, James Perry used the book's advice to murder Mildred Horn, her quadriplegic son and his nurse (p. 239). Perry committed the murders for Horn's ex-husband who wished to inherit a $2 million settlement from the accident that paralyzed his son. Perry's acts resembled several of the methods outlined in the book and he admitted using the book for guidance. In a very strange turn of events, the publisher of the book later admitted that he knew it was likely the book would be used for actual murders. The publisher apparently made these statements believing the book's contents were safely within First Amendment protection. That belief turned out to be wrong.

Even though the book included several disclaimers, the courts ruled that the detailed content went beyond mere advocacy of murder and amounted to a teaching manual for murder. As such, the book was not protected speech and the publisher did assume a civil liability for the murders. The court also distanced the book from other media products that have been accused of causing copycat crimes by emphasizing the truly unique circumstances of this case. The 4th U.S. Court of Appeals wrote:

> In the "copycat" context, it will presumably never be the case that the broadcaster or publisher actually intends, through its description or depiction, to assist another or others in the commission of violent crime; rather, the information for the dissemination of which liability is sought to be imposed will actually have been misused vis-à-vis the use intended, not, as here, used

precisely as intended. It would be difficult to overstate the significance of this difference insofar as the potential liability to which the media might be exposed by our decision herein is concerned. And, perhaps most importantly, there will almost never be evidence proffered from which a jury even could reasonably conclude that the producer or publisher possessed the actual intent to assist criminal activity.... Moreover, in contrast to the case before us, in virtually every "copycat" case, there will be lacking in the speech itself any basis for a permissible inference that the "speaker" intended to assist and facilitate the criminal conduct described or depicted. Of course, with few, if any, exceptions, the speech which gives rise to the copycat crime will not directly and affirmatively promote the criminal conduct, even if, in some circumstances, it incidentally glamorizes and thereby indirectly promotes such conduct [pp. 265–266].

The case was eventually remanded back to the U.S. District Court although Paladin ultimately settled out of court with the victims' families.

The courts' clarification of incitement and foreseeability was important in distinguishing these cases from ones in which a defendant merely claimed that they were inspired to lawlessness by a media product. Inspiration and incitement are very different conditions and only expression that actually incites users to criminal behavior may be actionable in the courts.

Time, Place and Manner Restrictions

Although most media products are protected by the First Amendment, there is the potential for harm from mature or violent content. These products can't be banned but it is possible to impose time, place and manner restrictions on media. These restrictions do not ban the media product or censor the content but they do restrict access for those who are most likely to be harmed by the product. In most cases that would be children. All time, place and manner restrictions (TPM) must meet four conditions in order to be constitutional. First, the TPM restriction must be content neutral. That means that all restrictions must be applied equally and may not be based on viewpoint or ideology. For instance, in the interest of public safety a city may require groups wanting to stage a protest to apply for a permit in advance. What it may not do is then award or deny a permit based on the ideology or political viewpoint of the group. Second, any time, place and manner restriction may not ban speech altogether. It may restrict the manner in which a protest may take place (e.g., between certain hours, with or without a loud speaker, confined to a specific location) but it cannot ban the protest if the group receives a permit and acts in a lawful manner. Third, government must have a substantial reason for wanting to restrict speech. In the example of protests, a city's responsibility to protect public safety is certainly an important rationale for restricting public protests. Finally, all restrictions must be narrowly tailored as to advance the government's rationale in the least restrictive manner possible. If the city is concerned that protests may endanger or inconvenience its citizens, it can impose the above-mentioned restrictions to protect everyone's welfare. It can't simply ban all protests. That would certainly attain the goal but it would also be more burdensome than needed to protect its citizens.

Among the most common examples of time, place, and manner restrictions are those imposed on pornographic material. In this country we do not ban pornography altogether; we simply restrict access of minors who may not be mature enough to handle explicit representations of nudity and sexual relations. Consequently, there are age restrictions to buy or rent pornographic films, age restrictions to buy pornographic magazines, and display restrictions requiring magazine covers to be obscured or placed out of public view. Pornography is still available for consenting adults to enjoy without imposing sexually mature themes on children and unsuspecting adults.

Broadcasting, for instance, is a unique medium with special legal restrictions. Because public airwaves are used to transmit the broadcast signal, the industry has a special responsibility to operate in the best interest of the public. Broadcast stations are private enterprises that rely on public property to transmit their signal and they lease their frequency through the licensing process. Congress mandated that because of this unique relationship broadcasters must operate their stations in a manner that serves the public's interest, convenience, and necessity, dubbed PICON. Of course, in today's media environment few consumers make a clear distinction between broadcast and cable television networks. Since so many people get their local broadcast stations as part of a cable or satellite subscription, the distinction between broadcast television and cable is becoming less significant in the consumer's mind. The distinction is probably easier with radio because satellite radio is still relatively new and most people continue to get "free" radio with a simple tuner.

Content regulation of media is essentially based on access. The easier it is to get a medium (e.g., broadcast radio and television), the more its content is regulated. Likewise, the harder it is to get a medium (e.g., satellite radio and pay-per-view television), the less the content is regulated. The logic is simple: the more effort you need to get access to a media product the less you need to be protected from its content. For instance, in order to watch a pornographic film in your home, you need to go through several steps. You have to subscribe to basic cable and to an upper tier of cable that includes pay-per-view. Then you have to order the specific pornographic film and confirm that order. That's a lot of effort and a significant investment of time, dollars and equipment just to be able to view that film. You can even block access to those channels so that no one can order the films without entering a password first. In contrast, broadcast television and radio are easy media to get and it is even easier to stumble upon programming that you might find objectionable. Channel surfing and scrolling the dial are routine practices that make it easy for a child to accidentally see or hear something that is inappropriate. Most concern, of course, is not with adults, but with children and teens who might be exposed to material that is simply too mature for them.

Media Ratings Systems

Despite content regulation and the use of time, place and manner restrictions, many critics still believe that the level of violence in media has reached unacceptable levels. Oddly, the complaints of parents today are very similar to those protesting the "Ether Bogeyman" in the 1930s. Surveys show that parents believe that today's entertainment media is saturated with sex, violence and explicit language that makes it unacceptable for children. Parents wanting to make informed decisions about their child's media use often feel that they do not have enough information about the content of movies, music and video games. Ironically, assistance for parents comes from the media industries themselves, but only after a great deal of pressure was exerted by government regulators. For example, the Motion Picture Association of America developed a ratings system in 1966 as a response to threats of impending government censorship of movies. The self-regulatory measure was designed to protect a filmmaker's artistic freedom but also provide parents with a general description of the film's content and theme.

Motion Picture Ratings

G   General audiences
PG   parental guidance; for mature audiences
PG-13   parental guidance advised for children under 13
         years old
R   restricted; no one under 17 years old admitted unless
         accompanied by an adult
NC-17   no children under 17 allowed

[Source: Motion Picture Association of America]

The ratings are age-based with no explanation about the content of the film. Critics complain that the ratings are antiquated, having changed very little in the past forty years. A 2004 Harvard School of Public Health study also discovered that a "ratings creep" over recent years allowed much more violence into films without a change in rating (Oldenburg, online). For instance, the original *Santa Clause* movie was released in 1994 with a PG rating while the 2002 sequel was released with comparable violence and sexual situations but only a G rating. The researchers suggested this illustrates a loosening of the standards for assigning ratings. Former MPAA President Jack Valenti did not dispute that ratings creep but explained that it was merely a result of society's changing standards of acceptability. That may be true, but parents have no way of knowing which moral compass the MPAA review board is using from week to week. Enforcement has also been a problem with the movie ratings. A 2003 undercover operation by the Federal Trade Commission found that 36 percent of unaccompanied teenagers under 17 were able to buy a ticket to an R-rated film ("Results of nationwide undercover survey released," online). Although the number is down about 10 percent from the previous year, it is obvious that many theatre chains still are not enforcing the MPAA's age restrictions.

Music Ratings

In a similar attempt to avoid government-imposed sanctions, a ratings system was "voluntarily" adopted by the music industry. In 1985, Tipper Gore led a controversial campaign by the Parents Music Resource Center (PRMC) that demanded warning labels on music records and CDs that contained sexually explicit and violent lyrics. Amid cries of censorship, the Recording Industry Association of America (RIAA) worked with PRMC and the National Parent Teacher Association in 1990 to establish a standard warning label to be displayed on any music that contains explicit depictions of violence, sex or drug use. The small label simply states *Parental Advisory: Explicit Content,* and must be displayed in a permanent form on the CD cover. The parental advisory must also be listed by an album's or individual song's description on a music download site. All advertising for music with a parental advisory label must also include that information. Typically this is done by printing the *Parental Advisory Label* in the ad. If, however, the cover depicted in the ad is so small that the label is unreadable, the RIAA suggests including the words *"Explicit Content— Parental Advisory"* to warn consumers of the explicit lyrics. The decision to label an artist's music is made by the music label distributing the artist's songs. Although the RIAA does not have explicit rules as to what must be labeled it does offer the following guidelines:

The Recording Industry Association of America (RIAA) requires that all music with sexually explicit or violent lyrics be labeled with a warning sticker for parents.

• Whether, in light of contemporary cultural morals and standards and the choices and views of individual parents, the recording might be one that parents may not want their child to listen to.

• Context is obviously important: some words, phrases, sounds, or descriptions might be offensive to parents if spotlighted or emphasized, but might not offend if merely part of the background or not a meaningful part of the lyrics.

• The context of the artist performing the material, as well as the expectations of the artist's audience, is also important. In addition to profanity, "depictions of violence, sex, or substance abuse" must be considered when making a determination regarding the application of the *Parental Advisory Label.*

• Lyrics are often susceptible to varying interpretations. Words can have different meanings. Also, words cannot be viewed in isolation from the music that accompanies them. Lyrics when accompanied by loud and raucous music can be perceived differently than the same lyrics when accompanied by soft and soothing music.

• Labeling is not a science; it requires sensitivity and common sense. Context, frequency, and emphasis are obviously important; isolated or unintelligible references to certain material might be insufficient to warrant application of the label.

These guidelines apply to the case of a single track commercially released as well as to full albums (whether released in the form of a CD, cassette or any other configuration).

The RIAA works with the National Association of Recording Merchandisers (NARM) to educate retailers about the warning labels, but each retailer is free to develop in-store policies regarding the sale of labeled music. For instance, many retailers claim they don't sell music containing the *Parental Advisory Label* to anyone under 18, but federal investigators found compliance to be miserable. A report released by the Federal Trade Commission found that 83 percent of teenage secret shoppers (undercover shoppers under the age of 18) were able to buy music with the explicit label and only 21 percent of retailers posted any information about the RIAA's warning system. Even worse, only 13 percent of the secret shoppers were even asked their age when they attempted to buy explicit music

(Federal Trade Commission, "Results of nationwide undercover survey released," p. 2).

Some retailers, including Wal-Mart, refuse to sell any music with the warning label. Many artists bemoan Wal-Mart's policy as a form of censorship because the retailer refuses to sell their creative product. This limits the artists' artistic freedom, and their sales, since the public's access to their product is restricted. For many music labels the "Wal-Mart Effect" is more about economics than censorship. In many communities Wal-Mart is a major retailer of music, so a decision not to carry music with a parental warning severely limits the community's access to that music. One record company executive who was interviewed for a PBS program on the music industry estimated that Wal-Mart accounted for 20 percent of his company's sales. Without access to Wal-Mart's customer base a label's bottom line is threatened in a very significant way. One way to deal with the criticism of violent lyrics and being shut out from Wal-Mart is to sell two versions of an artist's music. One version features the artist's explicit lyrics and is appropriately labeled with the parental warning. The other version contains the same songs but with the offending words changed or deleted. Edited music versions must also be labeled as such to alert the consumer that another, more explicit, version of the music exists as the artist originally intended.

The RIAA's warning system is unlike other ratings systems because it has no age or content descriptors. Instead the warning merely informs parents that there may be explicit words or mature themes in the music that they might deem inappropriate for their children. On its Web site the RIAA encourages parents to use the advisory as one tool in their efforts to make informed decisions about their child's listening habits. Despite inconsistent use by music labels and the different age restrictions enforced by retailers, the label is useful to any parent totally unaware of their child's favorite artist. But beyond that initial alert the warning label offers very little information to parents. The label gives parents no clue if the warning is related to explicit language, sexuality or violence. Themes such as suicide or revenge are not even accounted for but could be potentially harmful to someone who is already depressed. The warning label is a little like driving down a road and seeing a sign that reads "Warning — Danger ahead." You know that something hazardous is out there; you just don't know exactly what you are looking for. The warning label basically alerts concerned parents that they need either to listen to the music before buying or to go to a music lyrics Web site to find out about the artist's message.

In 1995, C. Dolores Tucker, chair of the National Political Congress of Black Women, and former Education Secretary William Bennett teamed up to protest explicit lyrics in rap music that they claimed glorified drugs and violence against women. The campaign attracted a lot of media attention and Tucker encouraged music labels to reconsider the type of music they were producing. Ultimately the music industry didn't stop promoting rap music, which remains one of the most popular and profitable music genres today.

Television Ratings

The television ratings system is the most contentious industry labeling system adopted. The idea to label television programs for explicit language and violent content was formally introduced during congressional hearings in the 1980s. However, any real chance of developing and adopting a ratings system for television programs died from inaction after the hearings ended. In 1990, Congress passed the Television Improvement Act which released television networks from antitrust restrictions in order to work together on ways to reduce onscreen violence. Employing the "raised eyebrow" form of regulation, Congress didn't directly impose its will on the industry but expressed its desire for the industry to clean up its act by giving the industry immunity from antitrust prosecution. If television didn't act then Congress would step in and force regulations that broadcasters undoubtedly wouldn't like. As the years went by with no real reduction in violence Congress continued its threats to enact regulation. Senator Paul Simon led several investigative hearings on television violence in the early 1990s that led to further monitoring of the industry by outside research organizations. Even when faced with yearly reports that showed television violence was increasing, the industry responded with little action. The snub angered many in Congress and bi-partisan support for television regulation peaked during the 1996 presidential election as both candidates campaigned for less violence and sex on television. Both Bill Clinton and the Republican nominee, Senator Bob Dole, threatened action if the industry continued to ignore its critics.

Congress found an opportunity to force the issue with the expanding importance of digital technology in communications. With broadcasters absolutely giddy with excitement over the prospect of a 500-channel television universe, lawmakers knew that the one thing that broadcasters wanted most was the relaxation of current ownership rules that restricted the number of radio and television stations a company could own. The proverbial carrot had arrived. After nearly forty years of complaining about the level of violence and sexuality in programming, Congress had the leverage it needed to force broadcasters to do something. Passage of the landmark Telecommunications Act of 1996 loosened most media ownership restrictions, enabling companies to own more stations than ever before. When Congress and President Clinton first indicated their mutual willingness to pass the deregulation package, broadcasters were strongly encouraged to adopt self-regulatory measures to rid their programming of excessive violence and sex. The quid pro quo was obvious. Congress would open up the media markets in exchange for more industry oversight of programming content and for development of a labeling program to alert parents to explicit content.

Embedded in the massive telecommunications bill was Section 551, which required the television industry to develop guidelines for ratings programs and eventually couple those ratings with an electronic blocking device known as the V-chip. The ratings are transmitted in the vertical blanking device similar to closed captioning and all televisions over 13" are required to include the blocking technology. The V-chip was obviously aimed at parents, who can program their V-chip with the rating that matches the level of content they accept. All programs carrying a more restrictive rating are subsequently blocked from viewing and adults can always override the blocking device by entering a password. Although broadcasters were encouraged to begin developing the ratings system immediately, the mandate for manufacturers to incorporate blocking technology in televisions was not expected to begin until the early 2000s. That gave broadcasters several years to develop an effective ratings system to be ready by the time television manufacturers perfected the V-chip technology.

Although the initiative was labeled voluntary, the FCC was required to approve the system and had full authority to develop its own ratings system if dissatisfied with the industry's efforts. The industry's first effort failed to win much support because it included only age-based descriptions, similar to those used in the motion picture industry. The system's format was not surprising given that the advisory committee was headed by MPAA president Jack Valenti. The age-based system suffered from the same problems as its movie counterpart. Both systems failed to give parents information about the content of programming in order to screen out specific elements including sex, violence and offensive language. Advocacy groups argued that parents were in the best position to determine what content was appropriate for their child, but how could they do that when the age-based ratings didn't provide any useful information? Parents already had experience with the inadequate movie ratings resulting in the frustration of taking a child to a PG-rated film only to find it full of explicit language and sexual references. A survey by the National PTA found that 80 percent of parents surveyed preferred a television content-based system over an aged-based ratings system (Cantor, Stutman and Duran, n.p.). Parents wanted content descriptors to provide more details about the substance of the programs so that they could assess the levels of violence, sex, and language they felt comfortable with. Other problems developed because use of the ratings system was voluntary and each network was responsible for rating its own programs. Without any oversight there was little incentive to critically evaluate a show's content. There also were few definitions to guide networks when assigning ratings, so there was little consistency among them.

A revised ratings scheme was approved by the FCC in March 1998. While not perfect, the ratings system did fulfill Congress's mandate to provide parents with information about the programs that come into their homes each week. This time the ratings were a combination of content and age descriptors that attempted to address the previous concerns of critics. The ratings divided all programs into six different categories according to the appropriate age of viewers: TV-Y (All Children), TV-Y7 (Directed to Older Children), TV-G (General Audience), TV-PG (Parental Guidance Suggested), TV-14 (Parents Strongly Cautioned), TV-MA (Mature Audiences Only). The ratings also included content descriptors for fantasy violence (FV), violence (V), sexual situations (S), strong language (L), and suggestive dialogue (D). The ratings are shown on the screen for 15 seconds at the beginning of every show, after every commercial break and at regular intervals throughout the show so that the V-chip will continue to block forbidden programming throughout the program. Although the ratings program remains voluntary, news and sports programming are exempt on all channels. News organizations argued that violence was a necessary part of truthful reporting and demanded uncensored presentation. Similarly, violence is such an inherent part of sports it is likely that every broadcast would be slapped with the most restrictive rating. But Americans don't typically equate sports violence with entertainment violence. Hitting, tackling and punching in sports programming is seen as part of the sport itself, with a valid, if not essential, function. A blood-filled beating in a boxing match is viewed by most as a realistic portrayal of the raw brutality of that sport. But the same portrayal in a fictional show such as *The Sopranos* or *The Shield* might be viewed as excessive to the storytelling and thereby deemed inappropriate for young audiences. Most cable channels were expected to participate in the new ratings system but many premium channels, such as HBO, indicated they would continue to use their systems that included ratings such as V (violence) and GV (graphic violence) before each program or movie. The NBC network initially refused to use the ratings, but later agreed to apply age-based rating without using any of the content descriptors. A few years later, the network quietly began using the full system.

The TV Parental Guidelines

TV-Y (All Children — This program is designed to be appropriate for all children.) Whether animated or live-action, the themes and elements in this program are specifically designed for a very young audience, including children from ages 2–6. This program is not expected to frighten younger children.

TV-Y7 (Directed to Older Children — This program is designed for children age 7 and above.) It may be more appropriate for children who have acquired the developmental skills needed to distinguish between make-believe and reality. Themes and elements in this program may include mild fantasy or comedic violence, or may frighten children under the age of 7. Therefore, parents may wish to consider the suitability of this program for their very young children. Note: For those programs where fantasy violence may be more intense or more combative than other programs in this category, such programs will be designated TV-Y7-FV. For programs designed for the entire audience, the general categories are:

TV-G (General Audience — Most parents would find this program suitable for all ages.) Although this rating does not signify a program designed specifically for children, most parents may let younger children watch this program unattended. It contains little or no violence, no strong language and little or no sexual dialogue or situations.

TV-PG (Parental Guidance Suggested — This program contains material that parents may find unsuitable for younger children.) Many parents may want to watch it with their younger children. The theme itself may call for parental guidance and/or the program contains one or more of the following: moderate violence (V), some sexual situations (S), infrequent coarse language (L), or some suggestive dialogue (D).

TV-14 (Parents Strongly Cautioned — This program contains some material that many parents would find unsuitable for children under 14 years of age.) Parents are strongly urged to exercise greater care in monitoring this program and are cautioned against letting children under the age of 14 watch unattended. This program contains one or more of the following: intense violence (V), intense sexual situations (S), strong coarse language (L), or intensely suggestive dialogue (D).

TV-MA (Mature Audience Only — This program is specifically designed to be viewed by adults and therefore may be unsuitable for children under 17.) This program contains one or more of the following: graphic violence (V), explicit sexual activity (S), or crude indecent language (L).

[Source: The Federal Communications Commission]

While the enhanced ratings were a step in the right direction, it didn't take long for problems with the new system to surface. There were immediate problems with consistency among networks in applying the ratings. Without explicit definitions of what words and violent images would fit a specific rating, broadcasters were left to develop their own definitions. This led to vastly different ratings for shows across networks, even within networks. In 1998 Kunkel et al. conducted a study of the ratings for the Kaiser Family Foundation to determine how well the new system was working. The researchers found mixed results and published the findings in "Rating the Ratings: One Year Out." In most cases the age-based ratings given shows were consistent with their content. For instance, 91 percent of G-rated shows contained no sexual behavior, 80 percent contained no adult language, and 80 percent contained no violence. In contrast, the highest rates of sex (56 percent), adult language (78 percent), and violence (70 percent) were found in shows appropriately labeled TV-14 (p. 1). However, the numbers were not as promising when it came to the all-important content descriptors. The researchers found that an astounding 92 percent of shows with sexual behavior and 91 percent of shows with adult language did not have the appropriate content descriptor. Seventy-nine percent of all shows with violence also were not labeled with the (V) content descriptor (p. 2). These omissions were particularly disturbing since the content descriptors were added specifically to help parents make informed decisions.

Another study found that broadcasters sometimes applied ratings inconsistently within their own networks based on conditions not even present in the rating descriptions. Cooper and Blevins (2000) discovered that the ABC network awarded the TV-14 rating to the sitcom *Ellen* and the gritty police drama *NYPD Blue* despite major content differences. The researchers coded several ABC programs for violence, sexual conduct, and suggestive and explicit dialogue. The results showed that *Ellen*, a sitcom with a lead gay character but virtually no violence and minimal sexual content or suggestive dialogue, was slapped with a more restrictive rating than *Spin City* and *The Drew Carey Show*, which both ranked much higher in sex and suggestive dialogue. The only other ABC show to get a TV-14 rating that season was *NYPD Blue*, which routinely featured explicit violence and language. It appears that ABC gave *Ellen* the more restrictive rating based on its lead character's sexual orientation, a characteristic not even listed in the ratings' definitions. The move caused concern for television producers and for gay rights groups as well because it underscored the arbitrary nature of awarding the ratings.

Critics also argue that programming content has sunk to new lows since the inception of the ratings system. With a restrictive rating in place what's to stop programmers from pushing the limits of acceptable standards? For instance, *The Jerry Springer Show* was one of the first programs to receive an MA rating for mature programming. Shortly thereafter, the show's staple of profanity and onstage fights only seemed to multiply. While the show's producers never admitted that the program consciously increased the violence with its MA rating, there certainly was nothing stopping it from doing exactly that. With a proper warning what's stopping any show from pushing the envelope as far as it can get away with? Because a program is rated for adult viewers there should, in theory, be no complaints. After all, the viewers were warned! Certainly, no parent should complain that a child saw too much mature material since the rating, coupled with the V-chip, should block the programming. Researchers also found that some viewers exhibited the "forbidden fruit" syndrome found to occur with other ratings systems. Some children are particularly drawn to what they know they aren't supposed to watch. Whether they learn the parent's password to override the system or merely seek out programming they know is aimed at an older audience, the unintended result is that children are drawn to the very programs parents don't want them to watch (Cantor 1998).

Other shows seemed to follow Springer's example with nudity, sexual content and violence more abundant and explicit than ever before. Of course, there are potential repercussions of receiving the MA rating because a percentage of the audience may block all programs with that rating. It also could get dumped by a network affiliate if it determines that an M-rated show doesn't match its audience. Because cable networks are less regulated they can show programs with more restrictive ratings. But this also means that these shows reach less of the total audience since cable viewership still lags broadcast networks. While a hyper-violent show like *The Sopranos* is a cable hit, its reach will never be as large as possible with the broadcast networks. But this really is exactly the way it should be. A premium channel like HBO requires a much greater effort to receive than an over-the-air broadcast network; consequently it's the perfect medium for more explicit programs. Although MA-rated programs on broadcast networks are still relatively rare, some have been successful in overcoming the stigma of the rating. For example, *Schindler's List* was broadcast with minimal editing and only one commercial break to an estimated audience of 65 million viewers. The violence and explicit language remained in the televised version because it was important to the film's realistic portrayal of the Holocaust.

It should come as little surprise that polls found that few parents were using the ratings system. An Annenberg Public Policy Center survey found that six months after the ratings system was introduced 66 percent of parents were not using it (Levin, p. E1). An Associated Press poll also found that 70 percent of parents showed little interest in the ratings system (Flynn, p. E6). Within a few years that number had increased slightly but few parents were actually using the rating system in combination with the V-chip to block objectionable programming. Some parents liked the idea but hadn't found the time to program their televisions. Others believed the ratings didn't reflect their values so the blocking by ratings category was not useful. Many simply reported they did not know the system even existed. Another Kaiser Family Foundation report (2001) found that 64 percent of parents who owned a television equipped with a V-chip didn't use it. Parents explained that they didn't need to use it because they were typically nearby when their children were watching television or that they trusted their children to make their own decisions (p. 14). In a follow-up study, the Annenberg Public Policy Center provided 110 families with a television equipped with a V-chip. Seventy percent of parents did not use the V-chip at all and only 8 percent were actively using it after a year (Jordan and Woodard, 2003).

The lack of use by parents spurred a massive public relations campaign by the networks in 2005 that offered information about the ratings system and how to program the V-chip. Even reluctant NBC got its favorite news personality Katie Couric to record a public service announcement encouraging parents to become more proactive in their children's viewing habits. The networks' campaigns underscored the importance of parents using these tools but indirectly scolded them for not using something they lobbied for. The underlying message was clear — use the V-chip or quit complaining about the content of television. Today, virtually every network's Web site has a link that lists the rating definitions and suggestions for programming the V-chip. The FCC also has an extensive section on its Web site to help parents control their children's viewing.

Video Game Ratings

The newest medium to be rated is video games. It's clear that this industry benefited from the problem with other media systems because it developed the most detailed system thus far. All new video games are submitted for review by trained evaluators of the Entertainment Software Review Board (ESRB). The company submits a detailed description of the game and a video representation of the game's most extreme elements. Each game is rated by a group of evaluators and the company's packaging and marketing are later checked to make sure they are accurately depicting the assigned rating.

ESRB Video Game Ratings

EARLY CHILDHOOD— Titles rated **EC (Early Childhood)** have content that may be suitable for ages 3 and older. Contains no material that parents would find inappropriate.

EVERYONE— Titles rated **E (Everyone)** have content that may be suitable for ages 6 and older. Titles in this category may contain minimal cartoon, fantasy or mild violence and/or infrequent use of mild language.

EVERYONE 10+— Titles rated **E10+ (Everyone 10 and older)** have content that may be suitable for ages 10 and older. Titles in this category may contain more cartoon, fantasy or mild violence, mild language and/or minimal suggestive themes.

TEEN— Titles rated **T (Teen)** have content that may be suitable for ages 13 and older. Titles in this category may contain violence, suggestive themes, crude humor, minimal blood, simulated gambling, and/or infrequent use of strong language.

MATURE— Titles rated **M (Mature)** have content that may be suitable for persons ages 17 and older. Titles in this category may contain intense violence, blood and gore, sexual content and/or strong language.

ADULTS ONLY— Titles rated **AO (Adults Only)** have content that should only be played by persons 18 years and older. Titles in this category may include prolonged scenes of intense violence and/or graphic sexual content and nudity.

RATING PENDING— Titles listed as **RP (Rating Pending)** have been submitted to the ESRB and are awaiting final rating. (This symbol appears only in advertising prior to a game's release.)

[Source: Entertainment Software Ratings Board]

The ratings also come with content descriptors that are more detailed than those used with the television ratings. These content descriptors give parents a laundry list of variables that may be encountered in the game. The ESRB's content descriptors indicate differences in mature elements and themes much like television ratings distinguish between different amounts of a variable (e.g., suggestive dialogue vs. intensely suggestive dialogue). But the ESRB's system goes a step further by giving definitions for each level so parents can really tell the difference between each category. For example, the definitions for the categories of Animated Blood, Blood, and Blood and Gore, are very detailed and useful for parents who really want to know what a child may encounter while playing a game.

ESRB Content Descriptors

Alcohol Reference— Reference to and/or images of alcoholic beverages

Animated Blood— Discolored and/or unrealistic depictions of blood

Blood— Depictions of blood

Blood and Gore— Depictions of blood or the mutilation of body parts

Cartoon Violence— Violent actions involving cartoon-like situations and characters. May include violence where a character is unharmed after the action has been inflicted

Comic Mischief— Depictions or dialogue involving slapstick or suggestive humor

Crude Humor— Depictions or dialogue involving vulgar antics, including "bathroom" humor

Drug Reference— Reference to and/or images of illegal drugs

Edutainment— Content of product provides user with specific skills development or reinforcement learning within an entertainment setting. Skill development is an integral part of product

Fantasy Violence— Violent actions of a fantasy nature, involving human or non-human characters in situations easily distinguishable from real life

Informational—Overall content of product contains data, facts, resource information, reference materials or instructional text

Intense Violence— Graphic and realistic-looking depictions of physical conflict. May involve extreme and/or realistic blood, gore, weapons and depictions of human injury and death

Language— Mild to moderate use of profanity

Lyrics— Mild references to profanity, sexuality, violence, alcohol or drug use in music

Mature Humor— Depictions or dialogue involving "adult" humor, including sexual references

Mild Violence—Mild scenes depicting characters in unsafe and/or violent situations

Nudity—Graphic or prolonged depictions of nudity

Partial Nudity—Brief and/or mild depictions of nudity

Real Gambling—Player can gamble, including betting or wagering real cash or currency

Sexual Themes—Mild to moderate sexual references and/or depictions. May include partial nudity

Sexual Violence—Depictions of rape or other violent sexual acts

Simulated Gambling—Player can gamble without betting or wagering real cash or currency

Some Adult Assistance May Be Needed—Intended for very young ages

Strong Language—Explicit and/or frequent use of profanity

Strong Lyrics—Explicit and/or frequent references to profanity, sex, violence, alcohol or drug use in music

Strong Sexual Content—Graphic references to and/or depictions of sexual behavior, possibly including nudity

Suggestive Themes—Mild provocative references or materials

Tobacco Reference—Reference to and/or images of tobacco products

Use of Drugs—The consumption or use of illegal drugs

Use of Alcohol—The consumption of alcoholic beverages

Use of Tobacco—The consumption of tobacco products

Violence—Scenes involving aggressive conflict

[Source: Entertainment Software Ratings Board]

If material is added or later revealed that would have resulted in the assignment of a different rating or content descriptor, the ESRB can impose sanctions including fines. The video game manufacturer may also be ordered to recall the product and repackage it with the correct ratings information and halt all advertising until the correct rating is printed. For example, hidden code dubbed the "Hot Coffee" program was found embedded in a version of *Grand Theft Auto: San Andreas* in 2005 that allowed players who downloaded third-party software to view nude characters. The ESRB had already rated the game as M for Mature, with accompanying content descriptors of Blood and

Gore, Intense Violence, Strong Language, Strong Sexual Content, and Use of Drugs. The M rating information appeared in all the print, television, and retailer ads for the game.

Advocacy groups and members of Congress, including Senator Hilary Rodham Clinton, called on the Federal Trade Commission to look into deceptive business practices by the game's publishers, Take-Two Interactive Software and Rockstar Games, since nudity was not a labeled element. The FTC investigated the incident and reached an agreement that called for the companies to release a patch that disables the "Hot Coffee" program (Federal Trade Commission "Makers of *Grand Theft Auto*"). The ESRB rerated *San Andreas* AO (Adults Only) and the companies agreed to relabel all existing inventory. The game no longer enjoys widespread distribution since many retailers have a policy against selling AO games. The rerating has cost the game's publisher an estimated $24.5 million in costs associated with returns of the game from retailers. The companies subsequently published a second, M-rated edition of *San Andreas*. In reaching the agreement, Lydia Parnes, the FTC's Director of the Bureau of Consumer Protection, reaffirmed that "Parents have the right to rely on the accuracy of the entertainment rating system" (p. 2).

Despite's the industry's best efforts to give parents all the information they need to make informed decisions, it appears that there are many problems with the accuracy of the ratings. A 2001 study of video games ratings found that two-thirds of E-rated games included acts of intentional violence and 64 percent rewarded players for inflicting injury on another character (Thompson & Haninger, p. 594). The researchers also found that most of the games were not rated with the appropriate content descriptors for violence. In 2005 Walsh et al. found evidence of "ratings creep," meaning that the ratings had not been updated to account for increases in the amount of mature content in games. M-rated games now contained more violence, sexuality and language than in the 1990s, making many worthy of an AO rating. The report concluded that:

> In the 90s only 16 percent of the M-rated games contained any kind of profanity at all and only 33 percent contained sexual content. By 2004 all (100 percent) of the M-rated games contained some level of profanity and sexual content. The actual figures shot though the roof. The games we analyzed from last year were 30 times more likely to contain profanity than those from

the 90s, and the average prevalence of sexual conduct increased a whopping 800 percent. Kids are six times more likely to see nude or partially nude figures in M-rated video games today than they were in the late 1990s. Yet the ratings haven't changed [p. 5].

Another problem occurs at the retailer end since many do not enforce the ESRB's ratings. While the ESRB sets the ratings it does not have the authority to force retailers to follow the recommendations. Some retailers, such as Wal-Mart, have written their own store policies requiring age verification for the sale of M-rated games, but other retailers freely sell or rent games to teens. Although the board strongly encourages sales based on the ratings recommendations, it has little power to force compliance by retailers. According to the 2005 study by Walsh et al., a yearly undercover operation by the advocacy group MediaWise found that 44 percent of all secret shoppers were able to buy M-rated games despite the fact that 94 percent of retailers claim to have a policy against such sales. In one incident a sales clerk even circumvented the store's computer system to sell the M-rated game to a young boy. When the clerk entered his real date of birth the register indicated that he did not meet the age requirement to buy the M-rated game. She simply changed the date to make it clear the computer (p. 2). The results were far worse in a three-year undercover operation conducted by the Federal Trade Commission. In 2003, 69 percent of teenage secret shoppers were able to buy M-rated games at major retailers and only 24 percent of cashiers asked the age of the buyer (Federal Trade Commission, "Results of Nationwide Undercover Survey Released," p. 2). No doubt this is hardly the type of compliance the FTC had hoped for.

The Future of Ratings Systems

A major problem with all of the ratings systems is that parents don't use them. Some parents explain that they do not understand the ratings; others simply don't take the time to use them. Regardless, surveys also show that parents aren't taking full advantage of the very programs that they lobbied Congress and the industries to create. Surveys also suggest that parents are not always as vigilant as they may believe. The MediaWise survey conducted by Walsh et al. in 2005 of parents and children found a lot of misinformation between the two groups regarding video game play. While half of all parents reported that they do not allow their children to own M-rated games, two-thirds of the children interviewed reported owning such games. Less than half of all parents reported that they understood all of the ratings and only 53 percent reported ever stopping a child from buying a game because of the rating. Children saw it very differently, with only 26 percent claiming that a parent ever stopped them from buying a video game (p. 3). The video game industry disputes these dire results and offers its own surveys that show that parents are quite pleased with the ratings systems. Dennis Wharton, president of the National Association of Broadcasters, rightly casts partial responsibility on parents. In an interview for *USA Today* (Oldenburg, online) Wharton said that "the ratings system that we have put forth is not meant to replace the role of parents, but it's a tool to empower parents."

For all the reasons outlined above, many experts now believe that the various media ratings systems are relative failures. Many blame the industries for putting a minimal effort into developing their ratings and Congress for failing to push for better ratings systems. Others have suggested that one system be used for all of the different media. That way parents wouldn't have to learn four different systems! The idea may be unworkable, however, since media are so different. In many ways these problems illustrate the fickle nature of media regulation and the inherent difficulties in linking a media product with larger societal issues. For 70 years parents, scientists, politicians and critics have blamed media violence for any number of perceived social ills. Yet, usage of media has remained high. In 1954, the average child watched 3.8 hours of television a day; today that number is virtually the same, at 3.7 hours viewed. A 2003 study by the National Association of Broadcasters reported that the typical family of three watches 60 hours of television per week. Shock jock radio hosts gain the highest ratings among radio listeners, all while pushing the limits of good taste and government standards. While teens comprise less than 20 percent of the total population, they purchase 30 percent of all movie tickets sold (Baran, p. 175). Finally, crime statistics show that American youth were significantly less likely to kill in the 1990s than they were in the 1960s and 1970s. This is not to say that media, especially violent media, have no impact on society. Nor is it true that media consumption is necessarily good for young people just because they continue to enjoy it in such high percentages. Nearly seventy years since the investigations and accusations began we seem no closer to fully determining its full impact or its value. And parents, armed with more tools than ever before, do not appear sufficiently alarmed to limit their children's consumption of media.

FOUR

Media on Trial

Courtroom debates over the influence of media violence generally fall into two overall categories: copycat crimes influenced by media violence and criminal insanity defenses claiming incitement to commit crimes by media violence. Typically, the media are blamed for influencing specific criminal acts by a defendant who claims that he or she was inspired by depictions of violence in a film, video game, television show or a song. Defendants usually make these claims during police interrogations or in interviews with news reporters while awaiting trial. While the claim of media influence is put out there for public consumption, these claims are rarely tied to a formal defense strategy at trial.

More commonly, defendants claim media influence in learning *how* to commit crimes. People with no previous criminal background often cite television shows and movies as providing them with explicit instructions to commit crimes or to cover up their acts. These admissions fuel the debate over the appropriateness of graphic portrayals of criminal behavior in American media. While some argue this provides a virtual blueprint for crime to an otherwise unknowledgeable mass audience, others counter that it merely portrays a realistic snapshot of our violent American culture and hardly amounts to an endorsement of such acts. Few defendants actually get to test these theories in court. While there have been a limited number of criminal trials implicating media influence, the strategy is relatively risky and, therefore, used infrequently. More common are civil suits brought by relatives of injured or murdered persons, accusing a media producer with negligence for failing to foresee the potential influence of its programming. In these cases, relatives typically blame injury or death of a loved one on copycat crimes of specific media depictions. These litigants seek compensation for their loss or merely want to change the programming practices of media producers.

To date, there have been no successful criminal acquittals due exclusively to media influence and very few civil awards granted for the impact of media violence on criminal behavior. However, a recent group of trials signals a revival of media violence defense strategies that could change the courts' treatment of media influence. These cases all involved defendants who claimed they were influenced by the popular film *The Matrix*, a highly stylized virtual reality film that posits that humans are being controlled by a group of evil machines. In each case, attorneys commented that their client was obsessed with the film and believed the film's premise to be true. In two cases, attorneys successfully argued for not guilty pleas due to reason of insanity because their clients were absorbed into the film's virtual reality plotline. Is *The Matrix* a judicial anomaly? Or do these verdicts open the door to other legitimate arguments for the mitigating circumstances of media violence?

Copycat Crimes

Long before the claims of influence by *The Matrix* a common reference to media violence in criminal proceedings is that of copycat crimes. Here, defendants claim a specific movie, television program, video game, or song inspired their own criminal behavior. While defendants often make these claims publicly, their truthfulness is never judged in a court of law since the defendants do not try to mitigate their actions via these media influences. Instead these claims often give rise to a new round of finger-pointing and debate surrounding the responsibility of media producers and consumers alike. The debates generally pit parents against media producers because it is generally believed that children are more susceptible to media effects. Do producers of violent programming have a responsibility to consider the possible influences of their programming, especially on impressionable young minds? Or is it the responsibility of parents to police their children's media consumption and to teach them appropriate media literacy skills?

The emphasis on the media's impact on teen behavior is not new. In fact, the desire to protect impressionable youth from the unintended consequences of reenacting fictional programming is often the driving force behind calls for increased media regulation. For instance, teen suicides are often been blamed on copycat acts. After the 1982 broadcast television debut of *The Deer Hunter*, officials nationwide reported more than 19 deaths of people who played Russian roulette after watching the film (Hanson, p. D3). In many cases alcohol appears to be a contributing factor (as it also was in the film), but the fact that so many people died in a manner consistent with the scene suggests at least mild media influence. Other suicides have been blamed on the music of Judas Priest and Ozzy Osbourne (Kunich, p. 1161) and on the animated television show *South Park* ("Boy's suicide note," p. E1). A number of student Web sites outlining methods and philosophies of suicide have also been cited in suicide notes or pacts by youths who killed themselves ("Web site back," 1998).

Other examples highlight a concern that youths are sometimes unable to distinguish the consequences of real-life violence from that of fictional violence in media programming. For example, a 7-year-old Texas boy killed his younger brother with a wrestling move he said he learned watching his favorite wrestling stars on television (Anderson, 1999). Another young boy died after role-playing the oft-killed character Kenny from *South Park*. When playmates told 11-year-old Bryce Kilduff that he would have to die just like the Kenny character he was imitating, Bryce reportedly responded, "That's OK, I'll be back next week" (*Today Show*, October 11, 1999). The next day Bryce died by hanging, an apparent accident while trying to imitate Kenny's death as described by his friends.

Youths have also claimed inspiration from the media regarding their own criminal behavior. Juvenile offenders have cited movies including *Helter Skelter* (Clark), *Menace II Society* ("Clips"), *Rambo* (Korber) and the *Basketball Diaries* (Grace, p. 25–26) as primary sources for information on how to commit a crime. When New York youths set fire to and killed a subway clerk shortly after the release of the film *Money Train* (which features a similar scene) obvious copycat connections were made. Although the clerks torched in the movie escaped unharmed the victims in the copycat crime did not ("Morning Report: Movies"). Critics refused to accept the different outcome as somehow diminishing any influence on the boys' behavior. The two acts, fictional and real, were largely identical; only the results were different. This case resonates with those who voice concerns over the unrealistic consequences of fictional violence. From their earliest viewing of

Police officials estimate nineteen deaths resulted from people who reenacted the Russian roulette scene from *The Deer Hunter*.

cartoons, children are exposed to countless acts of violence with unrealistic consequences. Unless they are taught by some other source (a parent, teacher or friend), the cartoons will leave them with incomplete knowledge about the potential outcomes of their actions. Of course that will change as they get older and more experienced, but that is little consolation to the sibling or other family member that just got hit by a three-year-old wielding a plastic bat.

This was precisely the argument made by the attorney for Lionel Tate, a 12-year-old Florida boy, who killed a six-year-old neighbor while recreating wrestling moves he claimed he'd seen on television. Tate's defense attorney claimed that Lionel did not fully grasp the potential danger of wrestling with his much younger, and smaller, friend because the wrestlers he viewed on television fought in a similar manner and always reemerged the next show healthy and ready to do it again. Tate's case drew national attention in part because he was only 12 when this happened. Critics used Tate's conviction of First Degree Murder to debate at what age children should know the difference between real and fake consequences. Absent this type of benchmark, it is difficult, if not impossible, to determine age-appropriate amounts of media violence. This presents a particular problem to advocates of program labeling since most systems are currently age-based. Tate's case suggests that a scheme for blocking violent programming may not be served best by age determinants, but rather by content codes. A detailed account of Tate's trial is presented in chapter five.

Media as Teacher for Youth

Youths accused of killing their parents have also claimed that they copied violent acts from media. Three California youths confessed to killing one's mother after watching the movie *Scream*, although no specific motive was given (Krikorian). Similarly, two California brothers (aged 20 and 15) killed their mother and dismembered her body as they reportedly saw done in an episode of the HBO hit series *The Sopranos*. While the boys never implicated the *Sopranos* episode as inspiring the killing, they did believe that copying the method of dismemberment would inhibit law enforcement from identifying their mother's body, masking their role in her death ("Police:

dismemberment had *Sopranos* inspiration," online). To some, the presence of media influence provides a *plausible* explanation for an otherwise unthinkable crime. Sheriff Michael Carona (p. 1) said that he was "comforted" by the boys' statements that they were inspired to dismember her body only after watching the *Sopranos* episode. The idea that they could have conceived that act on their own clearly was too much to take. The same was true when two young brothers cited an episode of the *Jerry Springer Show* as inspiring their assault of their 8-year-old sister. Although the show denied any such influence, people readily accepted that the boys could not have learned that behavior except through media influence ("Morning Report: Alleged rapists blame Springer"). This attitude does not diminish the seriousness of the youths' actions, and it probably wasn't even accurate, but it offers society an explanation that's easier than believing that they're just evil kids.

Sometimes media are described as a training agent for youth crime. Devin Moore of Fayette, Alabama, grabbed an officer's gun and shot him and two other law-enforcement officers while they were booking him on suspicion of car theft. Advocates for Moore, 18, claimed that he was merely reenacting a scene from his favorite video game, *Grand Theft Auto*. The game rewards players for stealing cars and killing police officers. When he was arrested four hours after the shootings Moore told police that "Life is like a video game. You've got to die sometime" ("Suit: Video Game Sparked Police Shootings," online). Moore pleaded not guilty and not guilty by reason of mental defect due to years of childhood abuse and the influence of *Grand Theft Auto*. This was very similar to the "TV Intoxication" defense used in Ronnie Zamora's murder trial in the 1970s. At his trial several mental health experts testified that Moore suffered from Post Traumatic Stress Disorder, but disagreed whether he was in a disassociative state when he shot his victims. Psychologist Brent Willis testified that Moore had a clear memory of the murders and demonstrated "goal directed" behavior in his attempts to escape the police station, indicating that he fully understood his actions at the time ("Experts say Moore has PTSD," online). His younger brother testified that their father often beat Devin with a belt and punished him by making him complete 1,000 pushups while naked. A jury deliberated for only an hour before rejecting Moore's claims, convicting him of capital murder. He received the death penalty in August 2005.

Media-Influenced Crimes and Suicides

Many times the issue is not copycat crimes but how media can influence someone's behavior, especially when he or she is depressed or angry. An alarming increase in teen suicides in the past several decades has led to increased scrutiny of music and its possible effects on depression and angst among impressionable young adults. Heavy metal music is particularly under suspicion because of its common themes of death, chaos, defiance and suicide. Many pediatric, mental health and child advocacy groups have released reports claiming a direct link between heavy mental music and teen suicide rates. These groups point most often to the angry, antisocial lyrics of Black Sabbath, Ozzy Osbourne, Megadeth and Slayer as leading teens, especially boys, down a path toward suicide.

The concerns over heavy metal music as a cause of suicide are misguided in many ways. In 1995 Scheel concluded that heavy metal fans tend to be a rather homogeneous group, mostly white males, with higher-than-average rates of substance abuse, depression, low self-esteem, strained family relationships, and lower socioeconomic status (p. 2). Many of these traits have also been identified by social scientists as common risk factors associated with suicide. So identifying heavy metal music as a direct cause of suicide cannot be substantiated. Other researchers have noted that heavy metal music has not cornered the market on themes of suicide and despair. Content analyses of different music genres have found an abundance of suicide-related themes in country music, rock, and opera.

In 1999, Canada's Centre for Suicide Prevention addressed the misconceptions of heavy metal's influence on suicide. In a report the group rejected claims that heavy metal causes suicide, instead believing that teens who are already predisposed to depression and suicide may be drawn to heavy metal's emphasis on isolation and despair (p. 1). In addition to citing research that disputes any cause-and-effect relationship between rock music and suicide, the group offered these general guidelines based on various studies:

• Heavy metal more often seems to become a problem for adolescents who are already disturbed and struggling with feelings of alienation. Those adolescents may also lack positive role models, come into repeated conflicts with authorities, family alcohol and drug abuse; and have a family history of violence and/or suicide.

• Far from placing adolescents at risk of suicide, heavy metal music may have a protective function for some.

• 45 percent of a sample of male heavy metal fans who were interviewed said that their music serve a purgative function, that is it helped to relieve feeling of anger. The music mirrored the emotional volatility brought on by the unusual crisis and conflicts of adolescence.

• Rock lyrics, including those said to advocate destructive acts, may in some cases provide a medium for dealing with issues of death and for managing anxieties these issues create.

A prejudice against heavy metal music is at the root of several civil lawsuits, including one of the first lawsuits to test media's culpability in a wrongful death case. The case involved Judas Priest and its album *Stained Class*. The parents of James Vance, 20, filed a lawsuit against the band, their record company and assorted executives after their son died from wounds he suffered in a failed suicide attempt. In 1985, Vance and his friend Raymond Belknap made a suicide pact after a day of drinking and listening to *Stained Class* and other Judas Priest albums including *Sin After Sin* and *Sad Wings of Destiny*. Both men had dropped out of school, drifted from job to job and had regularly used drugs including cocaine and crank. After getting in a fight with Vance's mother that afternoon, the two wrecked Belknap's room and went to a park with a sawed-off shotgun. There Belknap shot and killed himself. But when Vance tried to shoot himself the gun slipped, leaving him alive but with disfiguring injuries to his face (*Vance v. Judas Priest*, 1989). Three years later Vance died in a psychiatric hospital.

Vance's parents claimed in a wrongful death lawsuit that the suicide pact and their son's subsequent death were precipitated by subliminal messages embedded in songs on Priest's *Stained Class* album. Specifically the plaintiffs charged that the song "Better By You, Better Than Me," contained the subliminal message "Do It," and that "White Heat, Red Hot" contained a back-masked message "Fuck the Lord, Fuck all of you!" Finally, the plaintiffs claimed that "Sing My Evil Spirit" was embedded in the title song, "Stained Class," and Vance's parents believed that these subliminal messages caused their son's suicide attempt.

In a motion for summary judgment the musicians denied both the existence of any subliminal messages in their songs and the claims that their music was responsible for the two young men's deaths. Without determining whether subliminal messages actually existed on the songs as claimed, the court ruled that subliminal messages, if indeed present, are not afforded the same First Amendment protection as traditional lyrics. The court based its conclusion on three grounds: (1) subliminal communication does not advance any of the purposes of free speech; (2) an individual has a free speech right to be free from unwanted speech; and (3) the listener's right of privacy outweighs the speaker's right of free speech when subliminal speech is used (p. 2247). Presiding Judge Whitehead stated that he doubted the plaintiffs would prevail in proving that the subliminal messages contributed in any meaningful way to their son's suicide attempt. Still, Whitehead wrote that that was a matter for the grand jury to decide. Judas Priest's motion for summary judgment was denied and this court's opinion also had clarified the amount of protection afforded subliminal messages in music. The family's complaint was later rejected by the grand jury and the family subsequently dropped its lawsuit.

In the mid–1980s Ozzy Osbourne found himself at the center of two separate lawsuits blaming his lyrics for suicides by young men. In *McCollum v. CBS* (1988), the parents of John McCollum sued Osbourne and his record company after their son committed suicide after an evening of listening to Osbourne's music. On Friday, October 26, 1984, John, 19, listened to several of Osbourne's albums on the family's stereo system including *Blizzard of Oz*, and *Diary of a Madman*. The parents reported that John preferred the sound quality to the family stereo system but at some point retired to his bedroom to continue listening to music. Using his headsets to listen to the final side of a double album titled *Speak of the Devil*, McCollum shot and killed himself with a .22-caliber handgun. When found the next morning McCollum still had on the headsets and the stereo was running with Osbourne's record spinning on the player (*McCollum v. CBS*, p. 2002).

The plaintiffs claimed that Osbourne's music is often directed at the listener, giving the impression that he was singing just to you. They argued that the themes of Osbourne's music were particularly personal and attempted to connect with the listener as a peer who has the same problems and struggles as he does. The McCollums claimed that the overall theme of Osbourne's music is a world full of despair and hopelessness in which suicide is not only acceptable, but desirable. John had listened to "Suicide Solution" right before he went to his bedroom, which the McCollums alleged preaches that suicide is the only way out for a person with a drinking problem. The lyrics speak to the despair of alcoholism.

Included in a 28-second musical interlude in the song are some masked lyrics not published in the liner notes. They encourage violence.

The plaintiffs claimed that although these lines were sung at a very fast rate they were intelligible when the listener concentrated, as they said their son was doing that night. They alleged therefore that the defendants "knew, or should have known, that it was foreseeable that the music, lyrics, and hemisync (sound waves that impact a listener's mental state) tones of Osbourne's music would influence the emotions and behavior of individual listeners such as John who, because of their emotional instability, were particularly susceptible to such music, lyrics and tones and that such individuals might be influenced to act in a manner destructive to their person or body" (p. 2003). The McCollums also alleged that the record company acted negligently in releasing Osbourne's music, thereby aiding in John's suicide and creating an "uncontrollable impulse" in him to commit suicide (p. 2004). A final count of the complaint alleged that the defendants' conduct constituted incitement to commit suicide. Note that the plaintiff's complaint addresses all of the important issues in *Brandenburg*.

The California Court of Appeals rejected the plaintiff's claims because Osbourne's music is protected by the First Amendment. While many think of the First Amendment in traditional terms of protecting political speech and expression, the fact that an expression's primary value is entertainment or commercial affords it no less protection. The court also took exception with the plaintiff's claim that Osbourne's attention to suicide was particularly novel, citing a litany of classic works that focus on suicide including *Hamlet, Anna Karenina*, Sylvia Plath's *The Bell Jar, Death of a Salesman*, as well as the operas of Puccini, Menotti and Verdi. The court referenced the standards of *Brandenburg* and *Weirum* when it noted that in order to find incitement Osbourne's music must have intended to direct listeners to commit suicide, and that it was likely that such a result would occur. The court found no such evidence, writing that "Apart from the 'unintelligible' lyrics quoted above from 'Suicide Solution' to which John admittedly was not even listening at the time of his death, there is nothing in any of Osbourne's songs which could be characterized as a command to an immediate suicidal act.... Moreover, as defendants point out, the lyrics of the song can as easily be viewed as a poetic device, such as a play on words, to convey meanings entirely contrary to those asserted by the plaintiffs" (p. 2006). Indeed, Osbourne has explained in interviews that the song was about his own struggle to overcome alcoholism and the deep despair he felt about his addictions. Finally, the court ruled that CBS was not liable for McCollum's death simply by releasing and promoting Osbourne's records. There was no evidence that Osbourne or CBS released the recordings with the intent to harm John or any listener.

Osbourne's "Suicide Solution" was at the center of another lawsuit, again brought by the parents of a child who had committed suicide. Referencing the same masked lyrics, Michael Waller's parents claimed that their son shot himself in the head after repeatedly listening to Osbourne's song. The plaintiffs alleged incitement by Osbourne and also argued that subliminal messages were not a protected form of speech (*Waller v. Osbourne*, 1991). Consequently, they argued that the masked lyrics that encouraged their son to commit suicide were outside the scope of First Amendment protection.

In considering the status of the masked lyrics the court wrote that the "most important character of a subliminal message is that it sneaks into the brain while the listener is completely unaware that he has heard anything at all" (p. 1149). The court ruled that Osbourne's masked lyrics did not meet this condition and therefore were afforded as much First Amendment protection as the printed lyrics. The court also found that Osbourne's song failed to meet the *Brandenburg* incitement test and could not have produced the imminent suicide claimed by the plaintiffs. Despite ruling in Osbourne's favor the court chided the musician for his choice of themes, writing that:

> there is no evidence that defendant's music was intended to produce acts of suicide, and likely to cause imminent acts of suicide; nor could one rationally infer such a meaning from the lyrics ... the song "Suicide Solution" can be perceived as asserting in a philosophical sense that suicide may be a viable option one should consider in certain circumstances. And a strong argument can certainly be made that in light of the almost epidemic proportion of teenage suicides now occurring in this country it is irresponsible and callous for a musician with a large teenage following like Ozzy Osbourne to portray suicide in any manner other than a tragic consequence" [p. 1151].

Although Osbourne is English, he did live in the United States at the time, but it's not really accurate to imply that his primary audience was children.

In *Watters v. TSR* (1990) a mother whose son committed suicide filed a wrongful death lawsuit against TSR, the makers of the popular game *Dungeons & Dragons*. She claimed that her son was obsessed with the game and played it so much that he was driven to suicide. She claimed that TSR failed to exercise a duty of care in marketing the game and that it was negligent in not warning of its potential for physiological harm to fragile-minded children. Watters also claimed that her son's suicide was a direct result of his obsession with the game and TSR's aforementioned negligence.

A federal district court ruled that TSR was not negligent in marketing the game and that it could not foresee that playing *Dungeons & Dragons* could cause illegal or harmful behavior. Specifically, the court ruled that a company "cannot be faulted, obviously for putting its game on the market without attempting to ascertain the mental condition of each and every prospective player" (p. 389). To require such care would impose an undue burden and would effectively put every company out of business. The court also ruled that the company was not negligent in marketing the game because there was no proof the players of *Dungeons & Dragons* were any more likely to commit suicide than those who didn't play the game.

The court in *Watters* was clear that there was no foreseeability that Watters would commit suicide as a result of his playing the popular game. To hold any media company accountable for screening its customers is unreasonable. An even bigger imposition would be to require companies to restrict access to a product if someone might use it for crimes or harm to themselves. To expect TSR to screen users of *Dungeons & Dragons* for mental health issues would be comparable to holding the manufacturers of cars, baseball bats and even rat poison liable for anyone who uses their products in the commission of a crime.

Adult Crimes and Actions

Despite the attention given to the criminal actions of youths, adults have also been known to conjure up media images when faced with criminal charges. California robbers cited a recent television screening of *Cool Hand Luke* as inspiring multiple thefts from parking meters. In a memorable scene from the movie, Paul Newman's down-on-his-luck character is apprehended after smashing parking meters with a pipe to extract the cash. Police officials acknowledged that the crime was not new, nor was the influence of the film. Past television airings of *Cool Hand Luke* had resulted in similar outbreaks of parking meter crimes throughout the United States (Ryfle). Similarly, Nathaniel White, 32, attributed his murder spree to scenes in the *Robocop* films ("Family's stakeout nets suspect"), while no fewer than five murders were blamed on the influences of *Natural Born Killers* (Wharton, 1995). In *Byers v. Edmondson* (1998) two young adults were arrested on assault and murder charges after a drug-fueled shooting spree took them across three states. Sarah Edmondson and Benjamin Darrus, both 18, watched the Oliver Stone film repeatedly while partying and dropping acid in a cabin one night. The next day the two set out to recreate the murder spree of the film's two main characters, Mallory and Mickey, and began by shooting an elderly man in Mississippi to death. Next, Edmondson entered a convenience store in Ponchatoula, Louisiana, and shot the clerk, Patsy Byers, twice before taking some money and leaving (Rubenstein, p. 54). Byers was paralyzed from the neck down but later died from cancer. Edmondson and Darrus were sentenced to 36 years each in prison. Byers sued Edmondson and Darrus, as well as Oliver Stone, Warner Brothers Motion Pictures, and Time Warner for negligence, claiming that the film incited the teens' criminal behavior. Although Edmondson and Byers were the shooters, Byers' complaint asserted that "All of the Hollywood defendants are liable, more particularly, but not exclusively, for distributing a film which they knew or should have known would cause and inspire people ... to commit crimes such as the shooting of Patsy Byers, and for producing and distributing a film which glorified the type of violence committed against Byers by treating individuals who commit such violence as celebrities and heroes" (*Byers vs. Edmondson*, p. 684). In 1997, the trial court dismissed Byers' lawsuit on grounds that the law did not recognize a cause of action like hers, but that ruling was overturned by an appeals court. Four years later, Byers' claim was dismissed pre-trial when trial judge Robert Morrison ruled that the plaintiff had failed to discover evidence of incitement to commit violence by Stone and the film's producers and distributors.

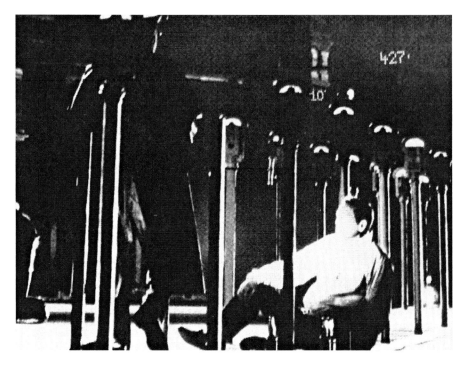

Police officials nationwide report parking meter break-ins after every broadcast of the film *Cool Hand Luke.*

Some adults seem to use claims of media influence simply to avoid accepting responsibility for their own misguided behavior. The 1984 television film *The Burning Bed* was controversial for its depiction of a battered wife who killed her husband after legal remedies failed to stop his abuses. The film sparked debate and allegedly spawned three assaults, including one man who beat his wife claiming that "he wanted to get her before she got him" ("A copycat assault?" p. 38). At least one notorious occurrence of military misconduct was also blamed on media content. In a newspaper interview regarding alleged sexual assaults at the infamous Tailhook Convention, Navy veterans blamed the debacle on the 1986 film *Top Gun* because, they claimed, it glorified "hard-drinking and womanizing in the Navy" ("Copycat Crimes," online). The officers, it seems, were merely living up to the standard of bad behavior portrayed in the film.

Evidence that media can indeed be an influencing force is seen in the

Patsy Byers was paralyzed from the neck down by a pair of gun-wielding teens mimicking Mickey and Mallory from *Natural Born Killers.*

reversal of Andrea Yates' murder conviction. Yates' case attracted international attention after she confessed to drowning her five children in the family's Houston home. At trial, Yates pleaded not guilty by reason of insanity and had five mental health experts testify that she was not able to tell the difference between right and wrong at the time of the deaths. In contrast, the prosecution offered one expert, Dr. Park Dietz, a forensic psychiatrist who testified that shortly before the murders the television show *Law and Order* featured an episode about a woman who killed her children and was found not guilty by reason of insanity. Dietz testified that he knew about this because he was a consultant for the show. His testimony was used to show that Yates merely copied the show's story line in her attempt to blame her actions on mental illness (Graczyk, p. A2). Yates was found guilty of murder and sentenced to prison.

The problem is that NBC never produced that episode of *Law and Order*. Although Dr. Dietz realized his mistake and informed the court before the sentencing phase, the 1st Texas Court of Appeals panel ruled that there was "a reasonable likelihood that Dr. Dietz's false testimony could have affected the judgment of the jury. Further we conclude that Dr. Dietz's false testimony affected the substantial rights of the defendant" (p. 1). Accordingly, Yates' conviction was overturned and she remains in a Texas psychiatric prison awaiting a new trial. Although critics often dismiss attempts to blame media for criminal behavior, the fact that jurors believed that Yates could have been influenced by *Law and Order* illustrates the growing acceptance of media as an influencing factor.

Media Self-Regulation

In the absence of regulatory measures, the mere claim that a program influenced harmful behavior can cause a media producer to take action. MTV moved its animated program *Beavis and Butthead* from an afternoon time slot to late-night hours after a young boy reportedly imitated an episode in which the characters celebrate setting things on fire. The boy ignited his bed, killing his younger sister. The incident attracted international attention, with thousands of protests lodged against the network. U.S. Attorney General Janet Reno echoed congressional calls for action during a Senate

Commerce Committee meeting Senate on media violence (E2788). The media had a field day with the image of Janet Reno taking on *Beavis and Butthead*, but ultimately Congress and the FCC took no action since MTV voluntarily moved the show to a later time slot. Later a journalist investigating the fire discovered that the family did not even have cable television, casting doubt that the MTV show had anything to do with the little girl's death. Similarly, Disney officials were quick to act after several teen deaths were attributed to reenactment of a scene in the film *The Program* in which characters lie down in a road to prove their courage.

It is important to remember that all of the incidents mentioned thus far represent only claims of media influence and not attempts to mitigate criminal liability. Consequently, it may never really be known the extent to which any of these criminal acts were really influenced by the media. Even though these incidents are often cited by politicians and advocacy groups to justify stricter regulation of media content, the actual occurrence of copycat violence and media-influenced violence is unknown. MediaScope, a well-known media watchdog group, released an eight-page report on copycat crimes in which it reminds readers that "The (copycat) events must be viewed within the context of thousands of violent crimes that occur where no one implicates the media as a source of inspiration. Copycat violence is unusual and uncommon, and is the least-occurring effect of media violence" (Copycat Crimes," online).

Court Cases Testing the Influence of Media Violence

Criminal cases in which a defendant attempts to mitigate guilt due to media influence have had little success, most never making it past pre-trial motions. More consideration has been given, however, to civil claims by relatives of persons hurt or killed through actions said to be influenced by media violence (either by their own actions or those of others). Plaintiffs typically seek compensation from the production and distribution companies for losses based on reenactment of some crime depicted in their media product. *Byers v. Edmondson* is a good example of a typical civil lawsuit involving media. The burden is high for plaintiffs who must prove that the media producer is responsible for the actions of the viewing public. Relying on the standards set forth in *Brandenburg* and *Weirum*, the defendant must have incited the audience to violent or illegal action and it must have foreseen that its media product was likely to incite such action. The argument is that media producers should foresee that audience members are capable of being influenced by the violent acts and false consequences often portrayed in fictional programming. Consequently, the person committing the crime is not fully responsibility for his or her behavior because he or she has fallen under the influence of powerful media messages. Savvy media producers should know better than to include such dangerous themes and messages in their media products. This fundamental argument is the basis for a number of criminal and civil complaints against media defendants and viewers alike.

The Niemi Sexual Assault Trial

One of the first examples of this kind of claim was in a case involving the sexual assault of a young schoolgirl. In 1976, the mother of 9-year-old Lisa Niemi filed a lawsuit claiming that Lisa was assaulted by fellow students who watched a similar attack in the recently aired NBC movie *Born Innocent.* Specifically, the family accused the network of negligence and reckless disregard for broadcasting the film at a time (7:00 P.M.) it knew juveniles were likely to be watching (*Niemi v. NBC*, 1976). The $11 million negligence complaint was originally dismissed by the California Superior Court as nonactionable, but was later revived when the California Court of Appeals ruled that the plaintiffs were afforded a trial by jury under state law (*Olivia N. v. NBC*, 1977).

The case captured national attention because of the brutality of the attacks by such young boys and because the case rested on larger issues such as media responsibility and censorship. Many media organizations voiced concerned that a verdict against NBC would expand media liability to the coverage of other violent content such as that naturally embedded in news and sports programming (see editorials in the *Washington Star, Atlanta Constitution*, and *Philadelphia Enquirer*). Ultimately, all the national debate and concern proved to be unwarranted. On the first day of the trial the judge dismissed the case after Niemi's attorney admitted in his opening statement that he would not be able to prove incitement by the defendant (NBC). The plaintiff's attorney told the jury that:

Nine-year-old Lisa Niemi was the victim of a copycat assault after NBC broadcast the film, *Born Innocent*, in which a girl was "artificially raped" by schoolmates.

At no time in this trial are we going to prove that either through negligence or recklessness there was incitement, which incitement is telling someone to go out encouraging them, directing them, advising them; that there will be no evidence that NBC ever told anybody or incited anyone to go out and rape a girl with an artificial instrument or any other way ... all of our proof will not be based on any type of incitement, but will be based on stimulation, foreseeability, negligence, and proximate cause [p. 1456].

The judge ruled that incitement to action was a requisite component if the television film was to be classified as unprotected speech under the First Amendment. Without this, Niemi's case had no merit. The dismissal was later affirmed by the California Court of Appeals and ended at that point (*Olivia N. v. NBC*, 1983).

Ronny Zamora's TV Intoxication Defense

At the same time the Niemi case was working itself through the California system, another landmark trial tested the influence of television in a Florida criminal court. Ronny Zamora captured national attention in the first criminal trial that allowed a defendant to advance a defense strategy involving media violence as a mitigating factor. In 1977, 15-year-old Ronny Zamora admitted killing 83-year-old Elinor Haggart, a neighbor who caught him and another youth in the act of burglarizing her home. At trial, Zamora's attorney, Ellis Rubin, entered a plea of not guilty by reason of insanity due to "prolonged, intense, involuntary, subliminal television intoxication," a consequence of Zamora's heavy viewing of crime shows ("TV on trial," p. 104). Rubin argued that television was an educational force in Zamora's life because his mother, a nurse, left him home in front of it each day when she went to work. Rubin called television Zamora's babysitter, and claimed that Ronny, a native of Costa Rica, learned English by watching his favorite programs. Rubin stated that because he learned so much from the fictional world of television Ronny was unable to understand the true consequences of his actions, including the consequences of violence. Zamora's mother testified at trial that Ronny was so intrigued with the show *Kojak* that he wanted to shave his head to look like the lead actor Telly Savalas. A psychiatrist also testified that after watching years of crime shows with thousands of fictitious crimes without adverse consequences, Zamora did not understand the true consequences of his actions when he shot Haggart ("TV on trial," p. 104).

The jury, however, did not accept the defense argument and deliberated just two hours before finding Zamora guilty of first-degree murder. Later Zamora was sentenced to life in prison. The jury's rejection of the television intoxication defense showed that they didn't accept that Zamora was incited to murder while millions of other viewers of violent television programming were not similarly affected. Rubin lost the appeal as well, prompting Zamora to hire a new defense team. In that appeal the defense argued that Rubin's TV intoxication defense strategy was a charade designed to get him attention and amounted to incompetent representation. Ultimately, all of Zamora's appeals failed and his conviction was upheld by a federal appeals court.

In yet another attempt to mitigate Ronny's actions, the Zamora family later filed a civil suit against CBS (home of *Kojak* and other crime shows) claiming that the network failed to use ordinary care to prevent Zamora from being "impermissibly stimulated, incited and instigated" to duplicate violent acts portrayed in its programming (*Zamora v. CBS*, 1979). The District Court dismissed the complaint, ruling that the plaintiffs failed to show cause of action and that imposition of such a vague standard of care would infringe on broadcasters' First Amendment rights.

Ronnie Zamora was so obsessed with Telly Savalas from *Kojak* that he wanted to shave his head.

Zamora made headlines 20 years later when the Florida Parole Commission granted him early release in 2004 (Farrington, 2003). Zamora was cited as a model prisoner who had completed college courses and even taught Spanish to other inmates. Upon his release in June 2004 Zamora was deported to his native Costa Rica where he reportedly was offered a job with the country's minister of justice. At the time of his release, the television intoxication defense was subjected to a new round of scrutiny. In interviews Ellis Rubin acknowledged criticism of his defense strategy from notable defense attorneys F. Lee Bailey and Alan Dershowitz. But Rubin stood his ground and said he would use the television intoxication defense again if the circumstances were right "because this time the scientific community does recognize television as an influence on our conduct" (Farrington). George Yoss, the attorney who helped Zamora receive parole, was less generous in his critique. Yoss told a CNN reporter that the defense strategy was "absurd" and accused Rubin of using the defense strategy to advance his own career rather than representing his client's best interest. Yoss claimed Rubin's self-promotion went so far that he went back into the courtroom to reenact his opening statements for a local television station that had lost footage of the event (Crumpler).

NBC's Tonight Show *and the DeFilippo Hanging*

NBC was sued again for negligence when a young boy died after apparently reenacting a segment from the *Tonight Show* with Johnny Carson. On May 23, 1979, Carson was "hung" by guest Dar Robinson, who was a professional stuntman. Before performing the stunt Robinson told viewers that this was a stunt and was "not something you want to go and try" (*DeFilippo v. NBC*). Several hours after the program aired, Shirley and Nicholas DeFilippo found their son Nikky hanging from a noose in his bedroom. The television set was still on and tuned to their local NBC channel. The parents sued NBC, claiming the network negligently failed to inform the plaintiff of the dangers, and aired the stunt with malicious intent and reckless disregard for the well-being of the viewing audience. Plaintiffs claimed that NBC should have foreseen that that televised stunt would encourage viewers to try it on their own.

Like those before it, this civil complaint never made it to trial. The Rhode Island Superior Court granted NBC's motion for summary judgment, ruling that the program was protected by the First Amendment (DeFilippo, p. 1876). The Rhode Island Supreme Court later affirmed the ruling and added that since Nicky was the only individual known to have imitated the fake hanging the broadcast did not constitute incitement to action. Like the Niemi and Zamora rulings, this court was reluctant to hold media producers accountable for the act of one viewer when thousands, if not millions, of others did not act similarly.

The Jenny Jones Show *and the Murder of Scott Amedure*

The next major case testing the foreseeability clause of media influence landed in courts nearly twenty years later. This case put *The Jenny Jones Show* on trial in criminal court as well as in the court of public opinion. In March 1995, Jonathan Schmitz murdered Scott Amedure just three days after the two taped an episode of the show focusing on secret crushes. Schmitz claimed to be surprised and humiliated to learn that Amedure was his secret admirer and killed him three days later while in a drunken stupor caused by this humiliation (*People v. Schmitz*). The case was widely dissected in the media because of its importance to future media regulation but also because it involved issues of class, sexual orientation and exploitation. Schmitz's attorneys argued that the show's producers blindsided him on national television to boost ratings of the show. The defense strategy was subsequently labeled in the media as a combination of media influence and the "gay panic defense." The jury, however, rejected both influences and convicted him of second-degree murder, for which he is currently serving a 25–50-year prison sentence.

After the criminal trial ended, Amedure's parents sued Schmitz, *The Jenny Jones Show*, Warner Bros. (the production company) and Telepictures (the distributor) in civil court for wrongful death. The Amedures hired high-profile attorney Geoffrey Fieger, who was most famous for representing Dr. Jack Kevorkian. The Amedures alleged that Schmitz killed their son as a direct result of an "ambush" since the show's producers withheld the true nature of the program — same-sex crushes — and never attempted to determine the impact this might have on Schmitz. The plaintiffs also charged that the producer "breached its duty, and foreseeably subjected plaintiff's decedent to an unreasonable risk of harm, ultimately resulting in his death" (*Graves v. Warner Bros*, p. 1). In this case the "unreasonable risk" meant that it was highly likely that someone would be pushed over the edge emotionally if it was implied that he or she was gay on national television. Jenny Jones testified at the trial that this claim was based on homophobia because it assumes that being called gay is so stressful that someone would be driven to murder.

Ironically, the complaint was similar to the defense used in Schmitz's own criminal trial. The so-called *trash* talk shows exploit unsuspecting guests for the sake of television ratings, but offer no follow-up or psychological support after the show is over. This time a jury agreed with the plaintiff's wrongful death claim and awarded Amedure's family more than $29 million in damages. However, the Michigan Court of Appeals swiftly overturned the award, ruling that the show had no responsibility for the subsequent actions of a guest and could not have reasonably predicted that the exposure of a secret gay crush would ultimately lead to murder. The court ruled that the blame for Amedure's death belonged to Schmitz. The court wrote:

> In sum, we conclude that defendants owed no duty as a matter of law to protect plaintiff's decedent from the intentional criminal acts of a third party, Jonathan Schmitz, that occurred three days after the taping of the *Jenny Jones Show*. While the defendants' actions in creating and producing this episode of the show may be regarded by many as the epitome of bad taste and sensationalism, such actions are, under the circumstances, insufficient to impute the requisite relationship between parties that would give rise to a legally cognizable duty [*Graves v. Warner Bros.*, p. 8].

The appellate court's ruling was upheld in July 2003 in a 5–2 vote by the Michigan Supreme Court, and the U.S. Supreme Court denied review in June 2004.

The Jerry Springer Show *and the Murder of Nancy Campbell-Panitz*

Just two years after the Amedure murder another daytime talk show found itself at the center of a murder trial. Although this incident bore some resemblance to *The Jenny Jones Show* trial (the program was about secrets), this time the audience watched the public dismantling of a love triangle that had a long history of violence. On May 7, 2000, Ralf Panitz, his ex-wife Nancy and his current wife Eleanor taped an episode of the *Jerry Springer Show* titled "Secret Mistresses Confronted." At the time Ralf, a German nationalist living in the United States, was reportedly going back and forth between the two women, often playing one off the other for money or a place to live. Nancy Campbell-Panitz told relatives that she thought she was going on the show to be reunited with Ralf, whom she had divorced just three months earlier. But that was not to be. Just one month after their divorce became final Ralf married Eleanor, whom he had met in an AOL chat room five months earlier.

Ralf had kept his marriage to Eleanor a secret from his ex-wife but their appearance on a show about mistresses still seemed odd. When it was revealed early in the program that Ralf had slept with his ex-wife the night before, the deception became clearer. A transcript of the show outlines how Ralf tricked his ex-wife into appearing on the show:

JERRY SPRINGER: What's going on here?

RALF PANITZ: Yes, I had sex with my wife yesterday, but I did it to keep her illusioned [sic]. I still love her but...

SPRINGER: Why? Why is it so important to keep an illusion that you love her if you don't?

RALF: I wanted Nancy to go on the show. A month ago I married Elli. I do love Eleanor. (He turns to look at Nancy.) But I care for you and don't wish you any harm. I just wanted to let you know. Please, let me go on with my life [*Jerry Springer Show*, May 7, 2000].

Later in the show the threesome argued over the facts of their relationships. Nancy leveled accusations that Ralf and Eleanor's so-called marriage wasn't legal, saying it "never was registered" at the local courthouse. This made it clear that she had been tracking Ralf's actions even after their divorce. Ralf's earlier statement that he didn't want to hurt Campbell-Panitz rang untrue when he admitted that he used the allure of national television to publicly disgrace Nancy:

ELEANOR: Are you ready to leave us alone?

NANCY: No.

ELEANOR: (getting up from her chair and walking over to Nancy) See. See, this is what I mean. You're not ready to leave us alone.

NANCY: You don't want me to. You love the game.

ELEANOR: I want you to leave us alone. I want a normal life. I want a normal life.

NANCY: No you don't, neither does Ralf. He loves the excitement.

Jerry: So basically you are saying that you don't want anything to do with her.

RALF: I don't want anything to do with Eleanor, uh, Nancy anymore.

JERRY: Well, you understand, and it is not my business, but you can say that all you want. But if you go over there and are sleeping with her, she is not going to believe you. (Audience applause)

RALF: Yep, I thought she might be humiliated enough to recognize that it's over [*Jerry Springer Show*, May 7, 2000].

But it wasn't over. Police reports show that just one month after tap-ing the show Ralf and Eleanor separated and he reconciled with his ex-wife Nancy. Again the two moved into a house together and were later joined by Panitz's nephew Markus (Steinhaus, online). But by July their reconciliation had soured and Ralf, once again, returned to Eleanor and even invited her to move into the house that he currently shared with Nancy. The prospect of this threesome living together under one roof led to a flurry of courthouse filings for protective orders based on accusations of stalking. On July 24, 2000, the three appeared along with Markus in a Sarasota courtroom for a hearing during which Nancy claimed that Ralf "is frequently violent. That morning he chased me with a knife and made threats about taking my life, ending my life, the way he was going to torture me" (Potter, 2002). Ralf, his nephew Markus, and Eleanor all made counterclaims of harassment and stalking by Campbell-Panitz.

The judge granted Nancy's request for a restraining order against Ralf and she also won an order allowing her to remain in the house. Later that same day, Ralf and Eleanor went to a local bar to watch the broadcast of the *Jerry Springer Show* episode they had taped two months earlier. On the same day that the threesome's dysfunction was aired before the entire television universe, Ralf and Eleanor were ordered to leave their home. The timing was purely coincidental but proved to be too much for Ralf. Police reports show that witnesses said that Ralf was drinking heavily and seemed upset throughout the program. A few hours later Nancy's body was found in a pool of blood in the home in which she had just earned the right to live.

Ralf and Eleanor fled Florida and were later seen in her home state of Maine. Sarasota police held a press conference because they believed that he was trying to reach the German embassy in Canada. Just four days later the couple contacted a Boston attorney and turned themselves in to Florida officials. News of Nancy's death immediately invited comparisons with the *Jenny Jones* murder, although the circumstances were quite different. Although more than two months separated the tape date from the air date, the program aired the same day Nancy was murdered. In that short period of time the love triangle took many turns, with no intervention from mental-health officials or law enforcement.

Many critics took the *Springer* show to task for cashing in on another tale of "white trailer-trash" drama but stopped short of blaming the program for murder. In a 2002 column Roanoke columnist Lana Whited wrote that the incident tarnished what precious little respect daytime talk shows had left. She also cited a poll that showed that viewership of the *Jerry Springer Show* dropped by 40 percent after the Panitz showed aired. But Whited reminded readers that this statistic revealed that 60 percent of viewers still watched the show. Applying H. L. Mencken's famous commentary on "stupid" voters, Whited warned that "Lest we be too quick to blame *Jerry* and *Jenny* for feeding us a steady diet of tabloid TV, we should remember that millions of us watch these programs regularly... Yes, perhaps our media should take some steps not to feed us such hooey, but we also have a responsibility to try and not be boobs." Andrew Wallenstein echoed that sentiment in a 2000 *Media Life* article in which he cautioned against blaming the *Springer* show for the murder:

> Accusing talk shows of exploitation is patently ridiculous. Guests volunteer to appear on the air, and yet we consider them victims for ugly reasons: condescension toward the underclass, who make up a high percentage of the talk-show guests. The assumption is that dangling perks like free airfare and hotel in front of them somehow renders them innocent of their moronic decision to appear on a talk show. You can deplore talk shows, but they aren't responsible for the behavior of the guests once they walk off the set [p. 21].

Jerry Springer himself did not comment on the murder but spoke often at industry conferences and on programs such as *Larry King Live* about the nonsensical nature of his show. Springer routinely labels the show stupid and pure entertainment with no educational value whatsoever. Speaking to a group of journalism students at Northwestern University just one year prior to the Panitz murder, Springer said his show's sole purpose is "to unwind to. No one is watching the show and saying 'Tomorrow I'm going to be a transvestite'" ("Springer hurls verbal chairs," n.p.). Despite Springer's comments there was evidence that the show had mandated a reduction in the amount of violence on the show. In 1998 the show publicly announced that fights, chair-throwing and other common *Springer* antics would no longer be tolerated. Critics were skeptical because it was widely known that Springer staffers often coached guests and helped stage fights. The first respite lasted only until the next ratings period when low ratings indicated that viewers had abandoned the tone-downed Springer Show.

After the killing, a representative for *Jerry Springer* called the murder a "tragedy" but declined further comment at the request of the Sarasota County Sheriff's Department (Grego, p. 11). That would be the last time the show offered any comments as producers tried to distance the show once the trial began. Panitz was charged with second-degree murder in an admission that prosecutors likely could not prove premeditation. Eleanor Panitz was initially detained as a material witness but ultimately was not charged with any crime. As if the case needed anymore attention Panitz was represented by attorney Geoffrey Fieger. While Fieger had represented the plaintiffs in the *Jenny Jones* case, this time he was on the side of the defendant. Prosecutors contended that the broadcast of the *Springer* episode on the same day Panitz was banned from living in Nancy's home only exacerbated his anger toward his ex-wife. The state presented evidence including 18 bloody footprints at the murder scene that matched Panitz's shoe, as well as his DNA under Nancy's fingernails. Fieger disputed that the evidence proved that Ralf murdered his ex-wife and presented several defense witnesses who testified that Nancy died of heart disease, not as a result of her beating. The jury deliberated for more than 18 hours over two days before convicting Panitz of second-degree murder and of violating the restraining order ("'Jerry Springer' Murder Conviction," online). In December 2004, Panitz filed a petition for a belated appeal based on ineffective counsel by his court-appointed attorney, Special Assistant Public Defender Judith Ellis. In his petition Panitz claimed that Fieger had identified at least 25 issues for appeal although Ellis presented only two. Panitz also claimed that Ellis failed to mount a rigorous appeal because she had stated to his wife in a telephone conversation that she believed he was guilty (Circuit Ct. Case 00–10578CF, Ex. J, 2004). Panitz has lost all of his appeals and remains in prison. His wife Eleanor maintains her husband's innocence on an online forum that she hosts and elicits a surprising number of supportive comments from people who believe the trial was rigged (Online Forum, www.voy.com, post November 8, 2003). The trial even sparked a following among members of the "Friends of Fieger," a Web-based fan club of attorney Geoffrey Fieger. Just months after Panitz was convicted, Jeffrey Campbell, son of Nancy Campbell-Panitz, filed a civil lawsuit against Jerry Springer, the *Jerry Springer Show*, and Studios USA, the show's distributor. Campbell claimed that Springer and the show's producers encouraged Panitz to lie to get his ex-wife to appear on the show to ensure a dramatic confrontation designed to humiliate her. The suit also claimed that Panitz was forced to share a hotel room with his ex-wife in hopes that it would lead to a sexual encounter to be revealed in a dramatic fashion during the show. Campbell's suit further claimed that "The Springer defendants knew or should have known that putting these three documented violence-prone people together on the show by deception and fraud would lead to further violence or worse" ("Murdered woman's son sues Springer," online). The lawsuit was similar to the one filed by Scott Amedure's family against the *Jenny Jones Show* earlier in the year. Campbell claimed that the show never thought past its own ratings grab when it purposefully encouraged animosity and betrayal among the Panitz threesome. The bigger the deceit, the bigger the confrontation and humiliation would be. *Springer* spokeswoman Linda Shafran quickly dismissed the lawsuit stating that "The murder of Ms. Campbell-Panitz transpired nearly three months after the taping of the episode. Many events occurred that were unrelated to the show, making it clear that neither the show, Jerry Springer, or the producers were responsible in any way for this tragedy, even if we are an easy and convenient target" (Cadorette, online).

Campbell was represented by Miami attorneys Ellis Rubin and Paul Vlachos, who called the lawsuit a declaration of war on the *Springer* show and all others that made money exploiting the human frailties of their guests. Rubin was a veteran of media violence cases having argued Ronnie Zamora's "Television Intoxication" defense 27 years earlier. Rubin told the *Bradenton Herald* newspaper that he was holding Jerry Springer personally responsible for Campbell-Panitz's death and that "I just want to say to Jerry Springer: 'Have a good time, because we're coming'" (Hass, 2002). Rubin and Vlachos vowed to sue the defendants for much more than the $25 million originally awarded in the *Jenny Jones* case. The attorneys' exuberance was short-lived, however, and they withdrew the lawsuit when a Michigan appeals court threw out the judgment in the *Jenny Jones* case. The appellate court ruled that a television show had no legal duty to protect guests once a program was complete. This ruling effectively ended any possibility of finding the *Jerry Springer Show* responsible for Campbell-Panitz's death. Eleanor Panitz reacted to the dropped lawsuit with a triumphant post on her Web site:

> Our situation was nothing like the Jenny Jones case. There was direct cause and effect there. Nancy's sons must be crushed that they are not going to

make millions off their mother's death. Oh well, but they did get our house-hold possessions, business equipment and our minivan, so they did not leave empty handed. Hope they enjoy. This news really set my New Year off to a good start. Now all we need is a new trial, and an acquittal, and my year will be made" [Online forum, post January 4, 2003].

Panitz did not get that acquittal and remains in a Florida prison today.

Lawsuits from School Shootings

In the mid 1990s a rash of school shootings gripped the nation. Advocacy groups and school officials both searched for answers to the inevitable question of *why*. Why were our children turning guns on one another? Why were they developing extensive and detailed plans to exact the greatest amount of harm in the most efficient way? Why were they compelled to do this and where were they learning the tactical and technical skills to pull off such elaborate attacks? The most common motivational force behind calls for regulation of media content is the protection of youth from the influences of violent media (Cooper, 1996). While any potential harm from media is worrisome, our society generally believes that adults are equipped with skills that allow them to mitigate media effects. Adults can, for example, distinguish between fictional and real violence and between fictional aggression and pro-social forms of conflict resolution. An adult can thoroughly enjoy a scene in an episode of *Family Guy* or *The Simpsons* in which a worker exacts revenge against a tyrannical boss, but know that they can't go to work and do the same thing. Children, however, may not be able to make a clear distinction between behavior as portrayed in television and the movies and that which is actually acceptable in society. Children also may also not be mature enough yet to fully appreciate the consequences of actions, whether physical or verbal.

The concern over access to violent media typically reignites with each and every instance of school violence. Dozens of congressional hearings, investigations and inquiries have been convened in the quest to find a definitive cause of youth violence. Typically these hearings come after a violent act attracts national attention, such as the rash of school shootings in the 1990s or the deaths allegedly inspired by the hit MTV show *Beavis and*

Butthead and the Disney film *The Program*. Despite the swiftness of these congressional inquiries, the committees typically fail to reach any definitive conclusion and public attention quickly wanes until the next violent act reignites the debate. But the families of victims of school shootings are intent on finding someone to blame for their child's death.

Victim's families often filed lawsuits against the parents of the shooter and against school officials for failing to thwart the attacks. For example, the parents of students injured and killed in school shootings by Mitchell Johnson (Jonesboro, Arkansas) and Luke Woodham (Pearl, Mississippi) filed lawsuits against their parents for negligence in supervising their children ("The Lawsuits," online). The parents of students shot by Kip Kinkle (Springfield, Oregon) filed lawsuits against the estate of Kinkle's parents since he had killed them, too. Others sued gun manufacturers and retailers for failing to impose required age restrictions that allowed the shooters to buy a weapon over the Internet.

Lawsuits against parents and schools only went so far in explaining why these school attacks were not prevented. Lack of supervision could possibly explain how it was possible to pull off such an attack, but it offered no insight into how these teens learned how to plan the attacks in the first place. As before, the media became a predictable target. What else could explain the high degree of marksmanship and the sophisticated plans used in many of the school attacks? As investigations of these crimes revealed disturbing trends in media usage by teen killers, attempts to hold media producers legally responsible intensified.

Columbine

No school shooting has been scrutinized more than Columbine. Within hours of the shootings national news networks set up camp outside the school to cover the unfolding investigation and, ultimately, the funerals of the 12 students and a teacher killed by Eric Harris and Dylan Klebold in April 1999. Much was made of the magnitude of the attack and how the two boys amassed such a collection of weapons and explosives without being detected. Law-enforcement officials were also interested in any connections to the media products the two boys enjoyed. Both favored long, black trench coats like the main characters in the film *The Matrix* and reportedly were fans of *The Basketball Diaries* and its scene of a student shooting teachers and fellow students. Both were also avid payers of the video game *Doom*. Some reports indicated that Harris and Klebold linked their personal computers so that they could compete against one another in an interactive version of *Doom*. After the shooting, police officials discovered a video made by the boys in which they compared their planned attack to *Doom* and Eric boasted that he had named his shotgun Arlene after one of the game's characters. A year before the rampage Harris wrote in his journal that the attack would "be like the LA riots, the Oklahoma bombing, World War II, Vietnam, Duke (the video game Duke Nukem) and Doom all together ... I want to leave a lasting impression on the world" ("Columbine lawsuit thrown out," 2002).

The decision to sue or not sue was a difficult one for many of the families because details of the investigation were slow to be released. Stories surfaced that Harris had previously been investigated by both the sheriff's department and school officials for threats to others, and for his authorship of a Web site that detailed planned bomb attacks. Famed attorney Geoffrey Fieger participated once again and filed lawsuits by some of the parents of the students killed that day. Other lawsuits were filed against the school district, the sheriff's department, and the parents of Harris and Klebold, and against the producers of media believed to have influenced the two teens. These plaintiffs filed claims of negligence, strict product liability and RICO activity against entertainment companies including New Line Cinema, Palm Picture, Island Pictures, Polygram and Time Warner (makers and distributors of *The Basketball Diaries*) and several video game manufacturers including Atari, Nintendo, Activision and Id Software, the maker of *Doom*. The lawsuit claimed that the content of the video games was not protected by the First Amendment and that these media producers were negligent in promoting violence to their audience. The plaintiffs believed that but for the actions of these media producers in promoting violent behavior the multiple killings at Columbine High School would not have occurred. The plaintiffs further claimed that the companies knew that children watching acts of violence and playing interactive violent video games typically act more violent themselves. Consequently the companies should have known that their violent products "had the potential to stimulate an idiosyncratic reaction in the mind of some disturbed individuals" (*Sanders et. al v. Acclaim Entertainment*, p. 10)

U.S. District Court Judge Lewis Babcock quickly dismissed the product liability and RICO claims and wrote that there was no way for the companies to foresee that their products would cause Harris and Klebold to attack the school that day. Relying on the previous rulings of foreseeability in *Weirum* and *McCollum*, Babcock ruled that there is "no basis for determining that violence would be considered the likely consequence of exposure to video games or movies. This factor weighs heavily against imposing a duty on the Movie and Video Game Defendants" (p. 13). Babcock concluded his ruling by writing that the producers of media and video games favored by the killers did not meet the *Brandenburg* requirement of inciting imminent lawless action. The judge dismissed all claims against the defendants.

Paducah, Kentucky

In 1997, Michael Carneal, 14, killed three students and wounded another five in an early-morning shooting spree at Heath High School in Paducah, Kentucky. Michael previously had complained of being bullied by fellow classmates but the victims, who had just attended a pre-school prayer meeting, were not among his alleged tormentors. School officials described Carneal as a quiet, socially immature teen who earned good grades and was liked by many fellow students. In statements to police after his arrest Carneal recounted that he was an avid player of violent computer games such as *Doom* and *Mortal Combat*. He was also reportedly a big fan of *The Basketball Diaries*, a popular film starring Leonardo DiCaprio. In one of the scenes DiCaprio's character dreams he is shooting his teacher and classmates to death.

Aside from complaints of bullying, Carneal offered few clues regarding his murder spree. Parents of the three girls killed agreed to a $42 million wrongful death settlement from Carneal although it was doubtful that they would actually receive any of the money ("Settlement in Kentucky School Shootings," online). Michael Breen, the attorney for the victim's families, claimed that they didn't care about the money; they just wanted to get as much insight as possible into why Carneal killed his fellow schoolmates. Breen also acknowledged the plaintiffs' strong desire to hold others accountable for failing to supervise Carneal and for influencing him and other teen shooters. The suit originally involved more than 50 defendants, including Carneal's parents, school officials, and fellow students who had advance knowledge of Carneal's threat of violence but failed to inform officials. "The shooting rampages at Columbine and Jonesboro made a strong statement about school violence all the more necessary," Breen said. "Because of this, the families came to believe this case could be used to teach others. This settlement sends a very strong message that all parents and school officials must be vigilant and ever aware of those children who would commit violence upon their classmates."

Breen's desire to send an even stronger message materialized when he and media violence crusader Jack Thompson filed a $130 million lawsuit on behalf of the victims' families against 25 media producers they believed influenced Carneal's behavior during the shooting spree. The suit named a pornographic Web site, Time Warner, Inc., Polygram Film Entertainment Distribution Inc., Palm Pictures, Island Pictures and New Line Cinema for producing and distributing the film *The Basketball Diaries*. The suit also named Atari Corp., Nintendo of America, Sega of America, Sony Computer Entertainment and Id Software, maker of the video games *Quake*, *Doom*, and *Castle Wolfenstein*, which Carneal played often ("Federal Judge Dismisses Lawsuits," online). The suit claimed that Carneal perfected his shooting skills by playing the video games and became desensitized to killing since that was a primary way to succeed in those games. Breen and Thompson supported their claims with transcripts from Carneal's trial in which an adolescent psychiatrist testified that he was "conditioned" to kill by constant exposure to violent media ("The Lawsuits," online).

Lt. Col. David Grossman, a former West Point psychology professor, noted that Carneal shot all eight of his victims in eight shots. Of those, five were shot in the head and three in the upper torso. Grossman claims that this level of "unprecedented marksmanship achievement" is directly related to Carneal's love of *Doom* and *Quake*, (Laidman, online). Grossman also points out that these games shared the same technology used in U.S. military simulators that train recruits to overcome resistance to killing. If shooter video games are used by the military to train soldiers, why wouldn't this technology have a similar effect on teens who typically play these games unsupervised? Would this not make the manufacturers of such games at least partially responsible for the deaths of those three girls in Kentucky because they helped Carneal become a trained killer?

Ultimately, the court ruled that the manufacturers could not be held responsible for Carneal's actions. The suit was initially dismissed by the U.S. District Court for the Western District of Kentucky and later upheld by the Sixth Circuit, U.S. Court of Appeals. On the claims of media influence the Sixth Circuit panel ruled that media (film and video game) producers cannot be held accountable for the criminal acts of those who enjoy their products. The court relied on its previous ruling in *Watters v. TSR*, Inc. (1990), a case brought by a mother who blamed her son's suicide on his obsession with the game *Dungeons & Dragons*. In both cases the court ruled that media producers can't foresee the actions of everyone who plays their games and that criminal behavior is not a likely outcome of using violent media products. In Carneal's case, the court wrote that "It appears simply impossible to predict that these games, movies, and Internet sites (alone, or in what combinations) would incite a young person to violence. Carneal's reaction to the games and movies at issue here, assuming that his violent actions were such a reaction, was simply too idiosyncratic to expect the defendants to have anticipated it. We find that it is simply too far a leap from shooting characters of a video screen (an activity undertaken by millions) to shooting people in a classroom (an activity undertaken by a handful, at most) for Carneal's actions to have been reasonably foreseeable to the manufacturers of the media Carneal played and viewed" (*James v. Meow Media*). The court also affirmed the First Amendment protection of the content of media, including that of video games and Internet sites. In January 2003 the U.S. Supreme Court refused to review the case further closing the door on any claim of direct influence by violent media on the consuming public (*James vs. Meow Media, Inc.*, cert. denied).

The Supreme Court's ruling did little to dissuade Jack Thompson in his crusade to hold video game manufacturer's accountable for training young men to kill. Thompson is a well-known critic of violent media who has spearheaded numerous lawsuits trying to establish liability of media producers. Aside from his work on the Carneal case, Thompson claimed video games influenced Lee Boyd Malvo in the Washington sniper case. Thompson is also well known for his indecency and obscenity complaints filed against *The Howard Stern Show* and 2 Live Crew. Thompson routinely offers his help to attorneys representing teen criminal defendants who were heavy users of violent video games. When attorneys for accused killers Dustin Lynch and Joshua Cooke refused to blame their client's action on violent media, Thompson petitioned to have them removed from the cases and offered to represent the defendants for free. Thompson is similarly hostile towards leaders in the video game industry. In interviews and articles posted on his Web site, Stopkill.com, Thompson likens Entertainment Software Association President Doug Lowenstein to Saddam Hussein and Nazi propagandist Joseph Goebbels. While Thompson has had some successes in court, his tactics have earned him widespread ridicule, especially among gaming online communities and free speech advocates. In 1992 the American Civil Liberties Union labeled Thompson one of its Top 10 Censors of the year and the Libertarian Party called Thompson's lawsuit in the Carneal murder case a blatant attempt to "dumb down personal accountability," for criminal behavior (Libertarian Party, n.p.).

Still, Thompson continues the crusade. In February 2005, he filed a lawsuit related to the fatal shooting of three law-enforcement officials by Devin Moore in Fayette, Alabama, two years earlier. Moore was ultimately convicted of murder and given the death penalty. Thompson believed that Moore's action were just another example of a teen being trained to kill through excessive playing of violent video games, in this case *Grand Theft Auto*. Thompson sued the game's publishers and Sony Computer Entertainment for its PlayStation 2 equipment on behalf on two of the victims' families. The $600 million lawsuit also accused Wal-Mart and another local retailer of selling the M-rated games to Moore even though he was under the recommended age of 17. Thompson stated that although a handful of companies participated directly in teaching Devin Moore how to kill, the entire game industry bore a special responsibility for producing the "murder simulators" that encourage violence against all law-enforcement officials. In an interview on CBS's *60 Minutes* in 2005, Thompson revealed how he intended to prove liability by the media producers despite the Supreme Court's dismissal of such claims in the Carneal lawsuit: "He bought it (GTA) as a minor. He played it hundreds of hours, which is primarily a cop-killing game. It's our theory, which we think we can prove to a jury in Alabama, that, but for the video-game training, he would not have done what he did." Thompson was relying once again on the popular notion that children and teens aren't mature enough to formulate violent thoughts (and actions) themselves so they must be influenced by some outside force. Thompson believes that Moore was simply repeating a scene from the video game in which a character escapes a police station by shooting an officer and fleeing in a stolen police cruiser.

The *60 Minutes* segment also featured child psychologist David Walsh, who believes that teens are particularly vulnerable to the potential effects of violent video games because their brains are not as developed as adults.' Repeated exposure to cop-killing play, like the hundreds of hours played by Moore, could "program" a teen to believe that shooting law-enforcement officers is acceptable. Walsh explained that "the impulse control center of the brain, the part that lets us think ahead, consider consequences, manage urges ... that's under construction during the teenage years. In fact, the wiring is not complete until the early 20s... And so when a young man with a developing brain, already angry, spends hours and hours rehearsing violent acts, and then he's put in this situation of emotional stress, there's a likelihood that he will literally go to that familiar pattern that's been wired repeatedly, perhaps thousand and thousands of times." Despite Walsh's claims of influence, courts and juries have not been as accepting of the idea that children can be indoctrinated to murder by a video game, film, or television show.

FIVE

Lionel Tate and the TV Wrestling Defense

In the fall of 1999 the stage was set for one of the biggest media influence cases ever. Many factors — the age of the defendant and victim, the brutality of the crime, the use of television wrestling in the defense strategy — came together to make this a widely watched and widely commented upon case. Cable television law shows loved to feature so-called experts debating the merits of media violence defense strategies. Long before the case made it to trial, the court of public opinion had weighed in heavily on the case of Lionel Tate, a twelve-year-old Florida boy who killed Tiffany Eunick, a six-year-old neighbor he was playing with. According to reports and Tate's own statements, the children were playing in his house one evening while his mother slept upstairs. At some point during their play Lionel began wrestling with Tiffany, during which he later admitted to striking her 35 to 40 times in the chest and throwing her across the room at least once. Tiffany died from her injuries.

The Investigation

Within two weeks a grand jury indicted Tate for murder in the first degree, a felony charge in the state of Florida that carried a possible sentence of life in prison with no chance of parole. At twelve years of age Tate was one of the youngest children ever charged as an adult and the media attention was immediate and relentless. Kenneth Padowitz, the Broward County prosecutor assigned to the case, was harshly criticized in the local and national media for filing adult charges against the juvenile Tate. Tate was initially charged with an open count of homicide that could have been adjudicated in the juvenile courts and would have resulted in confinement to a juvenile facility. Under Florida sentencing laws Tate would have faced a likely sentence of six to nine months in a juvenile facility which Padowitz believed was insufficient. Appearing on *The Montel Williams Show* in 2003, the prosecutor explained that "Six months is one month for every year of Tiffany's life, and that to me was not justice." Padowitz decided to present the case to the grand jury.

It was Tate's own statements to police, as well as those of his mother, Florida highway patrol officer Kathleen Grossett-Tate, that raised the suspicions of the grand jury. A police report entered at trial detailed some of the first statements made to police. The report read in part:

> On July 28, the defendant's first contact with the police, at the scene, was with Officer Arthur Chanard. Tate stated nothing about any physical contact with the victim. He did say that Tiffany was "rolling around on the floor, acting like a baby and had wet her pants." Tate then stated that the victim then went to sleep and instead of getting help, the defendant went back to watching television. There was no mention of professional wrestlers or wrestling or wrestling moves.
>
> It should be noted that Grossett-Tate (the defendant's mother) attempted to aid her son by stating to arriving paramedics that no one was present at the home with Tiffany Eunick except herself. Grossett-Tate then went into a detailed false story about hearing a noise and on her own, finding Tiffany's body, a story that did not mention the presence or actions of the defendant [Broward County Police report, case number 99–14401CF10A].

It's not necessarily unusual to consider, or even expect, that a 12-year-old would lie or be unable to recall details of an incident of such magnitude. Most adults would have difficulty recalling their actions with much clarity under the same circumstances. Law enforcement agencies often discount eyewitness accounts because they are simply too inaccurate. Jim Lewis, Tate's attorney, argued in pre-trial motions that Tate's changing statements were not an act of deception but rather the natural reaction of a teenager scared by his sudden involvement in a police investigation of a murder. But as Tate's statements continued to change every few days the lack of consistency seemed to be pointing to a calculated attempt to deceive the police by Tate and by his mother.

Two days later on July 30th, at approximately 7:45, Tate (already at Public Safety Bldg.) explained to his mother his involvement in Tiffany Eunick's injury. In his taped statement, Lionel Tate stated he was playing tag. He also described a "bear hug" and placing his hand under the victim's head while she was lying down and bumping her head into a table. There was no mention of professional wrestling or wrestling moves. Lionel Tate continuously denied or minimized the amount of force he used to cause the injuries to Tiffany Eunick. After the defendant's statement of July 30 the defendant was subsequently arrested and charged by the Broward Sheriff's office with an open count of homicide [Broward County Police report, case number 99:14401CF10A].

If the changing statements raised the grand jury's suspicion, the autopsy and the medical examiner's reports did little to reduce those concerns. Tate's statements ranged from him saying that he never touched Eunick to accounts that she bumped her head on a coffee table. But the autopsy suggested a very different story and one with a great deal more violence and trauma to the victim. Dr. Lisa Flanagan's preliminary autopsy report described Tiffany Eunick as a well-nourished, Black, six-year-old female child. She was 48 pounds and 50 inches tall. Dr. Flanagan listed 23 areas of injury and multiple blunt traumas including: extensive contusions on the frontal poles and left temporal pole of the brain; contusions of the superior right and left frontal lobes of the brain; multiple scalp contusions; extensive laceration of the liver; and extensive soft tissue hemorrhage of upper right abdomen. The scalp had several areas of hemorrhage and the skull had a thin, linear fracture. Evidence of brain swelling was also found (Flanagan, Autopsy #00–0911, Broward County Medical Examiner's Office).

Perhaps even more shocking was the severe damage to the pancreas and posterior liver. Dr. Flanagan's report stated that the right lobe of the liver had a 6 cm laceration that extended the full thickness of the liver from front to back. In addition a small portion of the liver was recovered from her abdomen. In short, the young girl was so badly beaten that a section of her liver had been severed. Dr. Flanagan's final opinion in the autopsy report stated that "Tiffany Eunick was a 6-year-old female who died as a result of multiple blunt traumatic injuries involving the head and abdomen. The injuries were sustained when the decedent was physically assaulted by another individual. The manner of death is determined to be homicide" (p. 2).

The severity of the young girl's injuries in no way matched Tate's account of the events that evening. Either something much more intense transpired between the two children or Eunick's injuries were sustained somewhere else. On August 5, 1999, Dr. Joshua Perper, Chief Medical Examiner of Broward Country released the following opinion:

> I reviewed the statement given by Lionel Tate on July 30, 1999 in reference to the death investigation of Juvenile Tiffany Eunick. It is my professional opinion, within a reasonable degree of medical certainty, that Lionel Tate's description of his physical contact with Tiffany Eunick and the description of the subsequent impact of Tiffany's head on the side of a coffee table does not match the severity and multiplicity of injuries substantiated at the autopsy of the above child.

Two days later the grand jury found that Tate acted "feloniously and from a premeditated design" to murder Tiffany Eunick and therefore indicted the 12-year-old of murder in the first degree (Broward County, case no 99–14401CF10A, Grand Jury Indictment).

From the outset, this case was not going to be just another murder trial. It wasn't just the ages of the victim and the accused that made it a natural oddity. There was the severity of the crime, a prosecutor staring down a 12-year-old boy in court facing adult charges, and the endless scrutiny of the defendant's mother — a law enforcement officer herself, who appears to have attempted to cover up her son's actions. As such, the case garnered an enormous amount of media interest. The defense and prosecution lawyers appeared on countless television shows while newspapers covered every motion, every filing and then every moment of the trial itself. And the public, particularly juvenile advocacy groups, criticized the state of Florida for prosecuting Tate as an adult. If ever there was a trial ripe for a media circus this was it.

Part of that media attention was by design. In a personal interview with me in 2005, Defense attorney Jim Lewis admitted that he courted media attention because he wanted to attract other law professionals who could assist him with his media influence defense. Lewis described Tate as a perfect example of the type of kid who could fall prey to the negative effects of media violence. Tate had no contact with his father and spent much of his childhood moving around to different homes with his mother. He was a boy of lower than average intelligence whose teachers reported was obsessed with wrestling and watched it every time it was on television. Lewis explained that Tate hero-worshipped several of the wrestlers and may have even seen them as the father figure he was missing in his own life. Since Tate had never been to a live wrestling match Lewis believed that Lionel could only have learned the wrestling moves that he used on Tiffany by watching television. And because the television world of wrestling rarely results in any real injuries, it was entirely believable that Tate did not understand the true consequences of his actions. The heavy marketing focus on children, Lewis explained, proved that professional wrestling purposefully targets children with programming that falsely portrays the consequences of physical aggression against others.

Shortly after the grand jury indictment, Broward County Prosecutor Kenneth Padowitz offered the defendant a plea arrangement that would involve no jail time. The offer solicited criticism from those who believed Tate should be prosecuted to the fullest extent of the law. The agreement involved three years confinement in a juvenile facility, 10 years probation with psychological therapy, and 1,000 hours of community service. Padowitz explained that the decision to offer Tate a plea agreement with such a short time of confinement was made with Tiffany's mother. Padowitz later described the case as "heartbreaking" because he had two children the same ages as Tiffany and Tate, but felt he had a moral obligation to consult the victim's mother with any plea agreement. While he said he was horrified by the brutality of the violence against Tiffany, Padowitz did not believe that Tate deserved to be sent to prison for life. In a display of uncommon compassion and forgiveness Tiffany's mother agreed to the deal and Tate was offered the plea agreement. Right before the case was set to go to trial the defendant and his mother declined the plea agreement and the case against Tate went forward. Tate's mother later defended her decision to discourage Lionel from accepting the plea by saying that she never really believed that he would be convicted, so she didn't see the need for a plea. Gossett-Tate maintained throughout that Tiffany's death was an accident and that her son should not be held liable for an accident. Lionel did not, she claimed, harbor any ill will toward Tiffany and he never intended to hurt her. And, she argued, in America, we do not put children away in prison for accidents.

The Pre-Trial Maneuvers

In September 1999, the prosecutor filed a motion to revoke bond and have Tate remanded to a state juvenile facility until trial. While Tate had not returned to his former school he was enrolled at a new school and was living at home with his mother. He was also monitored by an electronic ankle bracelet at all times. Because he was awaiting trial on first-degree murder charges there was concern that he might pose a danger to other students. At a bond revocation hearing the state presented two forensic psychologists who had interviewed Tate, and another psychologist who was consulted to interpret and analyze the transcripts of these interviews. Dr. Michael Brannon was appointed by the court to assess the risk posed by Tate to others while he was awaiting trial. Dr. Brannon testified that all the psychologists involved agreed to share the testing information from a Rorschach test and a Thematic Apperception Test. Brannon also spoke with Tate's mother and father once each and conducted a Behavior Assessment System for Children, which he described as measuring general psychological information (Brannon, personal interview). Brannon evaluated whether Tate had any psychological or personality disorders. Was he disconnected from reality or socially immature? He then looked at these factors to determine if Tate was a risk to the community in any way. Brannon testified that based on these test results he believed that Tate posed "a high risk or high potential for violence" (*Florida vs. Tate*, Bond revocation hearing, p. 7.) Specifically, Brannon testified that while he did believe that the risk was high, he didn't think that Tate posed an immediate risk of violence to himself or others. Brannon characterized Tate as quick to anger in their interviews even though he knew he was being evaluated, and reported that he made attempts to be dishonest in his answers. Brannon also cited concerns with Tate's impulse control testifying that "there were indications at times that he did have difficulty maintaining or putting brakes on his behavior" (p. 9). Tate's aunt and father told Brannon in interviews that Lionel did not always know how to "slow down his behavior" (p. 17).

Family members were not the first to raise the issue of Tate's problems. He had reportedly been suspended from school fifteen times and one of Tate's teachers even contacted the prosecutor when she saw news accounts of his arrest. In interviews Padowitz stated that the teacher called to tell him that Tate was a huge discipline problem in her class, often holding other students in a bear hug or other wrestling moves. The teacher also reportedly told Padowitz that each time Tate's mother was called to the school she defended her son and tried to focus blame elsewhere. She also came to the school in full police uniform and gun which many teachers interpreted as an attempt to intimidate school officials.

Brannon also testified that Tate had identified numerous violent images during the Rorschach test: a laser gun that had been split down the middle by a razor, a giant getting ready to squash a tree and a scorpion with its mouth open (p. 9). Brannon attempted to administer more objective tests, such as the Behavior Assessment System for Children, but found Tate's exam invalid because his answers indicated an attempt to minimize or deny the severity of problems that most children would agree were wrong or improper. In other words, Tate's failure to recognize examples of unacceptable behavior rendered his answers outside the acceptable range for validity (p. 11). All of these results led Brannon to state that he believed Tate did pose a threat to society and that he should be placed in a behavioral management program that provided a structured living environment (p. 12).

On cross-examination Jim Lewis, Tate's defense attorney, questioned Brannon's method of inducing anger in Tate and questioned whether it was unusual that the teenager would lie, especially given that the last time he was questioned about this incident he was arrested. Was it possible, Lewis asked, that Tate was merely scared to be interviewed by Brannon and not intentionally misleading him or lying to him? Of course it was possible, Brannon responded, but it was the cumulative effect of the dishonesty, the various test results and the defendant's past history of violence in school that led to his recommendation for confinement.

Tate's highly unusual answers during the Rorschach test were further explained by Dr. Edward Conner, a licensed clinical psychologist who was asked to review Tate's Rorschach and Thematic Apperception Test (TAT) results. Connor testified that he was surprised by the high level of aggressive responses in Tate's Rorschach answers. "You would expect a child this age to give approximately 1.08 aggressive responses in a test like this. Mr. Tate gave six aggressive responses" (p. 28). Connor went on to demonstrate that the standard deviation is .66 for aggressive responses for children this age. This means that a normal range for aggressive responses would be .42 to 1.74 (.66 below and above the mean of 1.08). Tate's six aggressive responses placed him way beyond the normal range for children his age. Conner also pointed out that Tate gave so-called morbid responses (those expressing damaged views or perception) four times. The median number of morbid responses for children his age is .67. The two measures on the Rorschach test led Connor to conclude that "these issues would certainly make me look for other correlates of behavior that suggest there is a degree of possible violence" (p. 29).

Conner found that correlative evidence in Tate's responses on the TAT exam. The exam is a projective test in which participants are shown a series of pictures. The participants then tell a story about the picture, what is going on, what is going to happen to the people, etc. Again, Tate's answers were highly aggressive and beyond the normal range expected. Three of the five stories Tate related involved violent crimes (kidnapping, burglary and murder) and two resulted in the perpetrator escaping any punishment for his crime (p. 10). The results of these two independent exams led Connor to testify that he was disturbed by the results of Tate's views.

Dr. Sherry Bourg-Carter, who was hired by the prosecution to evaluate Tate, also testified to the high level of aggressiveness in his answers. "On almost every percept he was asked to give there was some amount of anger, aggression, or damage — squashed butterflies, and a giant jumping on something and smashing something for no reason, a bug's face being peeled off with tweezers" (p. 38). As with Brannon, Bourg-Carter testified that the combination of the test results and Tate's behavior during his interview led her to believe that he was a potential danger to other children. She also was so concerned about the high number of violent answers made by Tate during his testing that she called in Dr. Connor, who is considered an expert in the field of child projective tests. She explained that at the time of her interview Tate stated that he was being home-schooled so she was less concerned that he could endanger others. Upon learning at the hearing that he was, in fact, enrolled in a private school with full access to other children, Bourg-Carter favored confinement for Tate.

On cross-examination Lewis again pressed the issue that Tate's alleged dishonest answers were the result of the pressure he was under in the face of a conviction. Lewis asked Dr. Bourg-Carter if it was surprising that a 12-year-old would lie and whether lying made Tate a danger to society. Bourg-Carter conceded that lying did not make him dangerous and explained that his psychological testing alone should not be the sole indicator for determining whether he should be confined or not. The incidence of morbid and violent answers, combined with the school reports of violence, built a profile of a youth capable of further violence. Tate's mother may have worsened the situation by minimizing his actions and trying to cover them up. When Bourg-Carter interviewed his mother as to why he had been suspended twice from school, Tate's mother said she could not remember. It was left to Lewis to explain during the hearing that Tate's suspensions were due to fighting with others at school.

The testimony presented by these psychologists was the first glimpse into Tate as the young man. And the picture painted thus far was not favorable. Tate's teachers and school disciplinary records described a bully who picked on others and appeared incapable of controlling his anger. Tate's story changed often when recited to police and psychological investigators. And while Tate may have thought he was clever enough to deal with school officials, he was not skilled in fooling the forensic psychologists. The defense called one witness who tried to show Tate's actions in a very different light, those of a frightened little boy who had no concept of the law-enforcement process. Dr. Joel Klass did not participate in the initial psychological testing of Tate, but the child psychiatrist reported that he had interviewed Lionel on three different occasions for a total of six hours. Klass testified that Tate initially lied to him about the circumstances surrounding his play activities with Tiffany the day she died but that he attributed this to fear over his earlier experiences of being questioned and then confined. Klass reported that it took awhile for Tate to trust him and that once he did he told the psychiatrist that he was roughhousing with Tiffany that day and that when he threw her for the fourth time she was hurt (p. 54). Klass also asked Tate to demonstrate for him how he was roughhousing with Tiffany that day, a task Tate was unwilling to do. Again, Klass reported that it took him several tries to convince Tate to use the full force of his strength as he would likely have done with the young girl. He was, Klass testified, too fearful of the consequences to replicate his acts until the fourth try. And Klass was convinced that Tate's roughhousing was directly linked to his love of wrestling. Once he was relaxed, Tate demonstrated great knowledge of the moves used by the professional wrestlers.

Although Klass painted a very different picture of Tate based on his interviews, he was quick to discount the types of test administered by the forensic psychologists. Calling such tests "dangerous" and the practice "ridiculous" to use to incarcerate someone, Klass kept reiterating that Tate's tests were invalid because he was scared and that Brannon purposefully agitated Tate, which did nothing to encourage him to be trusting during these interview sessions. Klass also believed that Tate had no idea that his size (165 lbs.) afforded him any unusual strength or that he had any intent to hurt his much younger and smaller playmate. Klass explained that "if he is playing with a younger child and he is into wrestling, I don't think he realizes that even just rolling onto or falling against a younger child, because that's in wrestling all the time, can cause serious and multiple internal wounds" (p. 59).

Under cross-examination Klass admitted that he could not determine with any real certainty whether Tate was telling him the truth. The doubt raised did little to resolve the conflicting views of Tate's testing. The absence of the psychologist chosen by the defense to administer the tests in the first place made it even more difficult to determine Tate's potential danger to society. Why that individual was absent was never discussed in the hearing transcript. So it can only be assumed that his testimony would not have been favorable to the defense and therefore was not presented.

Ultimately the judge determined that Tate did not present an immediate danger to society and allowed him to remain in the custody of his mother, under 24-hour monitoring through an ankle bracelet. The bond revocation hearing gave a hint of the strategies that would be used in the upcoming trial. The prosecution would present Tate as a bully, known for violent outbursts in school, whose teachers even predicted that someday he would seriously injure someone. Further, prosecutors would argue that after Tiffany was injured Tate did nothing to help her, even ridiculed her for acting "like a baby" and later lied to law enforcement to cover up his actions. The defense, of course, would present a very different picture. Tate was not a violent predator, just a television wrestling-obsessed kid who simply didn't understand how strong he was or how his play could harm another. The changes in his version of the events were not a calculated manipulation of the system but just the understandable inconsistencies of a young, frightened defendant. The false "reality" of television wrestling, where wrestlers appear to beat up one another but reappear unscathed the next week, led the impressionable Tate to believe that he could do the same. He wasn't a violent kid, just an oversized adolescent with a love of wrestling who never grasped the unrealistic consequences of the violence portrayed in televised wrestling.

Five. *Lionel Tate and the TV Wrestling Defense*

Kenneth Padowitz's tactics for prosecuting Tate were as unconventional as the crime itself. Padowitz used the charge of aggravated child abuse as the underlying criminal act with the felony murder indictment. A felony-murder rule applies when death is caused during the commission of another felony. A common example is an armed robber who shoots and kills a store owner as he reaches to push a silent alarm during the robbery. The robber did not enter the store with the intent to kill anyone. But because he did enter with the intent to rob and in the commission of that felony also murdered the store owner, a charge of felony murder may apply. Padowitz believed that Tate's physical harm to Tiffany and his subsequent indifference to her suffering met the definition of child abuse. This would be similar to any adult who does physical or mental abuse to a child, or neglects it to its physical or emotional detriment. As a general intent crime, aggravated child abuse provided evidence of intent to harm Tiffany, therefore the prosecution didn't need to prove any specific intent by Tate to murder in order to win a conviction of felony murder.

In our personal interview in 2005, defense attorney Jim Lewis called this a clear "bastardization of the child abuse statute." Lewis argued that child abuse laws were never meant to describe behavior between children and that it was completely improper to apply it in this situation. Since a plea of diminished capacity is not allowed in the state of Florida, Tate entered a plea of not guilty. Lewis actively courted media coverage because he intended to show that Tate was "intoxicated" by television wrestling and was immature in comparison with most children his age. In place of the diminished capacity defense Lewis would argue that Tate fell prey to the unrealistic world of television wrestling due to his immaturity and infancy. Infancy is a commonly accepted excuse defense that states that because of a defendant's young age he or she does not possess the maturity to make the decision to commit a crime. To prove this Lewis intended to call stars of television wrestling shows to testify and demonstrate how they train to make their fictitious moves look real. Lewis intended to convince a jury that professional wrestlers train extensively to trick the audience. What looked to us in the viewing audience as real violence was, in fact, a highly orchestrated and choreographed dramatic presentation designed to fool us. Wrestlers trained to make their violent acts look real while not actually hurting each other. And if someone in the audience, say an immature, impressionable child, did not fully understand the expert theatrics

135

involved in television wrestling, they likely would not understand the full ramifications of copying these violent wrestling moves either. As such, the television wrestling intoxication defense was born.

Lewis tried to subpoena several famous television wrestlers to explain the professional training wrestlers go through to support his defense strategy. But the stars of the wrestling world had no intention of getting dragged into the limelight of media scrutiny surrounding this child murder trial. Attorney Jerry McDevitt represented Dwayne Johnson, AKA The Rock, in arguing against his subpoena. McDevitt blasted the defense strategy as a desperate act to shift blame for Tate's behavior:

> From our standpoint of the law, it's been our position, expressed in the papers, this whole case is basically a factual and legal hoax. It has nothing to do with the facts of the case and there is no law whatsoever, not only in Florida, but anywhere in the country that supports the propositions being advanced by the defense, which is essentially asking this court to accept a new defense that's never been recognized in Florida courts, never been recognized by any courts, and I submit to your Honor, will never be recognized by any courts, which is, I saw on TV, so I go free defense, which is essentially an absolute defense that Mr. Tate is suggesting that he has available to him in this case. If he was engaged in some of the imitative behavior of something he saw on TV he can convince the jury he didn't mean harm and walk free out of the courtroom [*Florida v. Tate*, Supplemental appeal on behalf of defendant by Jerry McDevitt, p.4].

McDevitt argued that wrestling really had nothing to do with this case and that any attempt to designate professional wrestlers as experts regarding media effects was futile at best. This sentiment was echoed in the Affidavit of Terry Bollea (Hulk Hogan), another professional wrestler subpoenaed by Lewis. Bollea argued that he should not have to testify because he had no first-hand knowledge of the facts of this case and had never been qualified to testify as an expert on any manner relating to professional wrestling. Further, Bollea questioned the defense motives for compelling his disposition: "I believe the only purpose that would be served by allowing my disposition to go forward would be to embarrass and harass me by severely intruding and interrupting my private life and disrupting my job (*Florida v. Tate*, Supplemental appeal on behalf of defendant Terry Bollea, p. 2). An identical affidavit was filed by Steve Borden, who, like Bollea, was identified as an independent contractor with the World Wrestling Federation (WWF). Both claimed that they were not experts, were not witnesses to the case and did not have any connection to it, and therefore could not be compelled to testify.

Lewis responded with an admission that this "was an unusual case" with circumstances that "don't get anymore extreme than this in terms of a 12-year-old boy who is charged with first degree murder as an adult" (*Florida v. Tate*, supplemental appeal, p. 13). The fact that Tate had told Dr. Brannon during this interview that he idolized The Rock and Sting proved that these wrestlers were very influential on his behavior. Without their testimony it would be difficult to show that Tate was influenced by a group of professionals that, in essence, didn't really exist. These men were not truly engaging in the ancient art of wrestling, but rather were trained actors whose job it was to trick the viewer into thinking their actions were real. Further, Lewis argued that professional wrestlers were in no position to determine the appropriateness of a legal defense strategy. "It bothers me that the WWF thinks they can come here and either tag up with the State or somehow be involved with the State and say your defense has no merit.... That's the State's job" (p. 13).

While the wrestlers were fighting their subpoenas to appear, Prosecutor Padowitz responded by filing a Motion in Limine to exclude the testimony of professional wrestlers as experts and to disallow the television intoxication defense. Padowitz also called the intoxication defense a "hoax" defense and filed the motion to disallow expert testimony for the following four reasons:

1. A professional wrestling defense based on television intoxication is, in effect, a defense of diminished capacity, invalid as such in Fla.

2. The defense of television intoxication is not a "commonly understood condition."

3. The wrestling defense is in actuality irresistible impulse which is invalid in Fl.

4. Expert testimony opining a lack of intent, to-wit: the incident was an accident, is barred under Fl. Law.

Lewis' response argued admissibility for two reasons:

1. Any condition relating to the ability to form a specific interest is relevant; infancy is such an admissible condition.

2. Any evidence to show accidental killing is relevant, including immaturity [*Florida v. Tate*, case no. 99–14401CF10A, Order by Judge Joel T. Lazarus, 2000, p. 2].

Violence in the Media and Its Influence on Criminal Defense

A hearing on the motion to exclude the television intoxication defense was held on May 4, 2000. The key questions included the admission of expert testimony regarding the television intoxication defense strategy, the inclusion of testimony regarding the maturity of Tate, and the admissibility of a video reenactment of the incident performed by Tate and defense psychiatrist Dr. Joel Klass. While Dr. Bourg-Carter testified that Tate had, in her opinion, a maturity level just below a normal 12-year-old, Klass painted a very different picture. He testified that Tate was immature and completely "absorbed and fascinated" by the action and vividness of television wrestling (p. 2). In Klass's opinion Tate's low maturity was a direct result of Tate's high level of exposure to television wrestling.

Even more provocative was a video Klass shot in which he and Lionel reenacted the events that led to Tiffany's death. On the tape Tate admits to hitting Tiffany between 35 and 40 times in the chest and reenacts how she once narrowly missed hitting her head on a metal pole. The video was presented as an accurate representation of the events since Klass reported that he kept pushing Lionel to act in the same manner as the day of the incident, displaying the "same intensity" of play as he did with the little girl. This was a direct reference to Klass's testimony at the bond revocation hearing that Tate initially was holding back, and not truthfully demonstrating the force of his actions for fear of being jailed again. This time Klass was convinced the video was an accurate recollection of the events since he had worked with Tate and gained his trust.

But the judge was not convinced of the accuracy of the video reenactment. Judge Joel T. Lazarus wrote in his opinion that there was no mention or record of any verbal reactions by Tiffany throughout the incident. No cries for help, no pleas to stop, nothing. This strained credibility the judge wrote, "creating some doubt as to the label of 'accuracy'" of the video (p. 3). The judge ultimately delivered a split ruling that set the stage for the arguments that would be allowed at trial. The state's motion to deny the expert testimony as to Tate's infancy and maturity level was denied. The judge ruled that intent must be proven, whether it was of a general (aggravated child abuse) or specific nature. The defense was allowed therefore to present expert testimony as to Tate's mental age and maturity at the time of Tiffany's death. However, the judge did not allow the defense to mount a campaign to prove that Tate's mental infancy and immaturity were caused by television wrestling intoxication. The judge cited the ruling in *Frye v. US* (1923) that required that novel scientific evidence must be generally accepted by the scientific community as accurate and reliable.

> Just when a scientific principle or discovery crosses the line between the experimental and demonstrable stages is difficult to define. Somewhere in this twilight zone the evidential force of the principle must be recognized, and while courts will go a long way in admitting expert testimony deduced from a well-recognized scientific principle or discovery, the thing from which the deduction is made must be sufficiently established to have gained general acceptance in the particular field in which it belongs.

Lewis patterned his strategy after the unsuccessful "television intoxication" defense in Ronny Zamora's 1978 murder trial, and wanted to show that Tate's immaturity was caused by his excessive viewing of the unrealistic sport of television wrestling. But even the defense's own witness, Dr. Klass, admitted that there has been very little scientific research done on the effects of television wrestling on viewers, and on children in particular. Padowitz had also argued that wrestling intoxication was simply a clever redressing of the defenses of diminished capacity and irresistible impulse, both of which are invalid in Florida. The scientific evidence needed to allow such testimony was simply not established. The judge wrote that "at this point, no such proof, as required by Frye has been presented. It is the court's opinion that the impact of television professional wrestling on a preteen's infancy and maturity level is a novel science" (p. 7). As such the television wrestling intoxication strategy was out unless Lewis could prove in a separate Frye hearing that sufficient scientific studies existed to support this argument. At the trial Dr. Klass would not be allowed to opine that television wrestling caused Tate's immaturity, and the professional wrestlers ultimately would not be used to show that Tate was duped by their intentional acts of deception.

For Lewis, the ruling effectively "handcuffed his defense" (personal interview). Without being able to show how Tate was different and therefore capable of being influenced by this fictional violence, jurors would likely resort to the common comparison that millions of kids watch television wrestling every day and don't kill. Why did Tate?

The Trial and Verdict

Just five days before the trial began, the court held a plea colloquy during which Padowitz again offered Tate the plea bargain that guaranteed he would serve no time in an adult prison. The state offered Tate a deal of three years in a juvenile detention facility, followed by ten years probation. At the hearing Tate told the court that he understood the terms of the plea, and that he understood the implications of accepting the plea or rejecting the plea and proceeding to trial. After consulting with Tate and his mother, Lewis told the court that Tate wished to reject the plea and that he wanted to proceed to trial. Judge Lazarus questioned Tate and once again he stated that he understood the offer and the consequences of rejecting the offer and that no one had pressured him to reject it. To that the judge concluded, "I'm convinced that Mr. Tate has sufficient ability to make a decision in this very important matter" (*Tate v. Fl.*, Case no. 4D01–1306, p. 4).

The two-week trial was much like any other murder trial. Court testimony focused on the evidence and many of the experts who had testified at the pre-trial hearings reappeared to give insight into Tate's maturity, intelligence and actions. Some dramatic moments were provided by the prosecutor who showed a life-size model of Tiffany and all of her wounds as identified by the coroner. Tate testified that he thought Tiffany was acting like a baby because she was crying after he hit her and even urinated on herself. He left her lying there while he went back to watching television. Tate's mother testified that she heard Tiffany's screams and told Lionel to tell her to be quiet so she could go back to sleep. After a considerable amount of time passed Lionel realized that Tiffany was not breathing and he summoned his mother for help. By then Tiffany was dead.

On January 25, 2001, the court transcript shows that the jury was admitted into the courtroom at approximately 8:25 A.M. to receive instructions for the day. At 2:00 P.M. the jury buzzed that it had reached a verdict. After a short delay the jury foreperson delivered a verdict of guilty of murder in the first degree as outlined in the indictment (*Florida vs. Tate*, Transcript of trial proceedings, p. 40). Following a roll call vote by all jurors Judge Lazarus made a statement acknowledging the difficult environment surrounding this case and the intense public scrutiny. Lazarus (p. 45) praised both sides for their professionalism during such a controversial case and called Padowitz and Lewis a "credit to your profession." Lewis immediately asked that Tate be released to home confinement while awaiting sentencing but Judge Lazarus denied this motion saying that with "adjudicated Felony Murder in the first degree, I believe I have an obligation and I am remanding him to the custody of the Sheriff. I'm ordering the sheriff to treat Mr. Tate as a 13-year-old. And I would strongly recommend he be housed at the juvenile facility" (p. 44).

The reaction to the jury's verdict was swift and loud. Richard Rosenbaum, working with defense counsel Lewis, filed a motion for a new trial that listed numerous legal arguments for the verdict to be overturned. Along with several standard arguments (the verdict is contrary to the weight of the evidence, the verdict is contrary to law) the pair argued that aggravated child abuse was unconstitutionally applied to this case (*Florida v. Tate*, Motion for trial, 2001). They also alleged numerous procedural errors, including the trial court's denial to present testimony concerning media violence and professional wrestling and its effect on Tate's intent (part 23), and the denial of subpoenas to members of the WWF and the World Championship Wrestling Federation (part 24). Rosenbaum and Lewis also filed a motion to reduce the charge to second-degree murder or manslaughter based on the contention that Tate did not intend to kill Tiffany. Finally, Rosenbaum also filed a request for a competency hearing and evaluation on the grounds that Tate did not really understand the consequences of proceeding to trial and because of this and his documented immaturity was not able to assist his counsel in any meaningful way.

Juvenile justice advocates also worked quickly to look for a loophole in the state's mandatory life sentence for a murder in the first-degree conviction. Several would file formal petitions for dismissal of the conviction. Several jurors also told the press that they were upset that the guilty verdict would send Lionel to prison for life. Kathleen Pow-Sang described most jurors as "annoyed" that the trial was not adjudicated through the juvenile system. Juror Steve Danker told reporters, "I don't think anybody there thought that Lionel intended to kill her, but the state didn't have to prove that. I think it was too easy for them (with the underlying aggravated child-abuse charge)" ("Jurors felt decision was imposed," p. 8A). Even the prosecutor, Ken Padowitz, made statements to the media that he might approach Governor Bush about reducing the sentence or the charges against Tate so that he could avoid the mandatory life sentence. Padowitz explained that he would ask the governor "to consider reducing to a sentence that is more appropriate for all the facts in this case, taking into consideration Tate's age at the time he committed the crime" ("Enough blame to go around," online). The Reverend Dennis Grant, a long-time advocate for Tate, wrote a letter to Governor Bush asking that he intervene in the sentencing process as he blamed Tate's mother for not encouraging the young boy to accept the plea. He asked the governor to impose the conditions of the original plea bargain: "Failing this I offer myself to serve the time."

Judge Lazarus received dozens of letters from citizens around the nation who had heard about Tate's conviction and made suggestions for Tate's sentence. Most asked for leniency and pleaded for Lazarus to give the young boy another chance. Carlton Moore, a District III commissioner in Ft. Lauderdale, appealed to the judge to sentence psychological counseling for Lionel and as well as both sets of parents. Sue Britton of Illinois appealed to the judge as a mother of three. She recounted in her four-page letter that as a ten-year-old child she talked her little brothers into jumping off the roof, not fully understanding the potential consequences. She told the judge that "children don't think like adults," and encouraged him to give Tate a sentence of counseling, not prison. Cynthia Manning, who identified herself as a concerned citizen, submitted a petition with 125 names asking that Tate be treated as a child, not an adult. Manning wrote that Tate was "a child who made a misguided but not malicious mistake. Do not put him in an adult prison, please send him home." Still, others were convinced that the judge had it wrong when he declined to allow wrestling a greater role in Lionel's actions. These writers were convinced that it was possible, if not likely, that Tate fell prey to the fantasy world of television wrestling and could not have known the real consequences of his actions. Helen Smith wrote that "wrestling is truly having an alarming negative impact on young children," while suggesting a sentence of counseling and community service for two years. Smith further tried to deflect blame from Tate by raising the possibility that some of Tiffany's injuries could have been sustained prior to coming to the Tate home. Whether she was implying that Tiffany's own family caused the injuries or some other child was not clear, but it was apparent that the letter writer questioned the evidence and the verdict that followed. Others wrote that it was entirely understandable that Tate would think that his opponent would simply get up and walk away like they do on television wrestling (Cagle). Or that a child "thinks everything works just like on TV. Nobody ever really gets hurt" (Davidson). Some letters were sent from prisoners who wrote about the lack of rehabilitation in prison and asked the judge to give Tate a better chance at redeeming his adult life. Their suggestion was that Tate be given no jail time. Other letter writers didn't address Tate's guilt or innocence but merely encouraged the judge to impose the terms of the original plea agreement that Tate and his mother had declined. But not all appeals were for mercy toward Tate. Tom Matthews wrote on behalf of his family and laid blame for Tate's actions on his mother, not professional televised wrestling. Matthews asked the judge to "ignore the crying and pleas of Lionel's negligent mother" and grant no chance of parole for fear he would hurt or kill again (Matthews).

Some mental health groups asked the judge to be lenient based on the misinformation that Tate had been diagnosed as retarded. Michael Brannon explained that many of his evaluative findings were misrepresented to the public, especially when it came to Tate's intelligence. Brannon found that Tate's IQ was "low average — not retarded as many in the media reported. He had more than enough intellectual abilities to appreciate and understand what he was doing. So it was wrongly portrayed by the media that he had low IQ. There were no dispersions cast upon his intellectual ability by anybody other than the attorneys — the defense attorney" (personal interview).

At the sentencing hearing on March 9, 2001, Judge Lazarus immediately rejected defense pleas for a new trial and for a reduced sentence for Tate. Dozens of witnesses pleaded with the judge for leniency. Friends, relatives and clergy alike argued for a light sentence, some even asking for no jail time in favor of counseling instead. Deborah White told the judge that her own children, including an 8-year-old son with cerebral palsy, regularly played with Tate with no incidence of violence. Tate's own mother told the judge that she couldn't do anything to bring back Tiffany but "I have to stay here and fight for Lionel, because I know how he felt about Tiffany. So please be lenient" ("Governor Bush Open to Clemency," online).

Lazarus began his ruling by acknowledging the letters he received as well as the national and international attention the case had attracted. He admonished the public appeals to the media following the verdict and addressed the letter writers who asked for clemency directly:

Within sixteen hours of the verdict, opening statements were being made in a new forum... This was not the media doing its job or reporting; this was a calculated effort to try this case for a second time in a court not governed by the laws of the state of Florida but by the feelings of sympathy and compassion for a fourteen-year-old convicted of the highest offense known to mankind.

Most of the letters (sent to the judge pre-sentencing) and calls refer to the victim only as an afterthought. In the court of public opinion, Lionel Tate has turned into the victim. It is obvious what the purpose of these appearances in studios and on the pulpits by participants has been. If the purpose is to pressure this court to proceed with its heart rather than its mind, with all due respect, I decline [Sentencing order, p. 1].

The opening statement set the stage for the wrath of a judge who had presided over one of the biggest public legal spectacles in the Florida courts. Lazarus went on to dismiss the defense motion for a new trial ruling that there was nothing in the aggravated child abuse statute that precludes it from being applied to children, and was not, therefore, applied unconstitutionally in this case. He also dismissed the motion for reduction of the charges. The definition of child abuse is the intentional infliction, or an intentional act, that could reasonably be expected to result in physical injury to a child. Lazarus believed that the evidence supported Tate's intentional acts and his indifference to Tiffany's suffering.

Lazarus reserved some of his harshest criticism for those who lobbied for a light sentence or probation for Tate. He wrote that Florida law provided him no authority to impose the plea agreement that Tate himself had rejected the year before. Nor was he able to reduce the charges as had been done a few years earlier in the infamous "Nanny" murder trial in Massachusetts. After a jury found a British nanny guilty of murdering a child in her care, the judge reduced the charges to manslaughter which resulted in a much lighter penalty. Lazarus explained that Florida law did not provide for him to overrule the charges sought by the state. He also admonished Tate's mother for not encouraging her son to take the plea agreement and for her continuing protestations in the media that she didn't fully understand the legal quagmire her son was in. Lazarus wrote:

Testimony was received on March 2, 2001 and again today from Mrs. Grossett-Tate. She testified that she never knew or made inquiry as to the penalty for Murder in the First Degree. As a law enforcement officer, for her to say that she did not know the penalty for Murder in the First Degree is beyond credibility. For her to state that she did not ask if Lionel Tate would be facing that potentiality is unbelievable. Of course the issue is whether her son, the defendant knew. The court is satisfied that from early on, including his competency evaluation, he knew what he was facing.

Additionally, these statements made to the world by Mrs. Grossett-Tate as recently as a week ago state that no plea would ever be accepted; even now, in her words, this was an accident [p. 6].

Lazarus also admonished Padowitz for his willingness to ask the governor to set aside a conviction he had so skillfully and dutifully sought on behalf of Florida state law. The judge labeled such actions as dangerous and "totally inconsistent" with Padowitz's role in the prosecutor's office (p. 7). To those who believed Tiffany's death was an accident, Lazarus pointed to testimony that consistently showed that Tate knew, or should have known, that his actions were inflicting serious injury to the girl who was half his age and considerably smaller than him. The thirty wounds to her body could not have resulted from normal play or a one-time accidental use of excessive force. And, Lazarus wrote, any child would easily recognize when they hurt another and would stop their behavior immediately (p. 12). Tate did not do this and when his mother yelled at the children for making too much noise that night, he did not tell her that Tiffany was hurt and did not seek help until much later.

Lazarus also went into great detail to address those who laid blame for Tate's actions on the world of professional television wrestling. Although the television wrestling intoxication strategy was greatly limited in pre-trial motions, there was a concerted effort to advance this theory in the popular media. Lazarus responded by using Tate's own testimony to dispel any notion that television was to blame for his actions that evening.

It was shown, without dispute, that Lionel Tate was a fan of wrestling. Perhaps even zealous in his love for this type of "entertainment." But the facts on which the jury relied are deceptively simple in rejecting the involvement of professional wresting replication; thus, by necessary implication, (rejecting) accident:

1. In the two statements to the police, Lionel Tate's own words failed to indicate that wrestling played any part in Tiffany's brutal murder. The statements did not come close to explaining what happened in the townhouse.

2. In statements to EMS workers and the police by the defendant's

mother, she claimed neither accident nor wrestling played any part in Tiffany's fatality.

Not until there was a defense-initiated reenactment did actions imitating professional wrestling start to emerge as a defense. This reenactment totally failed to explain the extent and severity of the injuries to Tiffany Eunick. Even though the reenactment depicted a connection to professional wrestling, the testimony of Dr. Brannon shows that Lionel Tate disbelieved the authenticity of what he saw on TV.

Accordingly, the jury obviously then, and this court now, did not and does not accept that replicating what may or may not have been seen in various televised wrestling shows as a reason to call Lionel Tate's action accidental.

It should be noted that not only did the state's witnesses eliminate the possibility of accident but the defense's own expert, Dr. John Marracini, negated the argument of accident [p. 13].

Lazarus closed by summarizing his obvious frustration with the great amount of public comment, indeed even outrage, expressed by some citizens and advocacy groups who he believed did not grasp the legal intricacies of this case. The fact that Lionel Tate was charged as an adult was enough to garner the case national attention. The introduction of the TV wrestling defense just furthered the media frenzy. There was no shortage of politicians, pundits and advocates ready to debate the merits of the case in the media. The constant barrage of media attention, coupled with the involvement of groups such as professional wrestlers, rendered the legal freak show virtually unstoppable. Lazarus rejected these peripheral arguments and wrote that this case was not about race, nor professional wrestling, nor the treatment of juveniles in the adult court system. It was, he believed, about a little girl whose life was cut tragically short by a teenager who acted way beyond the years of childhood innocence. Lazarus leveled a harsh admonishment to those who offered commentary and criticism without the benefit of knowing the facts of the case.

> I am moved by the outpouring of concern for Lionel Tate. At the same time I am dismayed by the lack of concern for the child victimized by Lionel Tate. It is obvious that Tiffany Eunick will never have a second chance at life, and there are so many who plead for a second chance for the defendant.
>
> Only those who sat through the days of testimony can appreciate the nature of the acts of Lionel Tate.
>
> The acts of Lionel Tate were not playful acts of a child. The acts of Lionel Tate were cold, callous and indescribably cruel.

It is therefore the sentence of the court, in accordance with the laws of the state of Florida, that you, Lionel Tate, having been found guilty of murder in the First Degree in the death of Tiffany Eunick, be sentenced to incarceration for your natural life [p. 17].

The Appeal

Tate was taken from the courtroom in handcuffs and leg shackles and ultimately housed at the Okeechobee Juvenile Defenders Correction Center. Governor Jeb Bush held a news conference during which he expressed sympathy for both families and expressed his willingness to consider clemency once a formal request was filed by Tate's defense team ("Governor Bush open to clemency," online). Tate's defense team immediately began the appeals process. Richard Rosenbaum and his law partner Cheryl Zickler prepared an appeal based on no less than ten counts including alleged violations of Tate's due process because he was treated more harshly than other juveniles, a privacy violation because he was denied the confidentiality provision normally afforded juveniles, and the argument that life without parole was cruel and unusual punishment for juveniles. Ultimately, however, Gov. Bush declined the request for a clemency hearing, writing to Tate's attorneys that he "could find no compelling reason" to waive the standard two-year waiting period, especially in light of reports that Tate exhibited violent behavior while in custody, including an undocumented report that he stabbed another inmate ("Governor Bush Denies Clemency Hearing," online).

When Bush released his denial of the clemency, Rosenbaum began a public relations campaign to attract as much attention and legal firepower to the case as possible, as quickly as possible. Rosenbaum boasted of assembling his own defense "Dream Team" that included famed O. J. Simpson attorney Johnny Cochran. Cochran agreed to assist with the appeal and appeared on national television shows condemning Tate's life sentence. At the same time, Tate's mother was waging her own public relations spectacle. Grossett-Tate assembled a set of advisers, including her own attorney Henry Hunter and clergymen Thomas Masters and Dennis Grant. Grossett-Tate appeared on several national television programs after her son's sentencing explaining that she still believed that Tiffany's death was the result of an accident and appealed again to Gov. Bush for clemency. Masters, a bishop in the Greater Church of the Deliverance, became a staunch supporter and began a worldwide campaign to draw attention to Tate's sentencing. Masters is the founder of Under Our Wings, a nonprofit organization that helps juveniles who had been prosecuted in the adult court system. To garner support for Tate's clemency Masters brokered a personal meeting between Grossett-Tate and Pope John Paul II.

This was just one stop in the publicity machine that kept Lionel's case in the news. With each passing week the cast of characters got stranger and stranger. Grossett-Tate was escorted to every court proceeding by members of the Nation of Islam, and members of the Texas Black Panthers flew to Ft. Lauderdale to meet with Tate's defense team and pledged to raise $500,000 to help defray his legal fees ("Black Panthers Coming to help Tate," online). The Rev. Al Sharpton joined the Black Panthers for a clemency protest outside the Broward County Courthouse where Sharpton said he would ask Gov. Bush to hold a clemency hearing. Sharpton told reporters that he was consulting with Johnny Cochran on the case and that he told prosecutor Ken Padowitz that Tate never should have been prosecuted as an adult ("Sharpton Comes to Teen Convict's Defense," online). Observers remember the incident a bit differently. Press reports recounted Sharpton's charges of racism against Padowitz, while protestors marched with picket signs declaring "Padowitz is the Devil" and called for him to be fired.

Several juvenile justice organizations filed briefs urging the 4th District Court of Appeal to overturn Tate's conviction, based on procedural errors at trial because of his juvenile status. One Amici Curiae (friend of the court brief) filed by the Center on Children & the Law, et al., argued for dismissal of Tate's conviction because the organizations believed that Tate was simply too young to understand the complicated legal proceedings. The parties wrote that they "were dismayed by Lionel's case, which applied principles of adult criminal law in a context in which they were are so clearly inapplicable. The result was a miscarriage of justice that should be rectified on appeal" (Center on Children & the Law, et al., p. 1). The advocates went on to cite numerous specific constitutional grounds for reversal including arguments that the trial court's failure to consider Tate's age and documented immaturity violated the U.S. and Florida state constitutional protections of due process. They also argued that a mandatory life sentence without the possibility of parole applied to a 12-year-old amounted to cruel and unusual punishment. The friends acknowledged (p. 3) the emotional difficulty of a case involving such young children but wrote that Tiffany's death "should not deter us from the hard-headed thinking about the role of punishment and the appropriate balance of retribution, deterrence and rehabilitation in the life of a boy who was only 12 at the time. A system that ignores the laws of adolescent development is bound to be unfair... In this case the system stumbled because it sought to sidestep an American tradition of shaping justice to fit the blameworthiness and competence of young defendants."

Others petitioned the court to overturn Tate's conviction, primarily on the application of the felony-murder rule and the underlying felony charge of aggravated child abuse to this case. The Center for Florida's Children, joined by nine other parties, argued that the trial court erred when it applied the felony-murder rule to 12-year-old Tate who, by law, is presumed to be too young to form the needed criminal intent for such a crime. The felony-murder is predicated on liability when death occurs during the commission of a felony, which in Tate's case was aggravated child abuse. The group argued that Tate could not form criminal intent to commit a felony at such a young age and that the use of aggravated child abuse was incorrectly applied to Tate. They also argued Florida state statute § 827.03 (aggravated child abuse) was never intended to apply to children who hurt or kill another child during the course of play. By this logic, the group argued, every child whose school-yard scuffle ends in injury would be guilty of child abuse. Further, the group argued that Florida legislators wrote the law to protect children from a violent or negligent adult caregiver (p. 25). Although they stopped short of calling for criminal charges to be filed against Tate's mother, the group did write that the language set forth in the statute shows the "legislature's intent to focus on the culpability of the parent or caregiver who fails to supervise, rather than punishing the children who are left unsupervised. Under the statute, the key should be whether Lionel's mother, who was babysitting Tiffany, 'willfully or by culpable negligence neglected the children and in so doing caused great bodily harm' when she left them alone to play unsupervised while she slept" (Center for Florida's Children, et al., p. 33).

All of the legal arguments put forth on Tate's behalf were rejected by the appellate court except one, and one was all it took to overturn Tate's conviction. On December 10, 2003, the Fourth District Court of Appeal ruled that the absence of a court-ordered competency hearing did amount to a violation of Tate's due process rights. While the court acknowledged that Tate had stated several times throughout the proceedings that he understood the charges against him and the possible consequences of going to trial, the court ruled that Tate was not mature enough to make a self-determination of competency. At trial several mental health witnesses testified that Tate's IQ was 90, that he was immature and that he had the mental equivalency of a child 9–10 years old. But Dr. Sherry Bourg-Carter also had testified that she had performed a competency assessment during a pre-trial interview session with Tate and that she found him competent to stand trial. Although the assessment evaluation was not court-ordered, Bourg-Carter explained that the competency issue naturally emerged from the standard psychological tests administered and that Tate told her that he understood that going to trial could result in him going to jail for a very long time. Further, throughout the pre-trial motions and the trial itself the defense had never raised the issue of Tate's competency and none of their psychological experts testified to Tate's incompetence. Still, the appellate court ruled that Tate's age, his documented mental immaturity and the intricacies of the complex case warranted a competency hearing. The court overturned the verdict and ordered a new trial concluding that "due to his extremely young age and lack of previous exposure to the judicial system, a competency evaluation was constitutionally mandated to determine whether Tate had sufficient present ability to consult with a lawyer with a reasonable degree of rational understanding and whether he had a rational, as well as factual, understanding of the proceedings against him" (*Tate v. Fl.*, case no. 4D01–1306, p. 2.)

Florida state attorney General Charles Crist petitioned the 4th District Court to reconsider its dismissal of Tate's conviction on the grounds that no one, not even Tate's own defense team, ever raised any doubts about his competency until after he was convicted. Crist wrote that through two years of pre-trial motions and a trial "nothing about Tate's behavior triggered any questions" regarding his competency ("State asks for rehearing," online). But Richard Rosenbaum said one only needed to look at Tate's failure to accept the original plea agreement for proof that the youth was incompetent to participate in his own defense and that he didn't understand the judicial process in which he was embroiled. The ever-present Bishop Masters threatened "the largest demonstration Broward has ever seen" if the state decided to retry Tate on murder charges ("Justice for Juveniles, Massive protest planned," online). Juvenile justice organizations like the Youth Law Center heralded the news of Tate's successful appeal and used it as an indictment of all states that allow children to enter the adult system.

Ultimately the state decided not to retry the case against Tate and again offered him a plea agreement. Perhaps all the publicity and the original prosecutor's willingness at the time to petition the governor for clemency was enough to dissuade the state from proceeding with another first-degree murder trial against Tate. This time the plea agreement required Tate to plead guilty to second-degree murder in exchange for three years in prison, one year of house arrest and 1,000 hours of community service. Tate would be monitored with an ankle bracelet but would be allowed to leave home for school and church. He would remain on probation for 10 years. Observers believed the deal was a good one, offered again with the blessing of Tiffany's mother. Still Tate's mother stood in the way of her son accepting the plea because she believed that Tiffany's death was an accident and therefore warranted a plea of manslaughter instead. Her continued resistance to the plea did little to improve Grossett-Tate's public image. Editorials and public reaction cast her as an incredibly arrogant and reckless mother who would stop at nothing to save her own reputation. Critics charged that each time Tate accepted bad advice from his mother he paid the price by going to jail. Privately Tate's trial attorney Lewis (personal interview, 2005) acknowledged the difficulty in dealing with Grossett-Tate and her unwavering position that Lionel should receive no prison time. Lewis later wrote in a 2004 *Nova Law Review* article that the ABA Model Rules of Professional Conduct required that he communicate the matters of the case to his young client such that he could make an informed decision about his plea. But when that client is a child, and one regarded by some mental health experts as cognitively and emotionally immature, the child's parent will likely exert some influence on the child's decision. This, Lewis wrote, is often clouded by the parent's desire to protect a child from the severity of the possible legal punishment. There's also a natural inability to see one's own child as capable of such a serious crime as murder. Lewis concluded:

> As the Lionel Tate case illustrates, the role of the criminal attorney in representing a young teenager in adult court, charged with a serous crime, is

complex. The ultimate decisions must be made by the child client. However, the system is naïve if it believes children in this position will not be influenced, or even defer these decisions to the parent. All a lawyer can do is give good advice to the child client and the parent and hope the right decision will become apparent to all [p.484].

Tate did not need his mother's permission to accept the plea and this time Tate didn't let the chance pass him up. On January 29, 2004, Tate, in accordance with the new plea agreement, pled guilty to felony murder in the second degree. Deweese Eunick spoke at the hearing and told the court that she was relieved that Tate had finally taken responsibility for Tiffany's death. While she expressed forgiveness for Lionel, she blamed Grossett-Tate for not protecting her daughter that night.

> Lionel beat her so badly that no mother on this earth should ever have to live with the knowledge of these 35 injuries. No mother should have to live with the knowledge that her daughter cried out in pain and Kathleen Grossett-Tate would not come downstairs to help my baby. No mother should have to feel the pain every time she wears a police uniform and keeps up excuses for Lionel by crying that this was an accident ... Lionel's freedom is not a cause for celebration. My daughter is dead. There should be no celebration. My wish is that Lionel would grow up and never hurt another human being ["Victim's mother unloads," online].

This time Judge Lazarus sentenced Tate to the conditions of the plea agreement as well as psychological counseling and a requirement that he obtain his GED. It was to be a whole new beginning for Tate. Unfortunately things did not turn out that way.

Tate's New Beginning Is Short-lived

Within 10 months Tate was back in the news and it wasn't accolades for his accomplishments. Instead, Tate's picture was plastered on every area newspaper and TV news program because he had been arrested again, this time for violation of his house arrest and for a weapons violation. It seems that he was wandering the streets of Ft. Lauderdale at 2:30 A.M. with a knife in his pocket following Hurricane Frances. Once again the blame for Tate's wayward actions fell squarely on his mother. Richard Rosenbaum stated in court and in press interviews that Lionel's mother had thrown him out of the house following an argument but later lied to investigators that he was in the house all night ("Tate can return to mother's home," online). Former Prosecutor Padowitz called the accusations against Grosett-Tate troubling and suggested that the Florida Highway Patrol should investigate her ability to continue to uphold the laws of Florida ("Tate denies probation violation," online). Grossett-Tate and her attorney refused comment on the criticism leveled against her.

Tate's hearing went before Judge Lazarus, the same judge who had handled his murder trial. After prosecutors withdrew the weapons charge, the judge added five years to Tate's probation (for a total of 15 years) and allowed the young man to move in with another couple who were members of a church that had advocated for Tate's release and rehabilitation. The criticism of Tate's mother and the promise of a positive influence from others willing to add more structure and obedience to his life seemed to be a factor in the judge's decision not to revoke Tate's probation and send him back to jail for life. Lazarus allowed the teen to travel outside the house for work, school and church and promised zero tolerance for any new violation of his probation. But within a month the couple asked that Tate be removed because the constant checks by probation officers were "too stressful," so Tate returned to his mother's house ("Convicted child killer to return home," online). Despite the setbacks, Richard Rosenbaum was sure that Lionel could turn his life around, predicting that he "is going to become a beneficial member of society" ("Tate denies probation violation," online).

The prediction was short-lived. Just six months later, Tate was back in the national spotlight with predictions that the youth would be sent back to prison for life. On May 23, 2005, Tate was accused of robbing a Domino's pizza delivery man using a gun he stole from his mother who was out of town on a 10-day Army reserve assignment. Once again Grossett-Tate was front and center in the blame game. Reports surfaced that she had been told two months earlier by a neighborhood child that Lionel boasted of stealing her service revolver. Grossett-Tate told police that she did not report the theft to her superiors (or to probation officials) because she did not believe the neighbor's story was true and because Lionel "knows that he's not supposed to go in my room or touch my guns" ("Boy released from prison may be returned," online). But this time all three of her guns were missing and

Tate was positively identified by the Domino's delivery man who happened to be a police officer is his former country of Peru. Police later discovered a series of text messages sent by Lionel in which he talked in street slang about doing a robbery. Police also found a bullet and a handgun ankle holster under Tate's mattress. Detectives later testified that both the bullet and the holster belonged to Tate's mother ("Lionel Tate kept in jail," online).

Despite Lionel's claim of innocence few of his previous supporters were willing to speak on his behalf. Noticeably absent were the throngs of supporters advocating for him and for reform in the juvenile justice system. Gone were Al Sharpton and the Nation of Islam, and the Black Panthers for that matter. No comments, briefs or letters were sent by the advocacy groups that had previously pleaded with Judge Lazarus to spare him a prison sentence. Those who did speak out criticized Tate's mother and the juvenile system for failing to provide Tate with counseling. The Rev. Dennis Grant initially claimed that Tate had been set up and that "he would have to be the dumbest man ever to be born" to trade his freedom for $33 of pizza (Olkon, "Tate's latest arrest stuns supporters," online). But Grant, like other spiritual leaders who had tried to get Tate placed in a surrogate home, commented later that all of his offers to help Lionel were rebuked by Grossett-Tate. "It seems that the mother has contributed to all of this," he told reporters (Olkon, "Three guns missing from home of Tate's mother," online). Lionel never had a chance, supporters claimed, once he was returned to his mother's home in a crime-riddled neighborhood. While he received some counseling, it was not enough or for a long enough period of time to counter the drugs and crime that permeated his neighborhood (Lush, online). The Florida Highway Patrol eventually reprimanded Grossett-Tate for failure to report that her service weapon had been stolen. While the reprimand was a welcome act, years of finger-pointing directed at Grossett-Tate demanded more action. The *Sun-Sentinel* had covered every bit of Lionel's legal troubles and declared on the editorial page, "Tate is now facing prison again after being charged with an armed robbery about the time his mother's guns went missing again. Too bad there's no official reprimand for bad parenting" ("Lionel Tate's mother earns a reprimand," online).

Most who would comment were not at all surprised at Tate's relapse into crime. Michael Brannon, a forensic psychologist who evaluated Tate before his murder trial, blamed the defense team that he believes was more concerned with controlling public opinion rather than getting Tate the psychological counseling he needed.

> What happened here was very early on, as the court appointed doc, I identified for the judge that this young man had high potential for aggression and violence. And other evaluators corroborated that too. So early on if the defense had been listening to what the state was offering ... they could have maybe, and I stress maybe, have the window of opportunity to address someone in their formative stages of thirteen as opposed to waiting until multiple things have happened to him at eighteen. Would it have been different? We'll never know because no one intervened then. They were too busy trying to win a case as opposed to providing some assistance. In psychology we don't always do predictions so well... But we can speak in terms of probability, and what would have had the greatest probability of influencing him to turn out differently than he did now. That certainly would have been placement in an anger-management program with set rules, regulations and consequences for his behavior. The probability would have been greater had we intervened in that way than what had occurred. Which was excuse making and after every occurrence doing damage control instead of controlling the damage. It's my opinion that by the time he got to be eighteen he was so used to having others explain away his behavior that his acceptance of responsibility was nil [personal interview, 2005].

Brannon had testified at the pre-trial hearing that Tate needed intensive counseling for a long period of time to overcome his anger problems. Brannon explained to the *Miami Herald*, "His second grade teacher said Lionel was the worst behaved student she ever had in 30 years of teaching. He was a bully in the classroom. He had a bad temper. How many chances will he get, especially when he killed a girl with his bare hands?" (Olkon, online). News of Tate's rearrest moved quickly through Internet communities of wrestling and video game fans. For many, Lionel's continuing criminal problems were seen as a vindication of the sports they loved and merely shed light on the "hoax" TV wrestling defense. Posters on "Websleuths Crime Sleuthing Community" and "Gamufi," a site for video gamers, were in near unanimity that Tate's robbery charges proved that media had nothing to do with his criminal behavior. After three years in a juvenile detention facility where he presumably had limited access to media he still allegedly stole guns and committed petty crimes. This relapse proved, they believed, that it wasn't video games that "turned" Tate bad; it was something much more internal and familial at the root of his inability to function legally in society.

The stakes were higher than ever for Tate and for his mother. The state didn't need to prove that Tate committed any crime, only that he had violated the terms of his probation. Any violation, especially ones involving stolen weapons and robbery, could result in revocation of Tate's probation. And that could reinstate his original sentence of life in prison for the murder conviction. The bizarre drama that characterized so much of Tate's earlier murder trial surfaced once again. Despite the disappearance of all three of her guns, Grossett-Tate stood by her son and even accused the police of singling him out because of his past transgressions. But by now those willing to stand by Lionel and his mother's increasingly pathetic cries of foul were dwindling to those paid to advocate for them. When Grossett-Tate arrived at one of Lionel's court appearances she was accompanied by only her attorney. Nowhere in sight were the advocates and Nation of Islam representatives who stood so boldly by her side before. Jim Lewis resigned as Tate's attorney due to personal issues and the stress Lionel's rearrest put on his own family.

A few days before his probation violation hearing Tate wrote the judge a letter saying he was hearing voices and was contemplating suicide. Judge Lazarus postponed the hearing and ordered Tate to undergo psychiatric testing. There was no way Lazarus was going to chance any grounds for a reversal due to competency issues this time around. Both psychologists who interviewed Tate testified that he was faking his symptoms. Dr. Trudi Garfield testified that Tate would "bring his right hand up to his ear, he would slap his ear, and he would bring his fist up to his and then would turn his head and say 'Stop' to demonstrate that there were voices" ("Judge: Lionel Tate Competent," online). Garfield concluded that Tate's actions were completely inconsistent with any genuine hallucinatory episodes and that he was faking the symptoms. Later, Tate's new attorney, Assistant Public Defender H. Dohn Williams, admitted that the letter was also a fake that was actually penned by a fellow inmate who thought he could help Tate. "It was a desperate attempt by a young man," Williams told the judge (Burnstein, "Judge finds Tate competent to stand trial," online). Ultimately Tate decided to accept a plea bargain that would result in a 10–30 year sentence for the weapons parole violation and the pizza delivery robbery because it would allow him to avoid the life sentence.

Soon Tate looked a whole lot more devious than desperate as he embarked on a series of legal maneuvers that postponed his sentencing. Tate wrote another letter to the judge asking to withdraw his guilty plea claiming that he now wanted to fight the robbery charge. Tate returned to the only thing that had saved him before and claimed to Judge Lazarus that he didn't understand the ramifications of the plea agreement and that Ellis Rubin, his newest attorney, had not fully explained the plea agreement (Burnstein, "Tate asks judge to pull plea," online). Tate relied on the issue of competency to once again save him from a prison sentence. But Tate was now several years older, a veteran of the criminal justice system and nowhere near as naïve as he was during his first trial. Ellis claimed the letter to the judge was a complete surprise and asked the judge to order a psychiatric evaluation of Tate to determine competency. Ellis explained that Tate refused his legal advice and clearly was acting irrationally. Ellis claimed the psychiatric evaluation was needed to "determine why he does what I would call insane things. You don't put yourself in prison for the rest of your life for $33 worth of pizza" (Burnstein, "Judge orders mental evaluation," online).

But apparently Tate had done just that. As before, the mental health evaluators found that Tate suffered from no mental health disorders. Ellis quit; Williams returned as Tate's attorney. And finally, on May 18, 2006, Judge Lazarus sentenced Tate to 30 years for the parole violation of possessing a gun. Lazarus allowed Tate to withdraw his guilty plea to the robbery but even his own attorney later told the press that it was a bad idea for Lionel to chance conviction on the robbery charge. Williams blamed Grossett-Tate for telling her son that he could beat the robbery charge despite overwhelming evidence implicating him in the crime. While imposing the harshest sentence possible, Lazarus claimed that Tate has shown "disdain and disrespect" for the judicial system and, "In plain English, you've run out of chances. You do not get any more" ("Killer at 12 Tate returns to prison," online).

The Aftermath

Tate was hardly the only person affected. By all accounts the players in the Lionel Tate saga were all deeply affected by the sensational trial and his ultimate relapse into crime. Forensic psychologist Brannon recalled his disappointment when Tate's appeals attorney went beyond mere advocacy for his client by personally attacking Dr. Borg-Carter's credibility during an appearance on a popular cable television show. Brannon explained that:

> "We don't have a stake in the outcome (of the case) but we do have a stake that the data are being presented in an accurate manner. And it was through the misrepresentation of the data that it got appealed. And this was the period of time that Richard Rosenbaum was going on TV and [called Borg-Carter a 'state whore' five times of the 'O'Reilly Factor.'] There are unwritten rules (in the judicial system) that we are all in this together. This is an adversarial process but rarely does it get acrimonious. But the Tate case is the only one where I know there are still bad feelings" [personal interview, 2005].

Tate's original trial attorney, Jim Lewis, felt a few of those bad feelings himself after ending up having to defend himself against a two-year defamation suit filed by Vince McMahon, president of World Wrestling Entertainment (formerly the WWF). While Lewis had interjected television wrestling and some of the wrestlers themselves into his defense strategy, he was not the only one to decry the harmful affects of television wrestling. Perennial TV critic L. Brent Bozell, head of the powerful Parents Television Council, was quick to appoint Tate the poster boy for all the ills caused by violence in television wrestling shows. Bozell was a longtime critic of unbridled sex and violence in TV wrestling and found Tate the perfect example of what the shows can drive an unsupervised child to do. Bozell organized a boycott against advertisers on WWE programming and produced a video that claimed that four children had died nationwide as a result of viewers mimicking WWE programming. But Bozell was wrong in identifying some advertisers and inaccurately claimed that others had pulled their advertisements when, in fact, they had never advertised on WWE programs. Jim Lewis appeared in Bozell's video in which claims were made that Eunick's death was directly related to WWE shows and its stars. The National Association of Criminal Defense Lawyers came to Lewis's defense and cautioned against a slippery slope of allowing big business to sue a lawyer for simply mounting a competent defense for his client.

In the end Lewis was able to settle the lawsuit with an apology to the WWE but only after spending a significant sum of money to defend himself. Bozell bore much more responsibility for any defamation since he organized the boycott and waged an open war on the wrestling industry through his Web site and video. In a settlement agreement Bozell agreed to pay the

WWE $3.5 million and post a retraction on his Web site for six months. Bozell's retraction read in part:

> I now believe that professional wrestling played no role in the murder of Tiffany Eunick ... and am equally convinced that it was incorrect and wrong to have blamed WWE or any of its programs for the deaths of the other children. I want to be clear that WWE was correct in pointing out that various statements made by PTC and me were inaccurate concerning the identity and number of WWE *Smackdown!* advertisers who withdrew support from the program" [Krepel, online].

In the end, no one left the Tate trial unscathed.

SIX

The *Matrix* Murders

When the film *The Matrix* premiered in April 1999 it was celebrated as an inventive, artistically advanced film with a science-fiction theme like no other. The film posed important philosophical questions about the existence of life as we know it and introduced the idea that we're all living in a virtual reality. The real question, then, for the viewing public, is: How do we know what is real and what isn't? In one scene Laurence Fishburne's character Morpheus poses this very question to the main character Neo as he's trying to convince him of the existence of the Matrix. "Have you ever had a dream that you were so sure was real? What if you were unable to wake from that dream? How would you know the difference between the dream and your real life?"

After years of unsuccessful attempts to establish a legal causation between media violence and real violence, several cases involving the film *The Matrix* have changed the legal climate. Most criminal and civil complaints against the media fail on First Amendment grounds, or on an inability to establish incitement to violence. But cases involving *The Matrix* have succeeded for two main reasons. The first reason revolves around the film's unique premise that humans are living in an artificial world, a virtual reality world created and programmed by machines. Only those who have escaped the Matrix know of the constructed reality; all other humans are little more than disembodied brains "living" in a virtual reality. Mankind's only hope for survival is to kill the machines that are using us as an energy source. But most of us are totally unaware of our predicament, blissfully living in a computer-generated world.

A second important point to *The Matrix* hinges on the distinction between humans aware of the manipulated world within the Matrix and those who are not. In the film, there are only a "chosen few" who have figured out the truth about our virtual reality universe. In several recent murder cases, defendants have claimed to be among those who know about the Matrix and are merely trying to protect themselves (or others) from the evil, controlling machines. In other words, they killed because they were trying to save the human race from the machines, or as one defendant put it, to "kill before I was killed" (WCPO-TV Web site). So while they are cognizant of their criminal actions, they claim to be justified because they are simply following the call (the mission of the *chosen ones* in the film) to kill the machines who manipulate others. These defendants are not pleading not guilty. Rather, they are admitting they are guilty of murder, but believe it is a murder justified because they are actually living in the Matrix and are acting to save themselves and, ultimately, to save mankind. These defendants believe the premise of the movie, and believe they are among the chosen few who have escaped the confines of the Matrix. As such they must combat, if not destroy, the controlling machines.

Naturally, their attorneys seize upon this reasoning to argue for the insanity of their clients and the "Matrix insanity defense" is born. Not all states recognize insanity as a defense and many have requisite conditions that must be present in order to meet the state's definition. In general, insanity is a defense that claims some sort of mitigating mental factor or force that negates a person's responsibility for a crime. Based on an 1843 British case

The film *The Matrix* features the classic battle against man and oppressor. Several people who have murdered claim *The Matrix* made them do it.

involving a defendant name Daniel M'Naughten, the "M'Naughten Rule" identifies insanity in a person who does not possess the ability to distinguish between right and wrong. The federal courts and most states have adopted a modern update of M'Naughten called the "substantial capacity" test. This standard stipulates: "A person is not responsible for criminal conduct if at the time of such conduct as a result of mental illness or defect he lacks substantial capacity either to appreciate the wrongfulness of his conduct or to conform his conduct to the requirements of the law" (Model Penal Code, § 401, 1954).

Most defense attorneys will agree that insanity is not an easy defense strategy at all, some even dubbing it the "defense of last resort" because it is so unpopular with the general public and, consequently, with juries. Many people see it as a way to simply avoid taking responsibility for criminal behavior, especially when a famous defendant is caught faking insanity. There are, however, legitimate cases of crimes being committed by criminally insane people, although there is little consensus as to what may trigger violent or criminal behavior among those with preexisting disorders. When it comes to the cases of murder and *The Matrix*, the courts have to distinguish between defendants who are legitimately taken in by the virtual reality plot of the film and those who are merely using it as a scapegoat for their own criminal actions. Dr. John Kennedy of the University of Cincinnati's Institute on Law & Psychiatry explained the film's special appeal: "The concept behind the movie isn't new. But there may be a certain group of individuals who wouldn't have heard about the concept (that we are living in a constructed virtual reality) except for the movie, who are ripe for hearing it and running with it. They're people whose lives are so fractured or without meaning that *The Matrix* is a way to explain that without saying 'I'm sick,' or 'I'm different.' It's much more soothing than admitting you've got a problem" (Schone, p. D1).

Lee Boyd Malvo

As mentioned before, several police officials and news agencies have discussed a widespread belief that Columbine killers Eric Harris and Dylan Klebold were influenced by *The Matrix's* themes and philosophies. But their deaths make it virtually impossible to substantiate to what degree the movie actually impacted their plans. To a lesser extent, the same is true for Lee Boyd Malvo, the teen member of the infamous "Washington Sniper" duo who murdered ten people and wounded another three during a three-week shooting rampage in the fall of 2003. Malvo was tried in Fairfax County on two counts of capital murder and weapons charges and was suspected as the triggerman in the deaths of several others. He was arrested with John Allen Muhammad, a 42-year-old man whom Malvo frequently called his father although the two were not related. Malvo had lived with Muhammad and his family in Antigua before coming with him to the United States.

The Matrix was linked to Malvo's actions shortly after his arrest and remained an issue throughout his trial. During an interview with Fairfax County police investigators shortly after his arrest, Malvo reportedly referred to *The Matrix* several times and told them to watch the film if they wanted to understand his actions (Jackman, "Escape 'The Matrix,'" 2003). Later, handwritten notes and drawings were found in his cell that included references to the movie. In one drawing Malvo sketched a picture of himself in the crosshairs of a weapon with the phrases "Free Your Mind! The Body Will Follow!" written just above. The quotes are nearly identical to a line spoken by Morpheus, Neo's mentor, when he was trying to convince the skeptical Neo of the existence of the Matrix. Malvo also used the phase, "You are a Slave to The Matrix," another quote from the film.

In pre-trial interviews with mental health officials Malvo continued his references to the film. Carmeta Albus, a court-appointed forensic social worker who interviewed Malvo for more than 70 hours while he awaited trial, said he told her, too, to watch the film if she wanted to understand the motivation behind the sniper shootings. Albus did just that and later testified at his trial that she believed Malvo identified with the Neo character, who was guided through his odyssey by Morpheus. Albus explained: "Neo was 'the One,' who was going to contribute significantly to changing the system. Morpheus was to me the authoritative figure and mentor" (Liptak, p. 32). The defense later played scenes from the movie and showed several first-person shooter video games that Malvo and Muhammad played together. The demonstration was an attempt to show that Malvo had actually been brainwashed by Muhammad to participate in the killings. Muhammad used the video games to train Malvo to become a sharpshooter, while the film reinforced the notion that Muhammad knew the "truth" about the world. Clinical psychologist Dewey Cornell testified that Malvo told him he had watched *The Matrix* more than 100 times and, "he told me he was taught that right and wrong don't exist. Whatever Mr. Muhammad wanted him to do was the right thing to do" (Miller, p. B1).

Many court observers suggested that Malvo and Muhammad's real motivation for the killings was a belief that whites continued to enslave blacks, both economically and culturally. The film's theme that the only way to break this enslavement is by killing those who control you seems to offer Malvo a justification to murder his white oppressors. This theory fails to explain his actions, however, because many of the shooting victims were neither white nor powerful. Malvo was tried for the murder of an FBI investigator, which might fit Malvo's definition of an oppressor if he actually knew who she was. Malvo told investigators that the locations were scouted carefully but the victims were merely chosen because they happened to be there at the chosen time. A need to kill one's oppressors also fails to explain why the duo killed African Americans and children. Consequently, *The Matrix* as a motive is tenuous at best and offers very little explanation as to why these men killed so many people.

Vadim Mieseges

Two cases have successfully argued an insanity defense based on influence from *The Matrix*. In August 2002, a judge accepted a plea of not guilty by reason of insanity from Vadim Mieseges, 27, who killed and dismembered Ella Wong, his landlord, in San Francisco. Mieseges was a computer science student at San Francisco State University who came to the United States from Switzerland a few years after his parents were killed. The trauma reportedly sent Mieseges into a deep depression and he developed a drug problem for which he was institutionalized for a short time in Geneva. Police had little trouble apprehending Mieseges because he confessed to the murder and led investigators to locations where he dumped Wong's different body parts. Mike Maloney, an investigator with the San Francisco Police, initially questioned him at an area Macy's store for a routine investigation of vagrancy after he was identified as acting strangely. Maloney said that

Mieseges was talking fast and was very forthcoming with details about killing Wong. He detailed how he dismembered her body and told Maloney the locations where he dumped different parts of her body (*The Matrix Defense*, 2003). Police found Wong's torso at one of the locations but failed to locate all of her body because other dumpsters had already been emptied.

After his arrest Mieseges told police that he been "sucked" into the Matrix, a world he described as violent and dangerous. More specifically he believed that the United States and Taiwanese governments were plotting against him and that Wong was conspiring to suck him into the Matrix via his computer. For Mieseges it was a simple act of survival; he either killed Wong (a machine) or he would be killed. Police officials who interviewed Mieseges concluded that he was incapable of distinguishing between the real world and that portrayed in *The Matrix* (Jackman, "Escape 'The Matrix,'" 2003). They believed that his mental state made him susceptible to the themes and virtual reality plot of the film and fed his paranoia that external evil forces were now coming after him. A court-ordered psychiatric evaluation diagnosed Mieseges with paranoid psychosis. Mieseges's insanity plea was accepted by a judge and he was committed to a mental hospital for an undetermined period of time.

Tonda Ansley

Guilty by reason of insanity was the same verdict for an Ohio woman who also murdered her landlord. In a statement to police, Tonda Lynn Ansley said that on July 27, 2002, she walked up to Sherry Corbett and said, "'Hi Sherry, I want to talk to you' and then I walked around the car and shot her," ("Suspect: More targets on kill list," online). During that police interview Ansley made several references to *The Matrix* and claimed Corbett, Corbett's partner, Robert Sherwin, and Ansley's ex-husband were plotting to kill her. Sherwin and Corbett were both professors at nearby Miami University and Corbett was very active in the historic restoration of homes in the Hamilton area. Ansley had known Corbett for approximately eight years and had worked on the houses that Corbett refurbished and then rented out to tenants, including Anlsey. Sherwin described their relationship with Ansley as "friendly" and said that Ansley was very fond of them both (*The Matrix Defense*).

Ansley claimed that she was walking to Sherwin's house to shoot him, too, when police working undercover in the neighborhood apprehended her less than a block from the murder scene. Police described her demeanor as calm as she explained why she had to kill the three before they killed her. Ansley had been experiencing dreams in which the three appeared as vampires and other menacing characters. She explained that she soon discovered that these were not dreams at all; the events were real and Corbett had been drugging her. Ansley believed that Corbett and Sherwin were plotting to kill her because she had uncovered their involvement in a series of arson fires set to fraudulently collect insurance money. (Police never found any evidence of Corbett's involvement in the arsons.) Ansley realized that she was being drawn into the Matrix. She explained to police, "they commit a lot of crimes in The Matrix. That's where you go to sleep at night and they drug you and take you somewhere else and then bring you back and put you in bed and, when you wake up, you think it's a bad dream" (Bean, online). The parallels to the film were clear in Ansley's mind: Corbett and the others were committing the crimes of arson and fraud and now were trying to silence her because she had discovered their acts. Ansley's attorney explained that seeing *The Matrix* is what allowed her to awaken and see the "reality" of her dreams. "It resonated with her ... that's what appealed to her about the film. Things that you don't think are real — really are in *The Matrix*," explained Melynda Cook-Reich (*The Matrix Defense*). Dr. John Kennedy, director of the Institute of Psychiatry & Law, explained, "Someone who is already psychotic could use *The Matrix* as evidence of an alternative universe" (Ingrassia, online). Late one night Ansley found a migrant farm worker asleep in the bed of her truck as she left her job as a bartender. She believed that he had been sent by Corbett to kill her. Ansley said she contacted the National Security Agency with the evidence about the plot against her but when she never heard back from them she decided to kill them herself ("Suspect: More targets on kill list," online).

Ansley was indicted for aggravated murder with specification (carrying a concealed weapon) in August 2002 (*Ohio v. Ainsley* Indictment, Case #CR02–08–1227). Initially she was ruled incompetent to stand trial. After Ansley's court-appointed attorney filed a plea of not guilty by reason of insanity, Ansley petitioned to act as her own attorney. The judge denied her request and ordered a psychiatric evaluation. After several months of treatment at a state mental hospital Ansley told a psychologist that she now trusted her attorney and understood the expertise that someone trained in the law could bring to her defense (Morse, online). The judge ruled her competent and set a trial date for May 2003. But the trial never took place as three independent psychological evaluations declared that Ansley was too ill to know the difference between right and wrong, the standard of legal insanity in Ohio. One of the evaluators, Dr. Sherry Baker, said that Ansley saw almost everyone as a conspirator against her. She believed she was protecting herself and her son, and that killing Corbett was an act of survival (*The Matrix Defense*).

Ansley waived her right to a jury trail and Judge Keith Spath acknowledged that he was "duty-bound" to declare Ansley mentally ill after all three psychiatrist's reports supported the standard that Ansley "by a preponderance of the evidence, at the time of the commission of the offense, did not know, as a result of a severe mental disease or defect, the wrongfulness of her conduct" (*Ohio v. Ainsley*, Findings of not guilty, Case #CR02–08–1227). Ansley was remanded to the custody of the Moritz Forensic Unit of Twin Valley Behavior, a maximum security inpatient psychiatric hospital, for an indefinite amount of time.

Reaction to the plea was mixed among Corbett's friends and supporters. While some in Hamilton thought that Ansley had gotten away with murder, others found the verdict perfectly in line with Corbett's philosophy. An anonymous poster wrote in an online memorial created for Corbett, "What happened to Ansley. Probably just what Sherry (Corbett) would have wanted for her — Help" (Memorials to Sherry Corbett, msg. 14). In 2004, Ansley petitioned the court to be moved to a minimum security facility but Judge Spath dismissed her request because "there is clear and convincing evidence that the defendant remains a mentally ill person subject to hospitalization" (*Ohio v. Ainsley*, Entry, Case #CR02–08–1227).

Joshua Cooke

At first glance Joshua Cooke seemed like a typical teen. He lived in Oakton, Virginia, a suburb of Washington, D.C., with his parents and sister. The family lived in a comfortable home in an upper-middle-class wooded neighborhood where neighbors were cordial to one another. The façade of this "perfect" family was shattered on February 17, 2003, when Joshua walked into the basement of his home and shot dead both of his parents. He then got a Coke out of the refrigerator, dialed 911 and told the dispatcher, "I just shot my parents, just blew them away with a shotgun. Get your asses over here" (Moore, 2003). When police failed to arrive immediately, possibly due to the two feet of snow that had fallen that day in a huge winter storm, Cooke called 911 again. He explained again to a different dispatcher that he had just killed his parents and that he would be waiting unarmed for the police to arrive. Officers arrived and found Joshua's parents in the basement; Paul had been shot seven times; Margaret was shot twice.

After Cooke's arrest, the inevitable search for a reason he killed his parents began. Many journalists focused on the family in order to find some explanation for the crime in what many thought was a perfect family. Joshua floundered after he graduated from high school and searched for a career path. He flunked out of Virginia State University and was rejected by the Marines due to poor vision. This was believed to be a great source of concern to Paul and Margaret, he a financial manager with Lockheed Martin and she a former executive at IBM. One journalist reported that the parents were pressuring Joshua to succeed in school or work since his job at the Jiffy Lube "would be a big letdown in a family like this" (*The Matrix Defense*). A lot of attention was also given to the fact that the family was one of the few African American families living in a predominantly white neighborhood in Oakton. This alone led some observers to point out that the Cookes seemingly gave Joshua and his sister Tiffany opportunities not afforded many blacks. To many this made his crime all the more troubling. Neighbor Philip Terzian described Paul and Margaret Cooke as an "achieving pair" who were friendly, and often helped neighbors. Reporters and news stories always described the parents in terms of their achievements or that they were "successful African-Americans." In no other case studied for this work was the race of the victim or perpetrator discussed so prominently. The condescension underlying discussions of the Cooke's death reveals a double prejudice at work. First, the oft-repeated references to the family's race and the parents' successes reinforce the notion that these types of crimes don't happen in wealthy, suburban families. Second, the references imply that it *really* shouldn't have happened in a successful African American home because they were one of the few that made it out of the abyss of black suppression and hopelessness. If this was the reaction in death, it's easy to imagine the type of pressure put on the Cooke children to succeed given the perception that they had already been given an opportunity that many African American children do not have. If Joshua Cooke really did have all these advantages in life, why did he kill his parents?

Rachel Fierro, Cooke's lead attorney, believed that part of the answer could be found in Joshua's obsession with the film *The Matrix*. She announced her intentions in a pre-trial motion to defend Cooke's actions based on an insanity defense influenced by *The Matrix*. Fierro reported in media interviews that she went to Cooke's home a few weeks after the murders and was made aware of his fascination with the film the minute she stepped into his bedroom. She described that he had a poster of Neo on the wall and a black trench coat hung prominently in his closet, the same closet where he stored a shotgun identical to the one used by Neo in the film (personal interview, 2005). He also had a VHS copy of the film, which was his second copy since he wore out the first one from playing it so often. In a pre-trial motion for psychiatric evaluation Fierro wrote: "There's reason to believe that the defendant Cooke harbored a bona fide belief that he was living in the virtual reality of *The Matrix*. Defendant Cooke was obsessed with the major motion picture *The Matrix* at the time of the offense. It is imperative that this court have the opinion of a psychiatrist to evaluate his mental status." Consequently, Fierro explained in her motion for psychiatric examination, Cooke could not distinguish between reality and the world portrayed in the film.

The motion drew a lot of media attention and Fierro appeared on a number of national news shows defending the defense strategy. Fierro believed that much of the attention came since the second *Matrix* film was about to be released. In a CNN interview Fierro clarified that she was not saying that *The Matrix* made Joshua kill but that the film was more than just entertainment to him and it did influence his behavior. She explained it simply as "something just came over him that night." Warner Brothers Studios, which produced and distributed *The Matrix* film series, issued a statement after Fierro appeared on several national news programs. The statement was displayed during Fierro's CNN interview and in it the studio categorically denied any responsibility for Cooke's actions. Warner Brothers concluded by saying: "Our hearts go out to the families and friends of those who have been victims of violent crimes whenever we hear of such events. However, any attempt to link these crimes with a motion picture or any other art form is disturbing and irresponsible."

Cooke's fascination with *The Matrix* was no ordinary matter. He labels it his favorite movie and reported that he watched it almost everyday to the point that he wore out one copy and had to purchase another. He explained the cathartic effect of the film's violence, particularly as an outlet for his anger and frustration, in a 2005 letter. "I would pretend, when Neo shot his enemies, that *I* was killing *my* enemies, like the school bully or someone who called me names. It actually made me feel better. I bought a long, ankle-length trench coat and black Timberland boots and wore them to places like the mall. And I always had my headphones on my ears, playing my CDs, including *The Matrix* CD, which is the soundtrack to the movie." Just two days before the murders Cooke bought a shotgun at a local sporting goods store similar to the 12-gauge shotgun used by Neo.

Cooke also calls his love of violent video games an obsession, particularly those known as first-person shooter games in which the player can adopt the viewpoint of the character. Cooke reports that his favorite games were the various versions of *Grand Theft Auto*, *Doom*, *Quake*, *Metal Gear Solid* and *Max Payne*, which he admitted to playing for hours each day in his letter.

> I played these games for hours and hours every day. The worst thing about these ultra-violent video games is that you get more points for the more murder and mayhem you commit. There were literally days when I would play for 12 hours straight. I wouldn't even go to the bathroom because I didn't want to stop. I just peed in a large cup and I stashed food in my room so I never needed to leave. Therefore I could play non-stop. It was definitely a serious addiction.... Another thing about the violent video games is that when I got angry at something or someone in real life, I could go to the virtual reality and hunt or kill that person to release my anger. Especially since PlayStation2 is so life-like, it almost seemed real at times.

In interviews since his arrest Cooke is unable to offer any real explanation for his actions. With his sister away at college it was just Joshua and his parents in the Oakton house. Things had not been going well for him, especially since he had been turned down by the Marines. The day of the murders he did not go to his job as a technician at Jiffy Lube because of the storm. Instead he helped neighbors shovel out from the snowstorm. After dinner his parents went downstairs to do some work while he went up to his bedroom. He was listening to his favorite song, "Bodies," off the *Sinner* CD by the heavy metal group Drowning Pool. Cooke liked the song because it "fueled my emotions, particularly anger and hate" (Personal letter, p. 4).

Feeling like he "had nothing to lose" he said that he looked at the poster of *The Matrix*, put on his black trench coat and his wraparound glasses, grabbed his 12-gauge shotgun and ammunition and headed downstairs. With the song still blasting in his earphones he went to the basement and shot his mother, and then his father, who had jumped under his desk after the first shot. Joshua walked back upstairs to reload the shotgun but quickly returned to the basement to shoot his father several more times. Joshua's sister was on the phone with their father when the shooting began. When he picked up the phone Tiffany repeatedly asked him what was happening. Joshua told her that he couldn't talk, hung up the phone, went back upstairs, got a Coke out of the refrigerator, and called 911.

He would later describe his emotions that night to a *Washington Post* reporter, telling him, "I don't know. I kinda went into a zone. I had no emotion at that time. I felt like I was a kind of a zombie. And then I looked at my shotgun and I felt like there was nothing left in my life. I had all this anger building up and I guess I just felt like doing something. Anything. There was no sense behind it. It was just senseless" (Perl, W16). Police detectives remained baffled by a motive and couldn't find any apparent reason for Joshua to kill his parents. Homicide detective Robert Bond described Cooke as well-mannered and polite adding, "He really didn't have any reaction whatsoever ... he wasn't angry. He didn't show he was sorry for what he did. There were no tears... His statement was that nothing really provoked it. Everything was fine in the house" (Perl, p. W16). However, rumors that Cooke's parents were strict disciplinarians were confirmed by neighbors and friends in interviews with various media outlets. The Cookes, neighbors reported, were strict parents who often reprimanded Joshua for his behavior. Although his sister claimed that their parents never abused them she did concede that they could be considered strict.

Strict or not, Cooke himself never cited that as a reason he killed his parents. In fact, what sets Cooke's case apart from many others is that he didn't immediately offer a motive. Cooke never discussed *The Matrix* with investigators. The first time any reference to the film surfaced was in Fierro's pre-trial motion for a psychiatric evaluation. It is clear that Fierro still believes her client's actions could only be explained by a significant psychotic break triggered by his obsession with *The Matrix*. While Fierro admits that introducing *The Matrix* into her defense strategy was controversial, she still maintains, years after the trial, that his actions can only be explained by something out of the ordinary. In conversation she easily recounts that Joshua was an unremarkable student who received average grades but had no record of disciplinary problems at any level. That particular day was just a fun snow day in which Joshua shared an uneventful dinner with his parents. Fierro still believes that Cooke's family history directly impacted his actions that night. But because the adoption records had not been released to the Cookes they had no way of knowing about Joshua's mental health background or his need for help. "It's bizarre. The only logical explanation for his actions is an episode." While she took some heat in the media and from the film's producers, it was the right choice under these circumstances and a defense that many theorists agree was a solid defense strategy. What was not part of any legal strategy was Cooke's decision to plead guilty. As his attorney, Fierro supported him even though some media violence advocates pushed her to continue to trial so that she could continue the indictment of *The Matrix*. Fierro explained: "He still has horrible dreams and he has to reconcile himself with that. And part of that was accepting a guilty plea" (personal interview, 2005).

Obviously, the Matrix-influenced defense strategy was never tested in court as Cooke's attorneys abandoned the defense when he agreed to plead guilty to murder and weapons charges instead ("Guilty plea in 'Matrix' defense slayings," online). A judge granted Fierro's request for a psychiatric evaluation and in June 2003, Dr. Nadine Fakhrah, the staff psychologist at the Fairfax County Adult Detention Center, released her findings after a month-long evaluation of Cooke. Fakhrah determined that Joshua was mentally competent and capable of telling right from wrong. On June 24, 2003, Cooke pled guilty to murder, a move his attorneys claimed he felt very strongly about. "Mr. Cooke always wanted to take responsibility for his actions, said Mani Fierro, Cooke's co-counsel, and "as competent counsel, we needed to explore certain avenues, every possible defense" (Moore, 2003).

Although Cooke pled guilty, Fierro still fought for her client to receive a lighter sentence due to mitigating circumstances. The sentencing hearing was postponed when Fierro offered new evidence of familial mental health issues. Fierro sued to unseal Joshua's adoption records in Ohio and the 400-page adoption report revealed startling information. The adoption records showed that both of Joshua's birth parents had suffered from mental illness. Joshua's father had been diagnosed with paranoid schizophrenia while his mother also suffered from schizophrenia. Joshua's brother, who was not adopted by the Cookes, had also been diagnosed as suffering from paranoid schizophrenia. Both parents had been prostitutes and the father repeatedly beat Cooke's birth mother, resulting in the parents being declared unfit by the Ohio Department of Human Services when Joshua was just one. The possibility that Cooke's behavior the night of the killings was impacted by the newly revealed familial mental illness earned Joshua another psychiatric evaluation prior to sentencing.

At Cooke's sentencing hearing in October 2003, Fierro argued for leniency, arguing that his childhood trauma and inheritable mental illness made him particularly susceptible to the negative influences of *The Matrix* and the violent video games he played for hours each day. Brad Bushman, a researcher and psychology professor at the University of Michigan, testified that extensive research proved that exposure to violence in films, television and video games has significant physiological effects including increased arousal and anger that increase the likelihood of violent behavior. Child psychologist David Shostak also testified on Cooke's behalf. Shostak evaluated Joshua after the adoption records revealed a familial history of mental illness. Shostak testified that Cooke suffered from schizophrenia that was masked until adolescence, triggered by his failures academically and socially. Cooke's traumatic childhood inhibited his development of any attachment to his parents; a disconnect that then continued with his adoptive parents, Shostak explained. Shostak also testified that Cooke murdered his parents because they were the "only available targets" for his subconscious self-loathing, an act, in essence, of "deflected suicide" (Sentencing hearing). Shostak's testimony seems to make some sense of the haunting explanation Cooke gave to a *Washington Post* reporter for the murders:

> This may sound sick, but it didn't seem like a big deal at the time. It kind of seemed like, well, let me do this, you know. I mean, kind of like that. I had

given up on my life. Failing college was my fault, and then rejection from the Marines, and never having a girlfriend, and being antisocial, not having any friends. I mean, like, what is there left for me to do? I didn't really care. I didn't care if I died. I didn't care what happened to anyone [Perl, p. W16].

Prosecutor Robert Horan rejected the media influence claim, explaining that millions of other people saw the film and played violent video games but didn't kill people. Horan also cited the calm nature of Cooke's 911 calls and the methodical nature of his crime to dismiss Shostak's testimony of Joshua's disconnect from reality during the crimes. At the end of the day-long hearing, Judge Kathleen MacKay sentenced Cooke to 40 years in prison, a sentence at the higher end of the 26–46 sentencing guidelines. Since Virginia does not have parole, Joshua will not be eligible for release until he is at least 55 years old.

Cooke's calm, respectful demeanor belies his violent acts to this day. *Washington Post* reporter Peter Perl interviewed Cooke at the Fairfax County jail and described him as "polite and helpful, even as he quietly describes in graphic detail the night he shotgunned his parents to death" (Perl, p. W16). Cooke revealed potentially embarrassing details of his early sexual experiences to Perl with a humility and honesty rarely voiced by a 20-year-old man. Cooke's apparent naiveté reportedly prompted an older co-worker at his job at Jiffy Lube to encourage him to keep some things to himself. *Boston Globe* reporter Mark Schone met Cooke the day after his sentencing and pronounced him as "about as threatening as a churchmouse. Jut-jawed, muscled and 6-foot-2, he could fill the tiny cubicle (in the jail's visitors' room) if he wanted, but he's too meek and eager to be liked. It's easy to believe Cooke when he claims he's a nonviolent person — a polite, helpful, devout Christian who'd never even balled a fist before February 17" (Schone, p. D1). Indeed, in letters written since his incarceration at Wallens Ridge State Prison in southwestern Virginia, Cooke is well-mannered, direct and surprisingly open about his emotions. He's quick to offer more information if he didn't answer a question in enough detail and he apologizes for not answering a letter in a timely manner when he has no obligation to correspond in the first place. Cooke finds the inquiries from reporters and the college professor writing this book a validation that he has something to offer society.

In letters, Joshua's grammar and sentence construction are flawless, in sharp contrast to the descriptions by others that he was a slow learner and a poor student. And each correspondence ends with a blessing and pronouncement of his renewed faith in God. It would be easy to cynically believe that Cooke is perpetrating a clever manipulation of this interviewer if not for the "p.s.s. write back soon!" followed by a smiley face at the end of one of his letters. Cooke told both Perl and Schone that he was okay with his long sentence and even anticipated the structure prison would bring to his life, something that he had hoped to find in the Marines. He also told Perl that he was looking forward to going to prison because other jail inmates had told him that prison afforded more time for recreation and watching television. Just two years later, however, Cooke explained that his latest correspondence was delayed because he had been placed in isolation after problems with his cellmate (personal letter, p. 1). It's just one more example of his miscalculated expectations.

The truth of the matter is that Joshua Cooke is someone you never would imagine would kill his parents, or anyone else for that matter. And that is what makes some so eager to blame his undiagnosed mental illness for the crime. Of all the cases studied this is the one with the least clues or explanations for the crime. It is simply too difficult to accept that there is no reason that two people are dead and another will be in prison for 40 years. His undiagnosed familial mental health history is no small issue and likely played an important role in the decisions that Cooke made that night. But they were, nonetheless, his decisions and his actions. Cooke's willingness to take responsibility for his actions is rare in these days of avoidance. Cooke's case is a powerful reminder that there aren't always warning signs that people just failed to detect. And sometimes, there just isn't a good explanation for why things happen.

Matthew Lovett

In July 2003, Matthew Lovett, 18, and two teens were arrested in Oaklyn, New Jersey, just after 4:00 A.M. The boys had just attempted to carjack Mathew Rich's vehicle as he was on his way to work. Rich fled the scene and alerted police who stopped the boys, all dressed in long, black trench coats a few minutes later. Police confiscated a huge collection of weapons: rifles, several handguns, swords, a machete and 2,000 rounds of ammunition. The guns belonged to Lovett's father, who was out of town that weekend. Police later determined that the boys needed the car to carry out their plan to kill three teens and then randomly shoot others in Oaklyn. After that, Lovett planned to go to Missouri to meet with a girl he had been corresponding with via e-mail, who had complained to him a lot about her parents. Matthew wrote that he was going to go there and rescue her from them ("New slay plot in 'Matrix' case," p. 18). The day before his arrest she e-mailed Lovett and told him not to come; she didn't think this was a joke any longer and she didn't want to ever hear from him again.

Shortly after Lovett's arrest the stories of his obsession with *The Matrix* surfaced. Schoolmates said that Lovett dressed in black with his hair slicked back, and referred to himself as Neo, The One and The Mystic, all references to the main character in the film. He lived at home with his father and brother; his mother died several years earlier. Lovett was described in school as a shy, awkward loner who was bullied relentlessly and was greatly affected by the constant teasing of his younger brother, James, who has a speech impediment due to a cleft palate. The three teens targeted to be killed were identified as the biggest tormentors of the three defendants at school. Police discovered an e-mail from Lovett in which he said he believed that he actually was Neo and that there was a conspiracy against the human race that only a killing spree would end. In a note left for his father, Lovett wrote: "I thought you'd like to know that I am a warrior, I am fighting for mankind's freedom. Freedom from this society. Signed, Me. Matthew. The One. The Neo, the Anti-Christ, etc., etc., etc." (Valania, p. 17).

The three suspects retreated to Lovett's house often to play first-person shooter video games like *Grand Theft Auto* and *The Matrix* version of the film. The friends dubbed themselves the "Warriors of Freedom," after characters in their favorite online role-playing game. After the media reported the boys' penchant for violent video games the Entertainment Software Association released the following statement in 2003:

> From the media reports we have seen, the fact that this young adult — or any of those involved in this incident — played video games is incidental. One hundred forty-five million Americans play and enjoy video games each year. In other words, it would have been more extraordinary to find a teenage boy who does not play video games. The real difference between this individual

and others is that he had access to an arsenal of guns and was an individual who, according to media reports, seems to have had a history of psychological problems.

It's time to get past finger-pointing and scapegoating so we can focus on the real issues that give rise to youth violence in America, such as access to guns, untreated mental illness and dysfunctional families. A recent study by the National Institute of Child Health and Human Development found that 16 percent of all boys in grades 6 through 10 reported being bullied in school. These are the real issues, not the games we play.

Matthew's father, Ron Lovett, also took to the airwaves the day after the arrests to defend his son. He called it a moment of "*Matrix*-inspired stupidity" and claimed that his son never really intended to hurt anyone (Mulvhill, online). But in a later interview he placed some of the blame on the video games that Matthew reportedly played for up to six hours a day. Lovett said the games "brainwashed" the boys because they had play-acted these types of attacks so many times before with no real affects that it didn't seem so wrong to go out in the real world and do the same (*The Matrix Defense*, 2003). In the end Lovett's father never had a chance to test his claim that his son was fooled by the unrealistic consequences of video game violence because the case never went to trial. The two younger teens pleaded guilty to lesser offenses and Lovett pleaded guilty to carjacking charges and received a 10-year prison sentence (Wald, 2004).

Future of Media Influence Defenses

Many scholars wonder if the "success" of cases involving *The Matrix* signals an opening in the ironclad incitement and foreseeability clauses of media influence cases. That is not likely to happen because none of the defendants was able to escape punishment altogether for their crimes due to influence from the film. Two were declared not guilty by reason of insanity and the others never tested the film's influence in court, opting for guilty pleas instead. But what is it about this film that tapped into the psyche of so many people who described their own lives in terms of despair and isolation? Does Neo's reawakening to the virtual reality around him resonate with those with mental illness because it makes sense of their reality? It is as though they have discovered a kindred soul, someone whose life looks and feels very much like theirs. And if that character then makes it his mission to rid the world of the evil machines, these people feel they must follow his lead and do the same. If he discovers that the only way to save mankind is to murder the machines, they must do the same. The obvious problem, however, is that Neo's world is fictitious while theirs is not. A British psychiatrist explained that someone with paranoid psychosis may believe that something strange or sinister is happening to them. Then some event triggers this delusional thought and that serves to explain their anxieties. *The Matrix* taps into this belief directly and gives them a completely rational explanation for their paranoia (*The Matrix Defense*).

There are also some differences in the way *The Matrix* cases have been adjudicated. In "Murder and 'The Matrix'" Hilden points out two important distinctions: First, these cases have been adjudicated by judges, not juries. It's possible that jurors would be less accepting of the film's influence, especially if they saw the film themselves and did not commit any crimes as a result. Jurors were, for example, very quick to dismiss Ronny Zamora's claims of television intoxication, drawing on their own experiences of watching countless hours of television but never committing murder. Second, the unique plot of *The Matrix* sets it apart from other films accused of influencing criminal behavior. Because the film's plot revolves around a virtual reality theme it is more likely to adversely affect a fragile viewer's sanity. This becomes more pronounced when one actually believes in the constructed reality portrayed in *The Matrix*. If a few viewers truly believe *they* are living in the Matrix, they become compelled, if not duty-bound, to kill the controlling machines and help save mankind. As one of the chosen few with knowledge of the dual realities, they must act upon this sacred knowledge.

Regardless of any future cases involving the film and other virtual reality media products, the success of the Matrix insanity defense is groundbreaking and opens the door for other media influence strategies in criminal defense and insanity cases. The Matrix insanity defense succeeded because it satisfied the crucial legal standard of incitement to action; something that no other media strategy has achieved. It is important to understand however, that the scope of this incitement is very narrowly tailored to mentally impaired viewers who seem particularly vulnerable to the film's virtual reality premise. Whether this incitement will be found in more mainstream media products is, of course, purely speculative. Unfortunately, this legal standard cannot be further tested until someone commits a crime that harms or kills another and claims to have been influenced by a specific virtual reality media product. And while no one actively hopes for this to happen, history and human nature dictate that it likely will, and once again the courts will be charged with determining whether the media influence human behavior.

SEVEN

Lessons Learned
and Future Priorities

The stories of Joshua Cooke, Matthew Lovett and Lionel Tate offer sobering tales of the difficult times that teens confront every day. That entertainment products affected all three, who share a gender but few other characteristics, speaks to the power of media. Media impact young people's lives regardless of age, race, socioeconomic status or familial setting. Media are everywhere and no demographic characteristic can predict who will be affected more than another, or who is immune and who is not. The Secret Service analysis of school shootings found every race, family type and socioeconomic status represented among the young male gunmen. Most got guns from family members or ordered through the Internet. Many complained of bullying in school as precipitating the assaults; others claimed they were motivated to kill, because of a broken romance or a feud with a teacher or administrator. The divergent traits make it difficult to find any commonalities that could then be used to thwart future attacks.

What we do know is that media are a very important part of young people's lives. The surveys included in this text estimate that teens use media on average of 8 to 30 hours per week. For some, the numbers are significantly higher. That means that most teens make a very significant investment of time in their media of choice each week. Television, video games and music attract teens in such high numbers that much of the content in each is directly marketed to them. Films are more popular with teen boys than girls, and although they are willing to part with their precious disposable income to see the latest blockbuster once, if not twice, the high price of movie tickets still limits its audience. With children and teens devoting this much time each week to media, why is it that most adults still believe that media are bad for them? If we really believe that we should be restricting their use of television and video games. What lessons have adults learned to make better choices in the future?

There Is No Single Media Violence Effect

A good place to start is with dispelling the biggest misconceptions about media violence. Gerard Jones makes an excellent point when he chastises the research and advocacy communities for asking questions like *What is the effect of media violence?* Just as there is no one content or genre of media there can be no singular effect. If we accept that logic we must also accept that advertising affects all viewers equally and that music evokes the same emotions in all listeners. Intuitively we know that isn't true, because music is highly personalized. My favorite song that reminds me of a great memory or event could be your least favorite, simply because it reminds you of a horrible event in your life. We both share the same lyrics, but the meanings are very different, based on our personal experiences. That does not mean that research cannot pinpoint specific effects that are more prevalent than others or ones that are more commonly found in heavy users versus light users. It simply means there's a good reason that the magic-bullet theory of uniform and widespread effects was put to rest 50 years ago. Because it's not true! Even within media genres, products are very different. First-person shooter video games, for example, allow the players to assume the role of one of the characters and experience the action from their unique viewpoint. But who or what a player is shooting at varies significantly. Some games have players shooting people, prostitutes and police officers; in others a player's main enemy is a monster or creature of some alien form.

So the issue is not what media effect there is but what media violence effects are linked with conditions such as content, frequency, player demographics and with other contributing factors. Any study of human behavior is complicated so it must be approached with an equally complex protocol. As James Potter wrote, researchers have to stop arguing over definitions and methodological differences and share information in order to replicate the most promising studies. As there is no one methodology to study the effects of media violence there is no single effect on audiences.

Media Are Not the Scapegoat for All Social Ills

Since the days of radio people have been trying to blame a host of sociological and cultural problems on media violence. This trend continues today at an even faster pace because media such as video games are growing in popularity so quickly. Whenever an act of violence attracts national attention we begin the natural, yet often misguided, quest to find the cause of that violence. Most recently, school shootings and the Washington sniper case spurred a flurry of accusations because many of the perpetrators were teen men. What could cause these young men to commit murder?

Ideally these unfortunate events could result in increased funding for research on aggression, with violent media being one of the factors studied. Unfortunately, this rarely happens. Too often pundits jump on prominent crimes to push their agenda, and often they are wrong. Unfortunately the news media report these charges without checking the truthfulness of their claims. In the 1990s critics blamed MTV's program *Beavis and Butthead* for the death of a young girl. Her brother claimed that he watched an episode of the show in which the main characters set things on fire for fun. He repeated the act and set his bed on fire, killing his sister. Congress held hearings, Janet Reno vowed to clean up television and MTV bowed to pressure to move the program. The problem is that the children involved did not have cable television in their apartment. If the young boy really did see that episode of the show, it wasn't at his house where the fire was set.

L. Brent Bozell, head of the Parents Television Council, waged war against television wrestling after the arrest of Lionel Tate. Bozell teamed up with Tate's attorney Jim Lewis and blamed several deaths nationwide on television wrestling and started a boycott designed to scare sponsors away from the programs. Bozell bragged at the success of his boycott and claimed that a long list of sponsors had pulled their ads from wrestling shows. The problem is that no television wrestling shows were ever found culpable in any deaths and many of the companies that Bozell said had pulled their ads actually never advertised on those shows. Bozell was just plain wrong.

Critics of media violence often offer it up as the sole cause of aggression, neglecting the multitude of contributing factors identified by researchers. For example, most media coverage of Lionel Tate's murder trial centered on the so-called television wrestling defense and his claims that

Tiffany Eunick's death was really just an accident because he did not understand the consequences of play wrestling. Very few news stories explored Tate's past violent behavior or reported his multiple suspensions from school for fighting. Very few reported that one of his teachers said that he was the worst-behaved student she had ever had and that he bullied other students. By focusing only on the television wrestling angle, advocates missed an opportunity to explore why Tate watched so much wrestling in the first place and what other factors contributed to his aggression.

Critics often identify school shooters primarily with the violent media they used while ignoring other factors. For instance Joshua Cooke is identified with *The Matrix*; Dylan Klebold and Eric Harris with *Doom* and *The Basketball Diaries*; and Michael Carneal with *Quake* and *Final Fantasy*. Few media advocates look at another factor these teens all had in common, which is that they were bullied at school. Bullying is almost epidemic in American schools but it's rarely discussed; media violence is an easier target. As Jib Fowles points out, few people are willing to "stand up" for media violence, or argue that it is a good thing, so the scapegoating continues. Blaming teen violence on media, without looking at contributing factors such as bullying, socioeconomic status, and familial structure is too simplistic of an approach if we really want to discover the root causes of violent behavior.

Of course, the same is also true of those who dismiss all possibility that media violence has an affect on anyone. It's difficult, for example, to acknowledge that advertising affects viewers but violence does not. It is also difficult to praise a children's television show like *Sesame Street* for its educational value but not think that other programs can also teach children things, especially dangerous things. Certainly a show like *Sesame Street* is produced with educational techniques in mind, but isn't it possible that a child could learn, for instance, how to hit the dog with a bat after watching a cartoon character doing the same. How is it that only the good stuff is modeled by children?

There are also difficulties approaching media violence honestly when we impose our experience on others. We all model some behaviors from media even if we don't like to admit it. It may be the latest fashion from a reality show or a silly saying from a movie. How often did a colleague ask if "that's your final answer" in the course of a normal conversation? Or declare

Bonnie and Clyde was one of the first films to use slow-motion sequences to amplify violence. People continue to complain about the glorification of violence in films.

that she wanted to vote a co-worker off the island during a staff meeting? After the fifth time it's no longer funny. Those may only be annoying pop culture references, but we all do it at some point and then look down on others who don't know when to quit. Sometimes our sense of otherness is more pronounced. Several years ago I taught a senior seminar on media violence. The first night of class I posed a simple question for discussion: Does media violence cause aggression in people? Most of the students gave neutral answers: it affects some, but not all people; children are more likely than adults to be affected, and so on. But one student was adamant. He told us that he played 4–6 hours of violent shooter video games every day and that it didn't make him violence. And because he considered himself a normal young man, he extrapolated his experience to the larger population and concluded that it was ridiculous to think that media violence affects aggression.

Later in the semester he had to meet with me in my office because he had not turned in several assignments. While discussing this obvious problem he became agitated, balled his fists, paced the room, cursed and raised his voice to me. It was not a normal reaction from a student, even in this stressful situation. A few weeks later he graced the front page of the local newspaper after taking part in a riot at a campus event. Needless to say, he did little to advance his supposition that media violence has no effect. Perhaps he was just a very aggressive and angry young man who found a cathartic release in playing the games. Or maybe the games fed his anger and he was simply unable to set boundaries between appropriate aggression in game-playing and in interpersonal communications.

The media can't be so lopsided to affect users with one type of content but not another. If media are capable of inflicting bad things on people they must also be capable of doing good things for people. Media technologies themselves are relatively neutral; it's the content that has the ability to affect users. Although neurophysiologists are discovering some negative cognitive effects with newborns and toddlers who are exposed to fast-paced media like video games and television, the field does not condemn media altogether. Moderation is today's rallying call. It's not necessary to shield children from all media, but their viewing time should be limited to reasonable amounts each day.

Parents Are Well-Intentioned, But Clueless

Every survey cited shows that parents are not taking advantage of the ratings systems designed for television, video games, movies and music. In fact in most cases parents don't even know what the ratings are for each medium or what restrictions apply to each. Many parents raise the valid complaint that ratings don't always reflect their values so they do not find them very useful. Others doubt the accuracy of ratings, and studies by the Kaiser Family Foundation and MediaWise show that there are indeed major concerns with the application of the ratings by media producers. That is why some parents use other ratings systems, like those created by advocacy groups, religious denominations, and professional companies to monitor programming. Parents can use these reviews in combination with the existing V-chip to block programming.

Other parents simply say that they don't have the time or interest to mess with the ratings. Typically these parents say that they don't need the ratings because they "trust" their children to follow the rules they have put in place. In fact, I hear this a lot. But the MediaWise study showed that parents may want to rethink this trust issue a bit. While half of all parents reported that they do not allow their children to own M-rated games, two-thirds of the children interviewed reported owning such games. Parents need to take a greater role in reviewing their children's media habits. That means learning the ratings systems and applying them in whatever manner makes sense for their family. It's no longer acceptable to ignore the tools that are available and expect government to impose its police powers on the media industry.

More Regulation of Media Is Not Needed

The answer to continued concerns over media violence is not more regulation. Media products are protected from censorship by the First Amendment and by §326 of the Communications Act of 1934. Restricting access to violent media is permissible through passage of time, place and manner restriction, when these are found to be constitutional and narrowly tailored to address the media problem, but not censor content. Parents can impose their own time, place and manner restrictions, like allowing only 1–2 hours of screen time as suggested by the American Medical Association. Parents can also network with other parents to agree not to let young kids buy and play games rated higher than is acceptable. This way parents work together to present a united front, something that kids will take notice of.

Decisions about restricting access to violent media really are best made in individual settings, rather than through sweeping media reform. In 1996, Congress agreed to loosen media ownership rules in exchange for a concerted effort by broadcasters to develop a television ratings system to be paired with a V-chip blocking device. Broadcasters held up their end of the bargain but developed a ratings system that many find unusable. Instead of creating new regulation why not force broadcasters to redevelop the system? If parents still don't use it then it's their own fault. But jumping from a "voluntary" system to imposing FCC fines for violence is too extreme.

The same is true with video games. Although the Entertainment Software Review Board instituted one of the most elaborate ratings systems, many parents still don't use it. There is little incentive to change anything, or to take much criticism, if the games are being rated, the information is clearly printed on the box, but parents don't pay any attention to it. Currently there is no regulation mandating that retailers sell games based on the recommended age restrictions. Perhaps instituting such a law is warranted if social science research proves a definitive causal link between video game violence and aggression in children and teens. Like cigarettes, the sales could be restricted because society believes the teens are simply to immature to encounter the violent images and sexual themes in M-rated games. But this mean that retailers would have to enforce the suggested age restrictions. A three-year undercover operation conducted by the Federal Trade Commission found that in 2003, 69 percent of teenage secret shoppers were able to buy M-rated games at major retailers and only 24 percent of cashiers asked the age of the buyer. If the video game industry is serious about helping parents it will better educate retailers to the importance of upholding their own policies.

One of the biggest stumbling blocks to any content regulations on media is the continued popularity of television, video games, movies and music by the public. It's hard to argue that one of the *Grand Theft Auto* games is dangerous to society when it is a top seller every year. How can government determine that something is bad for a child if their own parents don't see it that way? It really can't and Congress is unlikely to try to impose any further regulation until parents quit buying their kids violent video games and a definitive link to real-life violence if found. But this reality doesn't negate the fact that the type of violence in these games is totally unnecessary and over the top. It's not necessary to have graphic portrayals of fighting and gunshots tearing apart bodies in order to enjoy a shooter game. The new-found popularity of sports games proves that video games don't have to be this violent to be appealing. Should publishers produce lifelike ultraviolent video games? Probably not. But can they? You bet. As Justice

Potter Stewart once said about journalists, "You are all confused about what you have the right to do under the Constitution and the right things to do." As long as there is a market for these games, publishers would be crazy not to produce them. If they don't some other company will. But all publishers could ratchet it back a little bit without fear of losing their consumer base.

Trust Your Instinct

The best advice to anyone is to listen to your own internal cues. Anecdotal evidence is the best resource in anyone's life. Despite the lack of overwhelming evidence supporting a causal relationship between media violence and aggression, there are some "warning signals" that indicate influence or correlation with anger. Trust in the experience shared by Joshua Cooke, who said that he was attracted to violent video games and heavy metal music because of his anger, not the other way around. At one time in his life he was playing first-person shooter video games up to 12 hours a day. That was a warning sign. Teens that are depressed or have been bullied or tormented often gravitate to violent movies and music, becoming obsessed with a certain song or artist. That can be a warning sign. In other words, one of the most important things is simply being open to the cues.

Then, we have to act on our instincts, even when that makes us unpopular or uncomfortable. Although it's probably not a surprise, I am not a fan of graphic violence. I find that it gets in the way of a good story and does little to improve my comprehension of a plot. However, I still have to remind myself to listen to my internal cues sometimes. One night I went to see Martin Scorsese's *Gangs of New York* with some friends. I sat through the first two hours of the film completely turned off by the constant barrage (at least to my mind) of stabbings, blood and guts spilling everywhere. At one point I started internal negotiations with myself that I would stay for three, maybe only two, more whackings. After all, how many more could there be? This went on for another 10 minutes before I realized that I was no longer paying attention to the film. The next scene involved a main character pummeling an adversary to death with an axe. He hit him once, then again, and again, and so on. I got it after the second blow; he was a bad man who killed another in a gruesome way. Blows three, four and five did nothing for me. Except force me to trust my instinct. I left the theater and went to the Starbuck's next door for coffee and a *New York Times*. I was happy, my friends were happy and I made a personal choice without imposing my standards on anyone else. It really was the best form of media violence regulation: self-regulation.

References

Adams, V. (1962, April 19). Minow given Peabody Award for service to radio and television. *New York Times*, p. 43.

American Amusement v. Kedrick et al. No 00-3643, U.S. Court of Appeals for the Seventh Circuit, March 23, 2001, accessed at http://www.ca7.uscourts.gov/tmp/1Q0Q21DV.txt

American Medical Association. (1996, July). *Physician guide to media violence.* Chicago, IL: American Medical Association.

American Morning. (2003, December 11). Transcript No. 121104CN.V47. [Online]. Available: http://web-lexis-nexis.com.

Anderson, C. A., Berkowitz, L., Donnerstein, E., Huesmann, L. R., Johnson, J. D., and Linz, D. (2003). The influence of media violence on youth. *Psychological Science in the Public Interest*, 4, 81–110.

Anderson, C. A., and Bushman, B. J. (2001). Effects of violent video games on aggressive behavior, aggressive cognition, aggressive affect, physiological arousal, and prosocial behavior: A meta-analysis review of the scientific literature. *Psychological Science, 12*, 353–359.

Anderson, K. (1999, July 1). 7 year old kid kills his 3 year old brother with a wrestling move. *The Dallas Morning News*, 3.

Asimov, N. (2002, March 29). TV today, violence tomorrow; Study links viewing by kids to aggression later in life. *San Francisco Chronicle*. [Online]. Available: http://www.sfgate.com/cgibn/artic/cgi?file=/c/a/2002/03/29/MN65503.DTL.

Baran, S. J. (2004). *Introduction to mass media: Media literacy and culture* (3rd ed.). New York: McGraw-Hill.

Bean, M. (2003, May 21). "Matrix" makes its way into courtrooms as defense strategy. *CourtTV.com*. [Online]. Available: http://cnn.law.com.

Black Panthers coming to help Tate. (2001, March 16). *Local 10.com*. http://www.local10.com.

Blucher, F. K. (2003). *Perspectives in violence.* New York: Nova Science Publishers, Inc.

Boy released from prison may be returned. (2005, December 4). *CNN.com*. [Online]. Available: http://cnn.com.

Boyle, K. (2005). *Media and violence.* London: Sage.

Boy's suicide note cites "South Park" character who dies. (1999, January 8). *Daily News*, p. E1.

Brandenburg v. Ohio, 395 U. S. 444 (1969).

Brannon, M. (2005, August 8). Personal interview with the author.

Britton, S. (2001). Personal communication to Judge Joel T. Lazarus, Broward County, *Florida v. Tate*, case no. 99-14401CF10A.

References

Broadcasters act to curb "bogeyman." (1933, February 28). *New York Times*, p. 21.

Broward County Police Report, case number 99-14401CF10A.

Bryant, J., and Thompson, S. (2002). *Fundamentals of media effects*. New York: McGraw-Hill.

Burden of Proof. (2001, March 14). The case of Lionel Tate: Was justice served? [Online]. Available: http://transcripts.cnn.com.

Burnstein, J. (2005, December 20). Judge finds Tate competent to stand trial. *South Florida Sun-Sentinel.* [Online]. Available: http://www.sun-sentinel.com /news.

_____. (2006, March 22). Tate asks judge to pull plea: Recanting "not guilty" plea could backfire in case. *South Florida Sun-Sentinel.* [Online]. Available: http://www.sun-sentinel.com/news.

_____. (2006, March 28). Tate's mother rebuked over missing weapon. *South Florida Sun-Sentinel.* [Online]. Available: http://www.sun- sentinel.com/news.

_____. (2006, March 30). Judge orders mental evaluation of Lionel Tate as he tries to renege on plea. *South Florida Sun-Sentinel.* [Online]. Available: http://www.sun-sentinel.com/news.

Buschel, R. C. (2002). Editorial on Jim Lewis libel defense. National Association of Criminal Defense Lawyers. [Online]. Available: http://criminaljustice.org/public.nsf.

Byers v. Edmondson, 712 So. 2d 681.

Cadorette, G. (2002, July 11). Springer sued by son of murdered guest. *Hollywood.com.* [Online]. Available: http://hollywood.com.

Cagle, W. (2001). Personal communication to Judge Joel T. Lazarus, Broward County, *Florida v. Tate*, case no. 99-14401CF10A.

Cantor, J. (1998). Children's attraction to violent television programming. In J. Goldstein (ed.), *Why we watch: The attractions of violent entertainment.* New York: Oxford University Press, 88–115.

Cantor, J., Stutman, S., and Duran, V. (1996). What parents want in a television rating system: Results of a national survey. Madison: University of Wisconsin Communication Arts. Unpublished manuscript.

Cantor, J., and Krcmar, M. (1999). Effects of advisories and ratings on parent-child discussions on television viewing choices. *National Television Violence Study*, 1, 407–408. Thousand Oaks, CA: Sage.

Catholic code for television viewers. (1958, August 2). *America, National Catholic Weekly Review*, 99, 473–474.

Center for Florida's Children, et. al. (2001, March 2). Brief in support of Lionel Tate, Appellant. No. 4D01-1306, 2003 Fla. App.

Center for Media Literacy. Educational Philosophy. [Online]. Available: http://www.medialit.org/about_cml.html.

Center on Children & the Law, et. al. (2001, March 10). Brief in support of Lionel Tate, Appellant. No. 4D01-1306, 2003 Fla. App.

Centre for Suicide Prevention. (1999, September). Music and suicide, SIEC Alert #37, Calgary, Alberta, Canada: Center for Suicide Prevention.

Clark, B. (1995, April 3). Shattered lives. *People*, 16.

Clark, C. (1993, March 26). TV violence: Will Hollywood tone it down or face regulation? *Congressional Quarterly Researcher*, 3.

Clips. (1993, December 17). *Hollywood Reporter*, n.p.

Cohen, A. (2001, March 9). Enough blame to go around. *CBSNews.com.* [Online]. Available: http://www.cbsnews.com.

References

Columbine lawsuit against videogames, movies thrown out. (2002, March 5). *Associated Press*. Retrieved July 28, 2005, from http://www.fac.org/news/aspx?id=4161.

Convicted child killer to return home. (2004, November 29). *CNN.com*. [Online]. Available: http://cnn.com.

Cooper, C. A. (1996). *Violence on television: Congressional inquiry, public criticism and industry response*. Lanham, MD: Rowman & Littlefield.

Cooper, C., and Blevins, J. (2000). How fairly did ABC apply the TV ratings system to prime-time programming?: A content analysis. *Feedback, 41*,1, 16–29.

A copycat assault? (1984, October 22). *Newsweek, 38.*

Copycat crimes. (2000, March 6). *Mediascope Issue Briefs*. [Online]. Available: http://www.mediascope.org.

Crumpler, I. (2003, February 19). TV killer Zamora to ask parole board for freedom. *Stuart News*, p. B1. [Online]. Available: http://web.lexis-nexis.com.

Davidson, L. (2001). Personal communication to Judge Joel T. Lazarus, Broward County, *Florida v. Tate*, case no. 99-14401CF10A.

Dedman, B. (2000, October 15 and16). School shooters: Secret Service findings. Deadly Lessons, Parts 1 & 2. *Chicago Sun-Times*. [Online]. Available: http://www.secretservice.gov/ntac/chicago_sun/find15.htm .

DeFilippo v. NBC, 8 Med. L. Rptr. 1872 (1982).

Durbin, D. (2004, June 22). Michigan appeals court throws out $29.3 million damage award in Jenny Jones case. *Associated Press*. [Online]. Available: www.ap.com.

Educator's television code. (1958, August 2). *America, National Catholic Weekly Review*, 99, 467.

Entertainment Software Association. (2003). Press Release on videogame violence. Retrieved on June 5, 2005, from http://www.theesa.com/news/index/php.

Entertainment Software Ratings Board. Video Game Rating Symbols and Content Descriptors. [Online]. Available: http://www.esrb.org/ratings/ratings_guide.jsp.

Experts say Moore has PTSD. (2005, August 8). *Al.com*. [Online]. Available: http://www.al.com/newsflash/regional/index.ssf?/base/news.

Family drops lawsuit. (2003). Messages posted to Panitz Murder Trial Forum. [Online]. Available: http://www.voy.com.

Family drops lawsuit against "Springer." (2003, January 4). *Associated Press*. [Online]. Available: http://www.ap.com.

Family's stakeout nets suspect. (1992, August 7). *Los Angeles Times*, n.p.

Farhi, P. (1998, September 25). Most new TV ratings missing, study finds. *Washington Post*, p. B7.

Farrington, B. (2003, February 20). Florida panel reduces sentence for "TV intoxication" killer. *Associated Press*.

Federal Communications Commission. (1961). *27th Annual Report*. Washington, DC: U.S. Government Printing Office.

_____. (1975). *Report on the broadcast of violence, indecent and obscene material*. Washington, DC: U.S. Government Printing Office.

Federal judge dismisses lawsuits against movie, video game makers. (2000, April 7). *Associated Press*. [Online]. Available: http://www.fac.org/news.

Federal Trade Commission. (2000, September 11). *FTC releases report on the marketing of violent entertainment to children*. Washington, D.C.: U.S. Government Printing Office.

_____. (2003, October 14). Results of nationwide undercover survey released. [Online]. Available: http://ftc.gov/opa/2003/10/shopper.htm.

References

_____. (2006, June 2). In the Matter of Take-Two Interactive Software, Inc. and Rockstar Games, Inc. Agreement Containing Consent Order, File no. 0523158.

_____. (2006, June 8). Makers of *Grand Theft Auto: San Andreas* settle FTC charges: FTC alleged companies' game content claims deceptive. [Online]. Available: http://ftc.gov/opa/2006/06/grandtheftauto.htm.

Federman, J. (ed.). (1999). *National television violence study, executive summary.* Vol. 3, pp. 1–54. Thousand Oaks, CA: Sage.

Fierro, R. (2005, August 5). Personal interview with the author.

Flanagan, L. (1999). Broward County Medical Examiner's Office. Autopsy #00-0911.

Florida panel reduces sentence for "TV intoxication" killer. (2003, February 19). *CNN.com/Law Center.* [Online]. Available: http://www.cnn.com/2003/LAW.

Florida v. Tate, No. 99-14401CF10A, Circuit Court of the 17th Judicial Circuit, Broward County, Florida. Affadavit. Supplemental appeal on behalf of defendant by Terry Bollea.

Florida v. Tate, No. 99-14401CF10A, Circuit Court of the 17th Judicial Circuit, Broward County, Florida. Bond revocation hearing, September 24, 1999.

Florida v. Tate, No. 99-14401CF10A, Circuit Court of the 17th Judicial Circuit, Broward County, Florida. Grand jury indictment.

Florida v. Tate, case no. 99-14401CF10A, Circuit Court of the 17th Judicial Circuit, Broward County, Florida. Motion for new trial, February 2, 2001.

Florida v. Tate, case no. 99-14401CF10A, Circuit Court of the 17th Judicial Circuit, Broward County, Florida. Motion in limine to exclude the defense of television intoxication and/or exposure to professional wrestling on television by way of expert witness, March 10, 2000.

Florida v. Tate, case no. 99-14401CF10A, Circuit Court of the 17th Judicial Circuit, Broward County, Florida. Sentencing order by Judge Joel T. Lazarus, May 26, 2000.

Florida v. Tate, case no. 99-14401CF10A, Circuit Court of the 17th Judicial Circuit, Broward County, Florida. Sentencing Report, March 9, 2001.

Florida v. Tate, No. 99-14401CF10A, Circuit Court of the 17th Judicial Circuit, Broward County, Florida. Supplemental appeal on behalf of defendant by Jerry McDevitt.

Florida v. Tate, case no. 99-14401CF10A, Circuit Court of the 17th Judicial Circuit, Broward County, Florida. Transcript of trial proceeding, January 25, 2001.

Florida v. Tate, case no. 99-14401CF10A, Circuit Court of the 17th Judicial Circuit, Broward County, Florida. Verdict report, January 25, 2001.

Flynn, L. J. (1998, April 2). V-chip and ratings are close to giving parents new power. *New York Times*, p. E6.

Fowles, J. (1999). *The case for television violence.* Thousand Oaks, CA: Sage.

Freedman, J. L. (2002). *Media violence and its effect on aggression: Assessing the scientific evidence.* Toronto, Ontario, Canada: University of Toronto Press.

Frontline. (1995, January 10).Does TV kill? New York: Public Broadcasting Service.

Frye v. United States, 293 F. 1013 (DC Cir. 1923).

Gentile, D. A. (ed.). (2003). *Media violence and children: A complete guide for parents and professionals.* Westport, CT: Praeger.

_____, Linder, J. R., and Walsh, D. A. (2003, April). *Looking through time: A longitudinal study of children's media violence consumption at home and aggressive behaviors at school.* Paper presented at the Biannual Meeting of the Society for Research in Child Development, Tampa, FL.

Gerbner, G., and Gross, L. (1976). Living with television: The violence profile. *Journal of Communication 26*(2), 172–199.

References

Girl's mother wants Tate to admit killing was no accident. (2004, January 24). *Local10. com.* [Online]. Available: http://www.local10.com.

Good Morning America. (2004, January 30). Mother hears admission of murder for the first time. [Online]. Available: http://web-lexis-nexis.com.

Governor Bush denies clemency hearing for Lionel Tate. (2001, June 15). *Local 10.com.* [Online]. Available: http://local10.com.

Governor Bush open to clemency in wrestling murder case. (2001, March 9). *CNN.com.* [Online]. Available: http://archives.cnn.com.

Grace, J. (1997, December 15). When the silence fell. *Time*, pp. 25–26.

Graczyk, M. (2005, January 7). Andrea Yates conviction erased. *Washington Post*, p. A2.

Grant, D. (2001, January 30). Letter to Governor Jeb Bush, Broward County, case no. 99-14401CF10A.

Graves v. Warner Brothers, 656 N.W. 2d 195 (2002).

Grego, M. (2000, July 26). "Springer" couple sought for murder. *Variety*, p. 11.

Griffits, B. (2005, August 5). Personal interview with the author.

Guilty plea in "Matrix" defense slayings. (2003, June 25). *CNN.com LawCenter*. [Online]. Available: http://www.cnn.com/2003/LAW.

Gunter, B. (1987). *Television and the fear of crime*. London: John Libbey.

Haas, B. (2002, July 1). Lawsuit planned against talk show. *Bradenton Herald*. [Online]. Available: http://www.bradenton.com.

Hamilton, J. T. (1998). *Channeling violence: The economic market for violent television programming*. Princeton, NJ: Princeton University Press.

Hamilton woman waives right to trial by jury (2003, May 13). WCPO.com transcript. [Online]. Available: http://www.wcpo.com/news/butlerwarren/20c1643a.htm.

Hanson, K. (1983, May 30). Children of violence and TV violence. *New York Daily News*, p. D2.

Hass, B. (2002). Lawsuit planned against talk show. *Bradenton Herald*. [Online]. Available: http://www.bradentonherald/news/local/3572770.htm.

Healy, J. M. (1990). *Endangered minds: Why our children don't think*. New York: Simon and Schuster.

Hilden, J. (2003, June 2). Murder and "The Matrix": Has the movie caused violence and if so, what should we do about it? *FindLaw Legal Commentary*. [Online]. Available: http://writ.findlaw.com/hilden.

Hill, G. (1954, July 15). Crime themes get more time on TV. *New York Times*, p. 29.

Hines, M. (1993, October 19). Not like the movie: A dare to test nerves turns deadly. *New York Times*, n.p.

Horwitz, S., and White, J. (2003, April 6). From Malvo, hubris and contempt; Teen told of cold-blooded campaign to terrorize, documents say. *Washington Post*, p. A1.

Huesmann, L., and Taylor, L. (2003). The case against the case against media violence. In Gentile, D. (ed.). *Media violence and children: A complete guide for parents*. Westport, CT: Praeger Publications.

Huesmann, R., Moses-Tius, J., Podolski, C., and Eron, L. D. (2003). Longitudinal relations between children's exposure to TV violence and their aggressive and violent behavior in young adulthood, 1977–1992. *Developmental Psychology*, 39(2), 201-221.

Illson, M. (1954, October 3). Real curb sought for delinquency. *New York Times*, p. 72.

Impact of interactive violence on children: Hearings before the Senate Commerce Committee. (2000, March 21). Testimony of Craig A. Anderson.

References

Ingrassia, Robert. (2003, May 21). "The Matrix" and murder. *New York Daily News.* [Online]. Available: http://www.nydailynews.com.

Jackman, T. (2003, May 17). Escape "The Matrix" go directly to jail. *Washington Post,* p. B4.

_____. (2003, June 25). Virginia teen pleads guilty to murdering parents; During sentencing hearings attorneys to discuss role of the film "The Matrix" played in slaying. *Washington Post,* p. B4.

_____. (2003, October 2). Oakton son sentenced in slayings. *Washington Post,* p. B1.

_____, and White, J. (2003, March 16). Malvo writing found in cell, authorities say. *Washington Post,* p. A1.

James v. Meow Media, Inc., et al., 2002 Fed. App. 02070 (6th Cir.).

James v. Meow Media, Inc., et al., cert. denied, U.S. Supreme Court Order List, 573, 2003.

Jansz, J. (2005, August). The emotional appeal of violent video games for adolescent males. *Communication Theory, 15,* 219–241.

"Jerry Springer" murder conviction. (2002, March 27). *Associated Press.* [Online]. Available: http://www.ap.com.

Jerry Springer Show. (2000, May 7). Secret mistresses confronted. [Online]. Available: http://www.friendsoffieger.com.

Johnson, J., Cohen, P., Smailes, E., Kasen, S., and Brook, J. (2002, March 29). Television viewing and aggressive behavior during adolescence and adulthood. *Science,* 295, 2468–2471.

Jones, G. (2002). *Killing Monsters: Why children need fantasy, super heroes, and make-believe violence.* New York: Basic Books.

Jordan, A., and Woodward, E. (2003, June 3). Parents' use of the v-chip to supervise children's television use. Philadelphia: An Annenberg Public Policy Center Report.

Judge: Lionel Tate competent; Probation violation hearing will move forward. (2005, December 19), *Local 10 News.* [Online]. Available: http://local10.com.

Jurors felt decision was imposed by unjust law. (2001, January 26). *Miami Herald,* 8A.

Jury awards over $25 million to Amedure family in "Jenny Jones" civil trial. (1999, May 7). *CourtTV.* [Online]. Available: http://www. courttv.com.

Justice for Juveniles. (2003, December 15). Massive protest planned if Tate retried. [Online]. Available: http://justiceforjuveniles.org.

_____. (2003, December 31). Tate plea not a done deal. [Online]. Available: http://justiceforjuveniles.org.

_____. (2004, January 1). Tate accepts plea! [Online]. Available: http://justiceforjuveniles.org.

Juvenile Delinquency (Part 1-B) Television Programs: Hearing before the Subcommittee to Investigate Juvenile Delinquency in the United States of the Senate Committee on the Judiciary, 83rd Cong., 1 (1954).

Juvenile Delinquency, Television Programs: Hearing before the Subcommittee to Investigate Juvenile Delinquency in the United States of the Senate Committee on the Judiciary, 84th Cong., 1 (1955).

Kaiser Family Foundation. (2001). *Parents and the v-chip.* Menlo Park, CA: Kaiser Family Foundation.

_____. (2002, Fall). *Children and video games.* Menlo Park, CA: Kaiser Family Foundation.

_____. (2003, Summer). *Parents and media: A Kaiser Family Foundation Report.* Menlo Park, CA: Kaiser Family Foundation.

_____. (2005, March). *Generation M: Media in the lives of 8–18 year olds*. Menlo Park, CA: Kaiser Family Foundation.

Kallestad, B. (2004, January 28). Parole panel moves up release for "TV intoxication" killer. *Associated Press*.

Killer at 12, Tate returns to prison for 30 years. (2006, May 18). *CNN.com*. [Online]. Available: http://www.cnn.com.

Korber, D. (1992, June 21). Fantasy turns to tragedy: Teen pressure drives some to violence crimes. *Long Beach Press-Telegraph*, A14.

Krepel, T. (2002) Pro wrestling pins Brent Bozell to the tune of $3.5 million and public retraction. [Online]. Available: http://conwebwatch.tripod.com.

Krikorian, M. (1998, January 15). Son, Nephew inspired by "Scream" movies kill woman. *Los Angeles Times*, n.p.

Kunich, J. (2000). Natural born copycat killers and the law of shock torts. *Washington University Law Quarterly (78)*, 1157–1270.

Kunkel, D., Farinola, W., Cope, K., Donnerstein, E., Biely, E., Zwarun, L. (1998, September). Rating the ratings: One year out. Executive Summary.

Laidman, J. (1999, April 27). Video games figure in school shootings. *Block New Alliance*. [Online]. Available: http://www.post-gazette.com.

The Lawsuits. (1995, January 10). *Frontline*. [Online]. Available: PBS.org/wgbh/pages.frontline.

Leeds, J. (2001, January 17). Surgeon General links TV with real violence: Report finds repeated early childhood exposure to intense shows, video games cause aggressive behavior. *Los Angeles Times*, p. A1.

Levin, G. (1998, January 13). Even with V-chip ahead, system earns few fans. *USA Today*, p. E1.

Lewis, J. (2004). The aftermath of the Lionel Tate case: A child and a chance. *Nova Law Review*, 28, 479–484.

_____. (2005, August 9). Personal interview with the author.

Libertarian Party. (1999, April 19). Lawsuit against "killer" corporations could murder the First Amendment. Washington, D.C.: Libertarian Party.

Liebert, R. M., and Sprafkin, J. (1989). *The early window: Effects of television on children and youth* (3d ed.). New York: Pergamon Press.

Lionel Tate kept in jail. (2005, June 24). *Associated Press*. [Online]. Available: http://sptimes.com.

Lionel Tate's mother earns a reprimand. (2006, March 31). *South Florida Sun-Sentinel* [editorial]. [Online]. Available: http://www.sun-sentinel.com/news.

Liptak, A. (2003, December 5). Younger sniper suspect's lawyers press insanity defense. *New York Times*, p. 32.

Long, G., and Green, L. (2005, January 7). Guilty verdict tossed over phantom TV show. *New York Post*, p. 19.

Lush, T. (2005, May 25). Once again, trouble finds Lionel Tate. *St. Petersburg Times*. [Online]. Available: http://www.sptimes.com.

Males. M. (1999). Children. In *Encyclopedia of Violence in the United States*. In Gottals, ed., *Violence in America: An Encyclopedia*, vol.1. New York: Charles Scribners.

Manning, C. (2001). Personal communication to Judge Joel T. Lazarus, Broward County, *Florida v. Tate*, case no. 99-14401CF10A.

The Matrix Defence. (2003). [Documentary.] London, UK: 3BM Films.

Matthews, T. (2001). Personal communication to Judge Joel T. Lazarus, Broward County, *Florida v. Tate*, case no. 99-14401CF10A .

References

McCollum v. CBS, Inc., 15 Med. L. Rptr. 2001 (1988).

Media Awareness Network. (2005). Research on the effects of media violence. [Online]. Available: http://www.media-awareness.ca.

Media Violence. (2001, June 13). Messages posted to SIGCHI Kid-Computer Interaction

Memorials to Sherry Corbett. (2002) Online Tributes. [Online]. Available: http://www.twistofair.com/We_Love_You_Sherry.htm.

Message Board. [Online]. Available: http://listserv.acm.org/scripts/wa.exe?A2=ind0106b&:=chi-kids&P=1173.

Mestel, R. (2002, March 29). Adolescents' TV watching linked to violent behavior. *Los Angeles Times*, p. A1.

Methodists seek elevation of TV. (1954, October 11). *New York Times*, p. 31.

Miller v. California, 413 U.S. 15 (1973).

Miller, S. A. (2003, December 9). Malvo team cites role of violent media; Movie, video games seen brainwashing defendant. *Washington Times*, p. B1.

Minow, N. N. (1961, May 9). Address to the 39th Annual Convention to the National Association of Broadcasters, Washington, D.C. Unpublished manuscript.

_____. (1995). *Abandoned in the wasteland: Children, television and the First Amendment*. New York: HarperCollins.

Montell Williams Show. (2003, September 8).

_____Children behind bars for life. [Online]. Available: http://web-lexis-nexis.com.

Moore, C. (2001). Personal communication to Judge Joel T. Lazarus, Broward County, *Florida v. Tate*, case no. 99-14401CF10A.

Moore, K. (2003, June 25). No more Matrix defense. *The Connection Newspaper*. [Online]. Available: http://www.connectionnewspapers.com/article.asp?20478.

Morning Report: Movies. (1995, November 25, January 8). *Los Angeles Times*, n.p.

Morning Report: Alleged rapists blame "Springer." (1999, January 8). *Los Angeles Times*, n.p.

Morse, J. (2003, February 20). Ansley now competent to stand trial. *Cincinnati Enquirer*. [Online]. Available: http://www.enquirer.com.

_____. (2004, January 4). Killer to stay in tight security. *Cincinnati Enquirer*. [Online]. Available: http://www.enquirer.com.

Mothers protest "bogeyman" on radio. (1933, February 27). *New York Times*, p. 17.

Mulvhill, G. (2003, July 8). Father says son was probably playing, not planning to kill. *Associated Press*. [Online]. Available: http://web-lexis-nexis.com.

Murdered woman's son sues Springer. (2002, July 11). *St. Petersburg Times*. [Online]. Available: http://www.sptimes.com.

National Association of Radio and Television Broadcasters. (1956, July). Television Code (3rd ed.). Washington, D.C.: National Association of Radio and Television Broadcasters.

National Commission on the Causes and Prevention of Violence. (1969, December 10). *Final report*. Washington, D.C.: National Commission on the Causes and Prevention of Violence.

NBC v. Niemi, 2 Med. L. Rptr. 1831 (1976).

NBC v. Niemi, 3 Med. L. Rptr. 1785 (1978).

Niemi Trial. (1978, April 27). Editorial. *Philadelphia Enquirer*, p. E1.

Niemi Trial. (1978, April 27). Editorial. *Portland Express*, p. E1.

Niemi Trial. (1978, April 29). Editorial. *Washington Star*, p. E1.

References

New slay plot in "Matrix' case. (2003, August 12). *New York Post*, p. 18.

Ohio v. Ansley, Case No. CR02-08-1227, Court of Common Pleas, Butler County, Ohio. Findings of not guilty by reason of insanity, May 13, 2003.

Ohio v. Ansley, Case No. CR02-08-1227, Court of Common Pleas, Butler County, Ohio. Indictment for aggravated murder with specification, August 2, 2002.

Oldenburg, A. (2005, July 28). Ratings system runs adrift. *USA Today*. [Online]. Available: http://www.usatoday.com.

Olivia N. v. NBC, 3 Med. L. Rptr. 1454 (1977).

Olivia N. v. NBC, 7 Med. L. Rptr. 2359 (1981).

Olkon, S. (2005, May 25). Tate's latest arrest stuns supporters. *Miami Herald*. [Online]. Available: http://www.miami.com/mld/miamiherald.

_____. (2005, May 28). Three guns missing from home of Tate's mother. *Palm Beach Post*. [Online]. Available: http://palmbeachpost.com.

Padowitz, K. (2005, August 8). Personal interview with the author.

Panitz v. Crosby, Case No. 00-10578CF, District Court of Appeal (2d. Dist.), Petition for Writ of Habeas Corpus.

People v. Schmitz, 231 Mich App 521, 523 (1998).

Perl, P. (2005, November 30). Paul and Margaret Cooke didn't know the harrowing story of their son's life before they adopted him, or understand the rage and self- loathing within. If only they had. *Washington Post Magazine*, p. W16.

Perper, J. (1999, August 5). Medical examiner's report, Case no. 99-14401CF10A, Broward County, Florida.

Police: Dismemberment had "Sopranos" inspiration. (2003, January 28). *CNN.com*. [Online]. Available: http://cnn.com.

Potter, J. W. (1999). *On media violence*. Thousand Oaks, CA: Sage.

_____. (2003). *The 11 myths of media violence*. Thousand Oaks, CA: Sage .

Potter, M. (2002, March). Talk shows and murder. *CNN.com*. [Online]. Available: http://cnn.com/LAW.

Prince, S. (ed.). (2000). *Screening Violence*. Piscataway, NJ: Rutgers University Press.

Radio reforms for youth, aim of joint drive. (1939, April 30). New York Times, 4D.

Ratings have "forbidden fruit" effect–study. (1997, March 26). *Reuters News Service*.

Rice v. Paladin Enterprises, Inc., 128 F. 3d 233 (1997).

Rideout, V. J. (2004, Fall). *Parents, media and public policy*. Menlo Park, CA: Kaiser Foundation.

_____, Vandewater, E. A., and Wartella, E. A. (2003, Fall). *Zero to six: Electronic media in the lives of infants, toddlers, and preschoolers*. Menlo Park, CA: Kaiser Foundation.

Rivers, J. (2001). Personal communication to Judge Joel T. Lazarus, Broward County, *Florida v. Tate*, case no. 99-14401CF10A.

Roberts, D. F. (2000, August). Media and youth: Access, exposure, and privatization. *Journal of Adolescent Medicine*, 27, 8–14.

Rubenstein, D. (1999). Plaintiff attorney targets Warner Brothers, Oliver Stone after deadly rampage. *Corporate Law Times*, 54, 54.

Ryan, J. (1997, September 13). Accused teen killer deploys Pearl Jam defense. *E!Online*. [Online]. Available: http://www.eonline.com.

Ryfle, S. (1995, July 7). Movies may have sparked rash of parking meter thefts. *Los Angeles Times*, C1.

Sanders, et. al. v. Acclaim Entertainment, et al., Civil Case no. 01-B-728 (CO. March 4, 2002).

Scheel, K. R. (1995). Preference for heavy metal music as a potential indicator of increased

References

suicidal risk among adolescents. Unpublished master's thesis, University of Iowa, Iowa City.

Schenck v. U.S., 249 U.S. 47 (1919).

Schone, M. (2003, November 9). This week, accused D.C. sniper Lee Malvo may become the latest in a string of criminal defendants to plead not guilty by reason of "The Matrix." *Boston Globe*, p. D1.

Senate Commerce Committee meeting on Media Violence, *Congressional Record*, 103rd Cong., 1993, E2788.

Settlement in Kentucky school shootings. (2000, August 3). *CBS.com*. [Online]. Available: http://cbsnews.com.

Sharpton comes to teen convict's defense. (2001, June 17). *Local 10.com*. [Online]. Available: http://local10.com.

Slack, S., and Gundlach, J. (1992). The effect of country music on suicide. *Social Forces*, 71, 211–218.

Smith, H. (2001). Personal communication to Judge Joel T. Lazarus, Broward County, *Florida v. Tate*, case no. 99-14401CF10A.

Snider, M. (2005, June 15). Video games help spies, soldiers learn their craft. *USA Today*, p. D4.

Springer hurls verbal chairs at news profession. (1999, February 2). *Inside Medill News*. Evanston, IL: Medill School of Journalism.

Springer show guest found dead. (2000, July 26). *Laredo Morning Times*, p. 5A.

Stafford. R. (2004, February 18). Violent video games could use limits. [Letter to the Editor]. *USA Today*, p. A10.

State asks for rehearing in Tate case. (2003, December 29). *CNN.com*. [Online]. Available: http://cnn.law.com.

Steinhaus, R. (2002, February 28). Florida v. Panitz: Talk show murder trial. *CourtTV.com*. [Online]: Available: http://www.courttv.com.

Stern, S. (2003, June 12). "The Matrix" made me do it. *Christian Science Monitor*, p. C3.

Sternheimer, K. (2003). *It's not the media: The truth about pop culture's influence on children*. Boulder, CO: Westview Press.

Stroh, M. (2002, March 29). TV viewing raises risk teens may turn violent: More than an hour worrisome, study says. *Baltimore Sun*, p. C1.

Substantial Capacity Test. (1954). Model Penal Code, § 401.

Suit: Video games sparked police shootings. (2005, February 15). *ABC News*. [Online]. Available: http://abcnews.go.com.

Surgeon General's Report by the Scientific Advisory Committee on Television and Social Behavior: Hearing before the Subcommittee of Communications, 92nd Congress, 2 (1972).

Suspect: More targets on kill list. (2004, August 28). *Cincinnati Post*. [Online]. Available: http://cincypost.com.

Tamborini, R., Eastin, M. S., and Skalski, K. L. (2004). Violent virtual video games and hostile thoughts. *Journal of Broadcasting & Electronic Media*, 48, 3, 335–357.

Tate can return to mother's home. (2004, November 29). *Local 10.com*. [Online]. Available: http://www.local10.com.

Tate denies probation violation. (2004, September 15). *Local 10.com*. [Online]. Available: http://www.local10.com.

Thompson, J. (2005, March 6). Interview on *60 Minutes*, CBS Broadcasting Network, News Division.

_____. (2005, July 14). An open letter to the members of the Entertainment Software Association. [Online]. Available:http://ve3d.ign.com.

References

Thompson, K., and Haninger, K. (2001, August). Violence in E-rated video games. *The Journal of the American Medical Association*, 286, 5, 591–598.

Times Mirror Center for People and the Press. (1993). TV Violence: More objectionable in entertainment than in newscasts. Washington, D.C., as quoted in Hamilton, T.

Today Show. (1999, October 11). News story on *South Park* suicide.

_____. (2003, December 11). Murder conviction of Tate overturned. [Online]. Available: http://web-lexis-nexis.com.

Too much bang bang. (1954, April). [Letter to the Editor]. *Christian Science Monitor*, p. E1.

TV: Dial anything for murder. (1958, October 10). *Newsweek*, 66.

TV on Trial. (1977, September 12). *Newsweek*, 104.

U.S. Supreme Court won't consider reinstating damage award in Jenny Jones case. (2004, June 21). *Associated Press*. [Online]. Available: http://www.ap.com.

Valania, J. (2003, July 6). The kids are not all right. *Philadelphia Weekly*, p. 17.

Vance v. Judas Priest, 16 Med. L. Rptr. 2241 (1989).

Van Taylor, D. (1992, August 2–8). The subject was suicide, series. *Los Angeles Times*, n.p.

Vedantam, S. (2002, March 29). Study ties television viewing to aggression. *Washington Post*, p. A1.

Victim's mother unloads in courtroom statement as teen pleads guilty. (2004, January 29). *Local10.com*. [Online]. Available: http://www.loacal10.com.

Video games don't breed violence (2004, May 14). Messages posted to Gamufi Discussion Board. [Online]. Available: http://www.gamufi.com/forums.

Violence on Television: Hearings before the House Committee on Interstate and Foreign Commerce, Subcommittee on Communications, 95th Cong., 1, (1977).

Violent video games: Psychologists help protect children from harmful effects. *Psychology Matters*. [Online]. Available: http://www.psychologymatters.org/videogames.html.

Vitka, W. (2005, February 25). GameSpeak: Jack Thompson. *CBS News*. [Online]. Available: http://www.cbsnews.com.

Wald, J. (2004, April 12). Teen gets 10 years in failed New Jersey murder plot. *CNN.com*. [Online]. Available: http://www.cnn.com.

Wallenstein, A. (2000). Another talk show killing, but don't blame television. *Media Life*, p. 21.

Waller v. Osbourne, 763 F. Supp. 1144 (M.D. Ga. 1991).

Walsh, D. A., and Gentile, D. A. (2001, June 6). A validity test of movies, television, and video-game ratings. *Pediatrics*, 107, 1302–1308.

_____, Walsh, E. Bennett, N., Robideau, B., and Walsh, M., et al. (2005, November 29). Tenth Annual MediaWise video game report card. A National Institute on the Media and the Family Report.

Wartella, E. (1996, November 23). The context of television violence. Carroll C. Arnold Distinguished Lecture, Speech Communication Association Annual Convention, San Diego. Unpublished.

Warton, D. (1956, April). Let's get rid of tele-violence. *Parents Magazine*, 93–94.

Watters v. TSR, Inc., 904 F.2d 378 (1990).

Web site back after boy's death. (1998, January 4). *The Daily News*, 13.

Weirum v. RKO General, Inc., 15 Cal.3d 40 (1975).

Wharton, D. (1995, June 30). New voice to rap Rap: Sen. Lieberman plans to join critics of Time Warner. *Variety*, 1A.

References

Whited, L. (2000). "Slime journalism" strikes again. *Roanoke.com*. [Online]. Available: http://roanoke.com.

Whitney v. California, 274 U.S. 357 (1927).

Who is Michael Carneal? (1997, December 3). *CNN.com*. [Online]. Available: http://www.cnn.com.

Winston, D. A. (1992, July 26). The bad news bank robbers. *Cleveland Plain Dealer*, n.p.

Williams, D., and Skoric, M. (2002, June). Internet fantasy violence: A test of aggression in an online game. *Communication Monographs*, 72, 217–233.

Winn, M. (2002). *The plug-in drug: Television, computers, and family life*. (Rev. ed.). New York: Penguin.

Wolfe Blitzer Reports. (2003, February 20). Transcript #022000CN.V67. [Online]. Available: http://www.cnn.com.

Writer's Guild of America West, Inc. v. FCC, 423 F.Supp. 1064 (1976).

Writer's Guild of America West, Inc. v. American Broadcasting Co., Inc., 609 F. 2d 355 (1979), cert. denied, 449 U.S. 824 (1980).

Yates' murder conviction overturned. (2005, January 6). *CNN.com*. [Online]. Available: http://www.cnn.com.

Youth's poems. (1998, November 10). *Cincinnati Post*. [Online]. Available: http://www.cincypost.com/news/1998/write111098.html.

Zamora v. CBS, 5 Med. L. Rptr. 2109 (1979).

Index

The Addams Family 16
Amedure, Scott 108–110
American Amusement v. Kendrick 30
American Medical Association 54, 187
Annenberg Public Policy Center 77
Ansley, Tonda Lynn 166–168

Bandura, Albert 33–35
The Basketball Diaries 89, 118, 120, 184
Beach Blanket Bingo 16
Beavis and Butthead 5, 102, 117 183
Behavior Assessment System for Children 131
Betty Boop 6
Black Panthers 148
Bollea, Terry 136
Born Innocent 104
Bourg-Carter, Sherry 132, 150
Bozell, L. Brent 158–159, 183
Brandenburg v. Ohio 61
Brannon, Michael 130–131, 143, 154–155, 158
The Burning Bed 100
Bush, Jeb 141, 147
Byers v. Edmondson 99, 103

Campbell-Panitz, Nancy 100–116
Carneal, Michael 24, 119–122, 184
Carson, Johnny 108
The Center for Florida's Children 149
Center for Media Literacy 45
Center on Children & the Law 148
Centre for Suicide Prevention 93
Clinton, Bill 71
Clinton, Hillary Rodham 82
Cochran, Johnny 148
Columbine 117–119
Communications Act of 1934 12
Cooke, Joshua 2, 122, 168–176, 181, 189
Cool Hand Luke 99

Copycat crimes 87–91
Corbett, Sherry 166–168
Couric, Katie 78

The Deer Hunter 89
DeFilippo v. NBC 108
Desensitization 41
Dietz, Dr. Park 102
Dole, Bob 71
Doom 24, 52, 118, 120, 171, 184
Drew Carey Show 76
Drowning Pool 172
Duke Nukem 118
Dungeons & Dragons 98

The 11 Myths of Media Violence 58
Ellen 76
Entertainment Software Association 122, 177
Entertainment Software Review Board 78–82, 188
Eron, Leonard 35–36, 38–39
Eunick, Tiffany 125–129

Family Viewing Hour 18
Federal Communications Commission 1, 14, 18, 73
Federal Trade Commission 82, 188
Fieger, Geoffrey 109
Fierro, Rachel 170, 173–174
Final Fantasy 24, 184
Fireside Chats 8
First Amendment 11, 59, 161, 187
Florida v. Tate 136
Fowles, Jib 50–51, 184
Freedman, Jonathan 39
Frye v. US 139

Gentile, Doug 37,
Gerbner, George 37–38

203

Index

Gore, Tipper 67
Grand Theft Auto 25, 81, 92, 122, 171, 177, 188
Grant, Dennis 142, 154
Graves v. Warner Bros 109–110
Grossett-Tate, Kathleen 126, 147 157
Grossman, David 120
Gunter, Barry 39

Hamilton, James 47–49
Harris, Eric 22, 24, 117–119, 184
Healy, Jane 54, 56
Helter Skelter 89
Hogan, Hulk 166
Hoover, J. Edgar 13
The House of the Dead 28
The Howard Stern Show 121
Howdy Doody Hour 8

I Dream of Jeannie 16

James v. Meow Media 121
Jenny Jones Show 108–110, 115
Jerry Springer Show 76, 92, 110–116
John Paul II (Pope) 148
Johnson, Jeffrey 36
Johnson, Mitchell 22, 117
Jones, Gerard 51–52, 182
Judas Priest 106, 112, 113, 253

Kaiser Family Foundation 75, 186
Kennedy, John F. 5, 16
Kennedy, Robert 16
Kinkle, Kip 117
Klass, Joel 133–134, 138–139
Klebold, Dylan 5, 22, 24, 117–119, 184
Kojak 106–107
Kunkel, Dale 75

Law and Order 102
Lewis, Jim 128–129, 131–140, 151–152, 158
Little Orphan Annie 6
The Little Rascals 9
Loukaitis, Barry 21, 23
Lovett, Matthew 176–181

Malvo, Lee Boyd 163–165
Martin Luther King 16
The Matrix 2, 88, 118, 161–180
The Matrix Defence 184
McCollum v. Vance 95–97
McMahon, Vince 158
MediaWise 83, 186
Menace II Society 89

Mieseges, Vadim 165–166
Miller v. California 30
The Milton Berle Show 8
Minow, Newton 14
M'Naughten Rule 162–163
Money Train 89
Montel Williams Show 126
Moore, Devin 25, 92, 122
Morpheus 161, 164
Motion Picture Ratings 67
Muhammad, John Allen 164–165
The Munsters 16
Music Ratings 67

Nation of Islam 148
National Association for Better Radio and Television (NAFBRAT) 9, 12
National Association of Broadcasters 13, 84
National Commission on the Causes and Prevention of Violence 16
National Council of Churches of Christ 8
National Institute of Mental Health 44
National Institutes of Health 18
National Television Violence Study 42–44
Natural Born Killers 1, 99
Neo 161, 171, 177
Niemi, Lisa 104
NYPD Blue 76

Olivia N. v. NBC 104–105
Osbourne, Ozzy 89, 93, 95–98

Padowitz, Kenneth 125, 129–130, 135, 137, 153
Panitz, Ralf 110–116
Parental Advisory Label 68
Parents Music Resource Center 68
People v. Schmitz 109
Potter, James 49–50

Quake 24, 52, 120, 171, 184

Rambo 89
Recording Industry Association of America 68–70
Reno, Janet 102, 183
Rice v. Paladin 63–64
The Rock 136
Rosenbaum, Richard 141, 147, 152–153

Sanders, et al. v. Acclaim Entertainment 118
Savalas, Telly 106
Schenck v. United States 60

Index

Schmitz, Jonathan 109–110
Scream 91
Secret Service 19
Senate Subcommittee to Investigate
  Juvenile Delinquency 19
Sharpton, Al 148
Shindler's List 77
Simon, Paul 71
60 Minutes 25, 122–123
Social cognition theory 33
Social learning theory 33
The Sopranos 74, 76, 91
South Park 89
Spin City 76
Sternheimer, Karen 46–47

Tailhook Convention 100
Tate, Lionel 91, 125–159, 181
Television intoxication 5, 106–108, 139,
  183
Television Parental Guidelines 73–74
Television ratings 71
Thematic Apperception Test 131–132
Thompson, Jack 120–133
The Three Stooges 9
Time, place and manner restrictions 64–
  66

Tonight Show 108
Top Gun 100
Tucker, C. Delores 71

U.S. v. Thoma 31

V-chip 72, 187
Valenti, Jack 67
Vance v. Judas Priest 94
Video game ratings 78–81

Wal-Mart 70, 122
Waller v. Osbourne 97–98
Wartella, Ellen 41,
Watters v. TSR 98
Weirum et al. v. RKO General 61–63
Whitney v. California 60
Winn, Marie 53–54
Woodham, Luke 22, 117
World Wrestling Federation 136, 158
Writers Guild of America West v. FCC 18

Yates, Andrea 102

Zamora, Ronny 5, 106–108
Zamora v. CBS 107